Hate Crime

The Elmer H. Johnson and Carol Holmes Johnson Series in Criminology

HateCrime

The Global Politics
of Polarization

Edited by Robert J. Kelly
and Jess Maghan

Southern Illinois University Press
Carbondale and Edwardsville

01 00 99 98   4 3 2 1

Library of Congress Cataloging-in-Publication Data
Hate crime : the global politics of polarization / edited by Robert J.
    Kelly and Jess Maghan.
        p. cm. — (The Elmer H. Johnson and Carol Holmes Johnson
    series in criminology)
    Includes bibliographical references.
        1. Hate crimes—Political aspects. 2. Hate crimes—Cross-cultural
    studies. I. Kelly, Robert J. II. Maghan, Jess, 1936–   .
    III. Series.
    HV6250.25.H39 1998
    364.1—dc21   97-44068
                                                           CIP
        ISBN 0-8093-2130-0 (cloth : alk. paper)
        ISBN 0-8093-2210-2 (paper : alk. paper)

The paper used in this publication meets the minimum requirements of American
National Standard for Information Sciences—Permanence of Paper for Printed Library
Materials, ANSI Z39.48-1984. ⊗

To
Gilbert Geis
Irving Louis Horowitz
Charles Winick

Contents

Preface

We like to think that we chose precisely the right time to publish *Hate Crime*. Any earlier, the systematic data collection that is now occurring would not have begun to disgorge its facts; any later, and the field would be awash with a spate of volumes whose repetitive claims and counterclaims could lead to more confusion.

As the essays illustrate, we have resorted to the widest spectrum of source material ranging across several continents, seeking clues to the truth about hate crimes and the historical, social, psychological, and cultural intricacies and contradictions behind them. The ubiquity of the phenomenon is clearly evident in its commonality across cultures, time periods, ethnic, racial, religious, and sexual groups.

The analyses in these pages serve to highlight two broad conclusions: that in times of social distress and economic uncertainty, tensions between groups become acute and find expression in hate crimes; and that the burden of guilt of these cannot be attributed to or blamed on entire groups of people. While individuals must ultimately bear the responsibility for their own behavior and criminal acts, the context and social climate in which these occur is quite relevant to their understanding.

Hate crimes are partly ad hoc and situational and partly a cynical extrapolation from the ethos and collective sentiments of various groups. Taking their cues from their communities, perpetrators of bias incidents may feel free to act without strong rebuke or sanction from the local neighborhoods and settlements in which these events occur.

In 1993, when *Bias Crime: American Law Enforcement and Legal Responses* was published, we began to gather new ideas about the general

relationships among race, ethnicity, sexual orientation, religious preference, and crime. A growing body of writing among legal scholars and
social scientists has developed arguments and perspectives on bias or hate
crime of which this collection is a part. We seek to describe a more general pattern of the relationships characteristic of phenomena whose mani-
festations reach well beyond the United States.

There are two tensions around which the essays in this book hover.
Even when the resources of modern states are purposefully applied to the
problems of ethnic, racial, and religious hatreds, the underlying rational-
ist dream of a community of reason is far too removed from a concrete
sense of the ethical life of pluralistic societies; and it has proven ineffective in solving these problems.

This is a book about what is, more than what might be. However, the
implications of the analyses, which involve some of our deepest and dark-
est instincts, may be thought optimistic. It is worth noting at the outset
that though moral and ethical principles are basic to the understanding
of the problem of hate crimes and instrumental in their resolution, it
should not be supposed that effective coping with these problems can be
done without social understanding. A purely moral/ethical stand and a
law enforcement response are necessary but not sufficient. Social scientific
research offers knowledge about the nature of social life in pluralistic
societies and the psychological realities of those living in heterogeneous
communities that may help to justify or create a disposition among culturally different peoples to accept certain ethical principles or guidelines
for social conduct.

The other great tension that exists worldwide and that has been a per-
ennial problem in the United States since its founding is the issue of
pluralism versus integration. The New England Puritans wrestled consciously with one form of this basic dilemma in their effort to maintain
a unified society while guarding the purity of independent congregations.

On another level, the issue of the one and the many crystallized in the
structure of the American Constitution. The Founding Fathers not only
left the problem of reconciling national supremacy with state and local
rights; they provided a matrix for dealing with it. The importance in the
United States and in many nations of reconciling ethnic diversity with
national unity is no less crucial, but it has been attempted less often. The
Constitution of the United States, which is viewed as a model of moral
and legal emancipation and protection, laid down no explicit guidelines
for adjudicating issues of social integration and tolerance. In short, there

are no courts of ethnic, sexual, racial, or religious rights in the United States, and the appreciation of the complexities in this troubled area is rarely met. Here the dilemma is both moral and sociological. It has to do with what societies are and wish to be; with the kind of identity we would like to have.

In the post–cold war period, the major East/West powers dismantled their empires. In their wake, a whole series of new states have emerged, as the traditional alignments forged in the aftermath of World War II came apart. *Hope* became the watchword. Many groups wished to reclaim their identities and participate in a nationalist, ethnic renaissance of cultural revival and political emancipation. Too often and too tragically, exhilarated promises and expectations have been betrayed and crushed, so that in many modernizing, newly liberated societies, the end of the cold war has meant a sense of bitter defeat, profound shock, and bewildering uncertainty. It has also meant, at the individual level, personal animosity and hate as peoples compete for scare resources, territories, and religious values.

This collection of essays is far from encyclopedic in coverage, though we trust that it is emblematic of the worldwide dimensions of the problem. As concerned students of hate crime, we have strived to keep the discussion above the testimonial level and have consciously sought to avoid the type of commentary that is simply a repetition of appalling clichés, most of which are unhistorical and hypocritical. There are victims and victimizers to be sure. But the amelioration of the problem is not just a police matter, deciding who is right and who is wrong. It begs for a political and moral resolution, and this entails a commitment to shared principles of accountability and solidarity to end the nagging inequities that promote exploitation and violence. A serious struggle against the causes of hate crime means a battle against poverty and ignorance, which we think must be joined seriously by victim and victimizers, who are in most instances interchangeable.

Our special thanks go to the Edward Sagarin Institute for the Study of Deviance and Social Issues.

Finally, we wish to thank editor Rebecca Spears Schwartz, whose queries were always enriching. Her editorial touch improved the entire manuscript.

Hate Crime

Introduction

Robert J. Kelly and Jess Maghan

*The object of one's hatred is never, alas, conveniently outside but is seated in
one's lap, stirring in one's bowels and dictating the beat of one's heart. And
if one does not know this, one risks becoming an imitation—and, therefore,
a continuation—of principles one imagines oneself to despise.*
           —James Baldwin, "Here Be Dragons"

With the end of the cold war in the 1980s, *terrorism* and *fundamentalism* emerged as two key terms in the analysis of political conflicts involving Sunnis and Shiites, Kurds and Iraqis, Tamils and Sinhalese, Sikhs and Hindus—the list could go on. The terms portray fearful images that lack discriminate definition or contents, but they signify moral power for whoever uses them and moral defensiveness and criminalization for whomever they designate. The fear induced by the overpowering images of *terrorism* and *fundamentalism* yields a third category connected to these—*hate crime.* Often the term is employed to describe local community conflicts that entail criminal acts motivated primarily by racism, homophobia, and anti-Semitic (or anti-Christian and anti-Muslim) attitudes and beliefs. This raises some questions: Is it that the emerging post–cold war societies and their social structures fuel strife among ethnic, racial, and religious communities? And to the extent that emergent communities are unassimilated and alien to each other, will the consequences

1

of nationalist fervor arouse anxieties that express themselves in hate crimes?

What might help to explain why ethnic, racial, religious, and sexual identities have become ascendant in the post–cold war era? What might explain how these identities can lead to brutal struggles among groups who are often neighbors? These questions are more compelling than ever, as Hutus battle Tutsis in Rwanda, Bosnians struggle savagely with Serbs, Azerbaijanis are at war with Armenians, and new tensions seem to flare up weekly around the world. Perhaps they were always there; conflicts of long-standing are not new but have been contained within the political structures of the cold war, which defined the terms of conflict more or less in the interests of the global imperial policies of the Soviet empire, NATO, and its key component, the United States. With the collapse of the Soviet Union and the unraveling of NATO, people are now freer to act on these ancient hates.

Hatreds based on identities, lifestyles, cultural values, and tastes appear to have a historic continuity and keep simmering across generations. Thus, a reservoir of biases and bitter memories are widely shared within groups. These can act as a flash point for violent antagonism in times of hardship where ambitious leaders seek to prod their constituencies into violence.

Unlike race as a category of reference and identity, ethnicity, religion, and sexual orientation are less matters of a common gene pool than of shared history, perceptions, and group affiliations. Indeed, some of the strongest and most dangerous ethnic and religious divides run between people of the same stock, whether in Bosnia, Rwanda, Northern Ireland, Somalia, Indonesia, Cyprus, India, Belgium, the former Czechoslovakia, the United States, Canada, or China, among others, where there are telling differences in history on all sides. It would appear that disdain and hatred are by-products of emotional investments in one's own social identities—which follows Machiavelli's sociological formula that when the differences between groups are small, greater impatience is placed on minor distinguishing features, a phenomenon Freud called the "narcissism of minor difference." And it seems that the closer the resemblance between neighboring groups, the greater the emotion they invest in maintaining small differences to the point of violence.

Potent sources of group identity are the collective memories, the *mythemes*, of past glories and traumas, especially when they are passed on to future generations and fire up animosities while also sustaining the group's identity. Jews after World War II coined the poignant phrase "Never Again" as a vivid, resolute reminder to themselves not only of the Holocaust but of a long, tragic oppression reaching back to the ancient biblical Maccabees. For the Serbs, their 1389 defeat at the hands of the Muslims at Kosovo has been rekindled in modern times and remains a bitter memory that simply defies the passage of time and logic. Every Serbian child learns about Kosovo as the beginning of five hundred years of Turkish oppression. Likewise, the Muslims of Bosnia revive for each generation the Serbian massacres of Muslims dating back to the nineteenth century and World War II. These folk memories persist powerfully because they are symbols of allegiance collectively shared.

Ascribing ethnic conflicts to ancient hatreds alone will not explain bias violence. What needs to come into play are the political forces that fan antagonisms between people who may have lived together, however restively, but without exchanging collective acts of violence. Major social and economic dislocations have resulted from ethnic conflicts, as in Rwanda, where a plunge in world coffee prices—a staple crop for the country—proved calamitous for the economy and indirectly contributed to a slaughter of Hutus by Tutsis in 1972. Similarly, the defeat of Germany in World War I and the humiliations of the Treaty of Versailles were factors that precipitated the rise of Nazism in Germany. Leaders who inflame old conflicts and rivalries (Hitler is the perfect example) typically generate visions of revitalizing their people, returning them to their historic glory; and where cultural traditions are rendered impotent and a people loses its psychological bearings, irredentist ideologies become most potent. In the case of Bosnia, the Serbs lived with the painful record of mass slaughter by the Nazis, sometimes with Croat help, and the loss of half their male population. Their modern leaders, who boast of a "Greater Serbia," do so at the expense of other ethnic groups— the Muslims and Croats—and call to mind the Nazi revitalization movement, which promised to restore Germany's heroic past and fulfill it in a Reich, a "Greater Germany" extending into eastern Europe, the Baltic, the Ukraine, and the Balkan states in southeastern Europe. Thus, reservoirs of hostility can turn into active antagonism in hard times, and few groups appear immune from this general trend.

Even within a group, vocal opposition to violence is often held in check or muted by the tendency of people to overestimate the strength and numbers of those committed to hate. Media presentations also play a crucial role in creating the impression that far more antipathy exists than is actually the case. The overestimation of bias works to weaken the resolve of those who might otherwise speak out against prejudice and bias.

Research on this very question of overestimations of ethnic, racial, and religious bias indicates that people perceive far more prejudice than exists, the net effect of which is to induce a reticence among those opposed to discriminatory policies and invectives against the "other." In turn, a silenced opposition to hate prepares the ground for escalations of bias and violence.

In 1961, the Berlin Wall was erected. Contrary to outraged interpretations as to its purposes, the wall did not close off the affluent and opulent West to the yearning, inquisitive eyes of those in the East (or "behind it," depending on your political ideology). Instead, it yoked the destinies of East and West together. The wall became a symbol of the incommensurability of ultimate ends and a perpetual reminder that the struggle between the two sides must be a war to the death. Over time, critics of the cold war articulated what used to be called the doctrine of moral equivalence—the belief that an open society willing to use nuclear weapons had no claim to moral superiority over a closed society willing to use the same kind of weapons. Western critics eagerly suggested that both sides shared the same fundamental political assumptions, meaning that the defense of communism or liberal democracy required in the end the same duplicity, the same willingness to exploit the exploitable, the same blind gamble that one's own side is history's side. The great conundrum for Western critics was that while they detested the selfish consumerism, the idiotic class invidiousness, the remnants of the Western imperialist mind-set, they also knew that a decadent democracy was preferable to a ruthless authoritarian state.

The end of the cold war exposed the ripe corruption of the communist states that had been cultivated by a venal political bureaucracy compromised and then overwhelmed by its conspiratorial partners of parasitic indigenous mafias. The bipolar world of two monolithic, cynical, self-aggrandizing establishments did not go down in a bitter but honorable battle. Instead, it gave way to a new world order that, whatever it is—unipolar, multipolar, or anarchic—has given rise to a whole new set of problems. The fusion of East and West Germany was nimbly achieved ideologically by a few heroic, sentimental speeches about a "new Germany." However, the actual mechanics of rapprochement, assimilation, and social reengineering in terms of jobs, housing, money, transport, infrastructure, social services, health, pensions, and so on has created massive problems. These are being lived out in the midst of a haze of felonious cruelties where the young especially, confused and threatened, have come up swinging with a political strategy whose shadowy existence ever since 1945 has lurked beneath the surface of German politics. According to Harnishmacher and Kelly's essay, the Skinheads and neo-Nazis experienced a resurgence in the streets of Germany whereby young men and women in former East German and West German cities and towns prowl about, marching with rekindled Nazi slogans about foreigners and predators on their lips; these street renegades demand a new *Lebensraum* of a purified Germany whose national essence and coherence will not be weakened and "contaminated" by ethnic and racial minorities. Urban guerrilla war in the name of a German culture of white racial purity is preached in the language of recovery and redemption to the disaffected who fear a life of economic drudgery closing in on them. The rhetoric describes the despised foreigner—Turks, Slavs, and even southern Europeans—as representing the interloper who is poisoning the commonweal.

The two groups, the neo-Nazis and Skinheads, are not always ideologically symmetrical; nor are they always organizationally interchangeable; but both are driven by an angry recall of the past that is racist, bigoted, heroic, triumphalist, and selective. The "Skins" and neo-Nazis reconstruct social history such that it is conveniently sanitized, not tainted with embarrassing recollections of the Holocaust; the latter bestial horror is simply denied as Zionist propaganda. And the carefully edited bravado of the Nazi era is disseminated with much macho overlay that plays to a varied audience, repulsing some, vindicating others, seducing many.

To say only that the Skins and neo-Nazis have a chip on their collective shoulder or that the "new barbarism," if it is that, validates the worst fears of anti-Nazis—fears that German culture is inherently flawed by political fanaticism, nationalist fundamentalism, and general xenophobia—ignores many of the problems Germany faces economically and demographically since the post–World War II recovery. For the Skins, the contrasts between the slum-ridden East and the high-tech West is an anxiety-ridden comparison between a society with one foot on the moon and the other stuck in a sewer.

The despondency of Germans, who are in other respects appalled by the violent tendencies of right-wing and left-wing militants, is deepened, such that hardly a week passes without some report of clashes between police and extremists. Many of these battles take the form of continuing vendettas between groups on the right and on the left. The conventional wisdom has it that the situation will not degenerate into a civil war because of Germany's history, geography, and the character of its national life. But there is widespread disillusionment with conventional politics. Increasingly, many people, not just from the poorer classes, look to the militants and extremists, not necessarily because they have acquired an interest in radical politics, but by way of protest against the status quo. And it is not comforting to be glibly told by mainstream politicians that compared to other countries, the situation is not bad. This is a view of official spokesmen, and it may be correct, as comparisons go, but the extremists do not make comparisons: they rage at what they see coming. And one can encounter in many German cities some shocking contrasts between squalor and opulence. It is this atmosphere of uncertainty and of rapid demographic and economic transformations that threatens to overpower the working classes; that breeds suspicion and distrust; that leads to contention and conflict.

For many emancipated African-Americans living in the aftermath of the Civil War, the grotesque image of night riders masquerading as threatening ghosts of the war had to be a frightful, haunting experience that instilled a fear of an enslaved past. Since the end of the American Civil War, the Ku Klux Klan movements intermittently emerged as national plagues and in reaction to major movements in immigration, war, civil rights, and racial/ethnic politics.

There is a "morphic resonance," it would seem, between the KKK and the German neo-Nazi Skinhead movement, with both dealing in the artificial currency of what Benedict Anderson describes as "imagined communities"—utopian pipe dreams and idealizations of ethnically cleansed communities.[1] The new Klan, closely resembling the Skinheads and neo-Nazis in its methods, targets groups and ideological orientations and deftly exploits a brittle, highly competitive job market in the United States weakened by massive restructurings in the economy; tensions over newcomers from Asia, Africa, and Latin America; and legislative reforms involving gay and feminist political programs.

Consistent with its sordid past, the modern Klan is committed to white supremacy and purveys fear of racial contamination through its loosely linked affiliations with the Christian Identity Movement.[2] The religious philosophy of the Identity Movement includes the beliefs that mythic Aryans are the true descendants of Israel; and that they, true to

Hitler's prophecies of a "master race," have been chosen to dominate the entire world. However, their current ambitions are focused on containing and controlling minority social mobility in the political economy of the United States. Many Klansmen and other white supremacists subscribe to the theological rationales that ministers within the Identity Movement promulgate as biblical truth; in this, the movement is similar to other radical groups prevalent in the Middle East.

In Palestine, Lebanon, and the Gaza Strip, to mention a few regions, there is a revival of terrorist activities—hate crimes—to support religions and political purposes.[3] In India, Sikh terrorists have been attempting to create an independent state;[4] and in Egypt, Al Jihad, an irredentist religious movement, has not hesitated to assassinate infidels and apostate Muslims.[5] As with other "sacred terrorists," Al Jihad believes that their ends and means are sanctioned by divine authority—the interpreting of the Koran—which humans have no right to alter. In Lebanon, Hizballah, "the party of God," consists of Shiite Muslims in Beirut who engage in sporadic battles with Israeli border forces and rival Muslim factions and militias.[6] As with Al Jihad, the declared aim of Hizballah is not only to improve its position as one of Lebanon's constituent communities but to make of Lebanon an ideal Islamic polity and society. In Hizballah's vision, Islam alone will redeem Lebanon from the ravages of civil war, Israeli interventions, and the ways of the despised West.

Israel and the PLO (Palestine Liberation Organization) have been locked in a struggle for rights and autonomy for more than two decades against the complicated background of the intertwined commercial and military relationships between the Arab Islamic world and the West. Ghada Talhami's essay on the homeless Palestinians shows that unlike other peoples who suffered from a colonial experience, the Palestinians do not primarily feel that they have been exploited but that they have been excluded, denied the right to have a history of their own. In the vast Palestinian diaspora, crimes against Palestinians are rarely motivated by economic factors alone; politics fuel the fury against a people who are stateless and stigmatized for being so. Within Israel and its contested contiguous territories, the conflict between the Jewish settler movement (which is inspired by early Zionist ideology) and the local Palestinian population bears an uncanny resemblance to anti-Semitic behavior in Europe and the United States. The Israeli Palestinians face a settler ideology that victimizes them through its mystical concept of 'Amalek. This,

Talhami tells us, refers to an enemy of the tribes of Israel; the term has now been appropriated to describe Palestinians whose destruction is justified through Old Testament invocations.

In 1969, Israeli Prime Minister Golda Meir set the general tone of the turbulent Palestinian/Israeli conflict by denying that the Palestinians existed at all. Compare this to the new anti-Semitism of the neo-Nazis, Skinheads, and Klansmen, which denies that the Holocaust ever occurred.

It took nearly twenty years for the Palestinians to debunk their image as a gang of skulking terrorists and to acquire the status of a dispossessed people trying to survive under a brutal military occupation.[7] What the Palestinians failed to appreciate early on was media power and its impact on opinion. Had they understood how the United States media operates, a good information policy could have emerged that would have effectively countered reporting in the United States that was astonishingly biased in favor of Israel. Until fairly recently, American media imagery of Israelis characterized them as pioneers, democrats, and heroes of a great struggle that commenced in Europe and continues in a different place with new antagonists. These new antagonists are dedicated to the destruction of Israel because they, the Palestinians, are inherently terrorist by nature.[8] In print and on television, the Palestinians are dehumanized, turned into a petroglyph of a frenzied mob determined to kill innocent Jews if for no other reason than the unregenerate desire for it. This image is rendered more cryptic in Europe where journalism is not as "valiant" as the American brand but at least more balanced.[9]

For Palestinians dispersed across Europe, the United States, Middle Eastern nations, and emirates, there are many different experiences that cannot all be assembled into one definitive description and explanation of their collective fate. In Kuwait before the mass expulsions during the Gulf War, Palestinians were a minority of workers, and when the offensive against Iraqi forces began, martial law was enacted causing mass deportations, establishment of internment camps, and an even less enviable status for a scapegoated people with nowhere to go. The 1994 Hebron mosque massacre attests to Palestinians' vulnerability. As victims of crimes, the plight of Palestinians seems more dependent on perdurable political conflicts than religious differences, though the latter often prefigure internal disputes within Palestinian and Israeli groups in the general regional conflict.

A situation where religious differences are primary stimulants of hatred and associated crimes may be found in modern India and Pakistan. Asad ur Rahman's essay begins with the great colonial hyperspace of the British raj as a machine of domination and control that profoundly affected the lives and institutions of the diverse groups making up the populations of the Indian subcontinent. From Rahman's perspective, at the core of hate crime is the symbolic status of the victim in a social setting where religious values are fluid and circulate dynamically among subgroups of believers; religious values are not static pieces of culture or rigid beliefs fiercely clung to by believers who ascribe transcendental qualities to them. The imposition of imperialist values on the rhythms of the religiously, ethnically, racially, and linguistically heterogeneous Indian life yielded a hybrid solidarity that was forged in opposition to colonial rule. This became evident on a worldwide scale in the period of Gandhi's resistance movement. Coalition politics during the time of heightened anticolonialism was carried on by diverse groups of religionists—principally Hindus and Muslims—that produced a powerful repudiation of British rule through its unified sense of purpose best exemplified by the political agendas of the early Congress Party. For reasons not entirely clear, in the postcolonial time, the invidious social differentiation of peoples by religious orientations returned with a vengeance; and since then, political and cultural tensions have been exacerbated. Here, Rahman describes the rearticulations and reconstructions of the symbolic "fictions," Hindu/Muslim and other essences that reemerged enabling individuals to retreat into the anonymity of religious identity and to embrace rhetorics of blame and grievance that ravage various parts of India and Pakistan today. While there is some psychological value in ethnocentrism for those wounded by history, the religious cultures that mold the way of everyday life are, according to Rahman, too intermingled, their contents and histories with one another too interdependent, for their surgical separation into those large, insular ideological entities—Pakistan and India. Indeed, the fundamentalist furor nurtured by separatist religious changes could not remain substantially intact were there a nationalist rapprochement embodying the ideal of communal solidarity and tolerance—an effort, unfortunately, that has so far failed.

Apart from intergroup conflicts that generate hate crimes, another distinctive source of hate crime is the state and its apparatuses of government. The state claims for itself an unconditional security rationale, a rationale whose historic origins are presumed to lay in the institutional structures of government.

With respect to the origins of state power, an influential school of sociological thought, structural functionalism, which derives much of its intellectual energy from the political philosopher Thomas Hobbes, conceived of state coercive power as necessary in maintaining a system of social order within a polity. (Actually, the very notions of "polity," "community," and "state" would be inconceivable in Hobbes's view without the concomitant authority of force and its sanctions.) For sociological theorists, Hobbes's view translates into the legitimation of a law enforcement apparatus and police functions whose goal is order maintenance. Other approaches to the problems of force and coercion in society see law and its implementation as expressions of prevalent power relations, as Antony Simpson puts it in his essay on punishment and hate in eighteenth-century England.

Thus, the grand "autonomy" of the law and its criminal justice ramifications concerning equity and consistency in its application are, at least, modern ideals. And these ideals are often violated or ignored when the apparatuses of the police are misappropriated in the interests of elite or influential segments of society, as happened in Colombia, where a form of hate crime known as *limpieza social,* or social cleansing, occurred. This is not unlike the notorious "ethnic cleansing" policy implemented in Bosnia. According to Suzanne Wilson and Julia Greider-Durango, the dreadful idea was to rid the streets of "disposable" people, including street children—a small, beleaguered world of abandoned children, runaways from pathological families and communities, and those marginalized, stigmatized, and labeled as undesirable by Colombian society. Other victims of social cleansings include prostitutes, homosexuals, the mentally ill, and social outcasts wandering the streets as homeless people. The hate crime logic seems to be that if one is deprived, different, or devalued, one is then expungable.

On a smaller scale, social cleansing is reminiscent of the "purification" program inaugurated by the Nazis during World War II, which was, among other things, a horrendous form of state oppression. Of course, such a comparison, even when implicit, invites skepticism, and while I do not wish to deny Jewish victims of the Holocaust the uniqueness of their experience, there are, from a sociological viewpoint, strong elements of continuity, as well as discontinuity, with smaller-scale versions of genocide where people are killed simply because they exist and inhabit undesirable social statuses that are more often ascriptive rather than selective, voluntary, or achieved. The Nazi Holocaust is the great tragic event of the Jewish people, scarcely comparable with other genocides; however, as Irving Horowitz observes:

> Those who take on exclusive positions [about the special nature of the Holocaust] are engaging in moral bookkeeping in which only those who suffer very large numbers of deaths qualify. Some argue that the six million deaths among European Jews is far greater than the estimated one million deaths among Armenians. However, the number of Armenian deaths as a percentage of their total population (50%) is not much lower than the percentage of Jewish losses (60%). Others contend that too few Ugandans or Biafrans were killed to compare the situation to the Holocaust, yet here, too, tribal deaths in percentage terms rival the European numbers. In certain instances, high death rates (for example, approximately 40% of all Cambodians, or three million out of seven million) are indisputable; then one hears that such deaths were only random and a function of total societal disintegration. Yet it has been firmly established that such violence was targeted against intellectuals, educators, foreign-born, and literate people—in short, the pattern was hardly random; anyone who could potentially disrupt a system of agrarian slave labor flying under the communist banners was singled out and eliminated. Even making the definition of "holocaust" a matter of percentages risks creating a morality based solely on bookkeeping.[10]

The uncomfortable fact is that genocide is the consequence of certain forms of unbridled state power. Though Colombia is not a totalitarian state as Nazi Germany was, the vigilante actions of its paramilitary groups is painfully similar to the "private justice" of the SS and Brown Shirts in the streets of German cities prior to Hitler's assumption of power. Colombia's paramilitary groups operate in an environment where, as in Germany, the middle and working classes seem indifferent to the social outcasts in their midst. One could add to the list of examples Rwanda, Somalia, and Haiti.

RWANDA: A LABORATORY OF HATE

With the outbreak of civil strife in Rwanda, the world stood aghast as the tribal animosities between the Hutu people and the Tutsis intensified into acts of widespread massacre and wanton slaughter. Other countries are not without blame in this cauldron of genocide: France, Egypt, and South Africa had been selling arms in Rwanda since 1990; and before the spring of 1994, the army, composed of Hutu extremists, had been expanding, training, and indoctrinating Hutus against the Tutsis while the United Nations stood by.

When the massacres began in earnest, radio stations promoting the extermination of the entire Tutsi ethnic group were not suppressed by the government. The spreading of anti-Hutu terror across Rwanda created a panic: a quarter million Hutus sought refuge in Tanzania and a half million in Zaire. The anti-Tutsi propaganda produced effects not anticipated—a mass movement of frightened and confused people who were no more than pawns in a vicious political power struggle.

The consequences of the Tutsi actions are simply staggering: In a land that was home to eight million people, between 200,000 and 800,000 have been killed; and between two or three million, most of them Hutus, have fled from their homes out of fear.

Still, the lessons from Northern Ireland, the Chiapas region of Mexico, Somalia, Bosnia, Iraq, and the republics in the former Soviet Union have not been learned. Rwanda's neighbor, Burundi, heavily populated with Hutus and Tutsis, is beginning to unravel as the fear and hatred spreads like a virus. In October 1993, more than fifty thousand people were killed in clashes between the Tutsi-dominated army and the Hutus. The gruesome fate of Rwanda should be a stern lesson for those political forces that recklessly ride ethnic passions to power. In the 1970s, the tiny East African country was a test site for international development strategies because it featured a cooperative government, a good transport network, and a small population, but then it disintegrated into the atrocities of tribal hatred. Likewise, politicians from Belgrade, Armenia, to Kashmir and beyond in the post-*perestroika* dissolution of the Soviet Union had been playing upon simmering ethnic divisions, and as in Bosnia, the results are tragic because international reaction is so timid. Indeed, this poses the question of whether international reaction could be other than diffident.

Simpson's essay goes directly to discussions of state power and its manipulations of hate and violence. For Simpson, an analysis of public spectacles involving crime in eighteenth-century England reveals that punishment served several functions that emphasized the links between the organization of criminal justice and the ruling classes, who monopolized government functions. As a ritual event, punishment mobilized public hate and, at the same time, reinforced the power of the sovereign and his functionaries.

The role of local and national authorities is one dimension of the phenomenon of hate crimes. State-sponsored hate crimes involve perpetrators acting on behalf of the law and state rather than outside it. In this sense, there are distinctions to be made between neo-Nazis, Klansmen, and the SS of the Third Reich. Colombian vigilantes, who operate "informally," cannot be wholly classified as state-sponsored; for they do not represent official agencies; nor are they part of those loosely organized in street gangs, who are presumably more difficult to discipline.

Simpson's analysis of the historical data, together with the observations of Talhami and Wilson and Greider-Durango, suggest that the psychological phenomenon of hate and its social consequences (which the Nazis mobilized and exploited tragically but brilliantly) can constitute one of the various instruments of state policy, albeit a very potent one. Another frightening dimension, which these authors uncover and penetrate, is the prosaic bureaucratic language such practices hide behind. Again, these linguistic deceptions are reminiscent of the muted parlance of Nazi bureaucracies that masked monstrous policies of systemic extermination—the Final Solution. There is no blaze of innuendo or public hectoring against this or that group all the time; rather, the hate talk and polemic is often subtly coded and transmuted as if to relieve the anxieties of the perpetrators from the ugly consequences of their repercussive implications.

Our chief interest is not only with the clever (or not so clever), devious language of "ethnic cleansing" or "social cleansing"; nor does it rest solely on the unleashing of degrading characterizations of undesirables; nor on challenges of a state that would single out some as "fools" or "morally depraved cretins." Our focus is on the sponsorship of expressive dramaturgy or duplicitous language and the shock effects of intimidating practices on the public. In a word, we are concerned in this set of essays with the spectacle of state-orchestrated violence against all oppositional tendencies and with the distancing strategies of reactionaries and fascists. Curiously, the Skinheads and neo-Nazis seem less concerned with the vituperative quality of their rhetoric, perhaps because they believe either of two things: first, that despite appearances and claims of outrage, the state's criminal justice system is sympathetic and therefore protective; and second, that the rawness of their hate messages and acts will dramatically awaken those who are disenchanted and in despair over the apparent betrayal of the state to affect desirable changes. If these rationales have any validity in Germany, the Skinhead neo-Nazi phenomenon may not reflect a crisis of social disconnection with the state and the public after all but a vanguard phenomenon of hardening social attitudes that are neither generous nor charitable.

In most cases, the alienated or state-sponsored hate groups adopt strategies that appear to reconcile their violence with seemingly sincere claims to be representative of values at large in society. And as we see, their arcane abstractions, which depersonalize their victims are, with exceptions, designed to achieve some distance between policy and pain and the flesh-and-blood effects of what they do. The language relieves and protects sympathizers from any tangible link with violence. It is a schizophrenic bargain, which doubtlessly offers some peace of mind for allegiance to evil. Every contented hater has struck such a pact, if only unconsciously.

In Jacobs's essay, the issue of language, of "hate speech," is addressed directly. The discussion by Jacobs of legal frameworks regulating hate speech on university campuses, in the workplace, and in other public domains raises other significant questions about conduct and the status of language in relation to hate crime. For example, is hate speech an action? Further, can offensive verbal conduct be considered a species of discriminatory conduct?

A current concern with hate speech seeks to establish, in part, that discriminatory conduct ought to include verbal conduct as one of its instances.[11] What this demand stakes out is the claim that the importation of rhetorical and philosophical accounts of language into the debate offers a view of speech that enables proponents to make sense of "hate speech." Strict adherents of First Amendment language (one is tempted to say First Amendment absolutists) take the view that unfettered freedom of speech is foundational to other rights and freedoms protected by the Constitution and that this proviso includes all "content-based" utterances as protected speech—even forms of threatening verbal conduct. This is challenged by an emergent perspective on verbal behavior in which the content of speech itself can be understood in terms of the very actions that the speech performs. In other words, racist epithets not only relay a message of racial disdain, but the act of "relaying" (or relating) in the narrative interactional context represents the verbal institutionalization of that very racial degradation and stigmatization. Thus, hate speech is understood not only as communicating an offensive idea or imparting negative personal characterizations but as enacting the very messages being communicated.[12]

Jacobs reviews these arguments concerning hate speech regulation and acknowledges implicitly that language indeed does "act," that it can be a form of injurious conduct but that—and this is an important qualifying exception—it does not directly or causatively "act on" addressees in quite the manner that proponents of hate speech legislation describe.[13]

The rationale for the regulation of hate speech is accomplished in part by conceptualizing utterances as both expressive of ideas and as forms of conduct in themselves: racist speech, in particular, both proclaims the inferiority of the race to whom it is addressed, and, it is argued, effects the subordination of that race through the utterance itself. To the extent that utterances of this sort enjoy First Amendment protection, this fact is construed as meaning that racism enjoys indirectly, but no less effectively, the backing of the state. The failure of the state to intervene is tantamount to an endorsement by the state. The utterance thus has the power to effect the subordination that it either depicts or promotes precisely through its free operation within the public sphere unimpeded by state intervention. By way of this argument, the state permits the injury of its citizens, and Matsuda concludes that the "victim [of hate speech] becomes a stateless person."[14] MacKinnon makes a similar argument concerning pornography and refers to it as a sort of "hate speech" wherein pornography "wounds" precisely because it communicates. Furthermore, pornography enacts a message of subordination that simultaneously proclaims and effects an inequality, in that it institutes the subordinated status of women.[15]

From an ideological standpoint, the works of MacKinnon and Matsuda are quite provocative and more so. Their vocabularies deliberately depart from standard usage and produce effects that subtly reshape our reactions to what first may seem odd formulations. For instance, in MacKinnon's politically loaded idiom (what idiomatic speech isn't?), the phrase "rape in ordinary circumstances" appears not as extraordinary but as a taken-for-granted construction.[16] The questions raised by MacKinnon's analyses of pornography and rape, which she declares to be "hate speech," are questions that go deeply into the network of our beliefs and values. Rape and pornography are surface issues (not superficial issues) that prompt many questions. Her interesting view in connection with hate crime is that she and others construe speech as behavior so that hate speech is a form or species of hate crime. As her essays illustrate, power resides in the vocabulary that permeates a culture or is projected into it so thoroughly that it seems merely descriptive of independent realities.

According to MacKinnon, change is produced not so much by creating an alternative to the pernicious gender dichotomy of male-versus-female thinking. Rather, change occurs when a rhetoric takes hold to such an extent that its elaborative flourish becomes normative and seeps into everyday linguistic practice. More often, change just creeps up on a community as a vocabulary makes its way into its every corner. It is the intellectual force of feminist theory and its slogans ("gender is social," and so on) that makes the impression and also the impossibility of avoiding feminist sensibilities, even if one rejects them. Actually, rejecting and repudiating them is what one cannot do: The man who refuses to substitute "he or she" for "he" is deluded; that he would refuse marks his conduct as different from the "he" that he referred to, without any conscious or deliberate awareness that it was a choice. Feminism "has" him in the sense of making him painfully conscious of his behavior no matter what he does. It is one small but nonetheless significant instance of what is now a cultural revolution in our political and social life. Wherever one turns—in the schools, corporate boardrooms, the family setting, factories, courts, the workplace—the pressure either to embrace a feminist perspective or to resist it, and by resisting it, to verify its power, cannot be avoided.[17]

Jacobs acknowledges the power of symbolically denouncing hate speech but warns about the counterproductive dangers of formalizing opposition to it through legislation. The phenomenon of hate speech is a vexing issue with ramifications and interconnections that bring up the conflicts and tensions of discrimination, racism, homophobia, religious-linked violence, affirmative action policies in businesses, in public and private employment, and in the assignment of admission slots in colleges. Especially on college campuses, hate speech and speech codes arouse the ire of students, administrators, and a bewildered public that must wonder about all the fuss.[18]

Those, like Jacobs, who question the wisdom of legally codifying the means of discouraging and frustrating harmful speech have only to point to the Salmon Rushdie affair. At the international level, the publication of Rushdie's novel *The Satanic Verses* and the stunning prohibitions and denunciations by Islamic clerical authorities—to be precise, Khomeini's "Fatwa"—took the world, especially the West, by surprise. This should not be understood to mean that the entire Islamic world acquiesced, but that its official agencies and spokespeople either blindly rejected or vehemently refused to engage with a book that the enormous majority of people never read.

The Ayatollah's condemnation went a good deal further than mere rejection: Rushdie was condemned to death. Rushdie's main offense was to deal with Islam in English and in fiction prose for a Western audience. Thus, it was the medium Rushdie used to reinterpret the Koran that constituted his crime. In the Muslim world, poetry is the traditional means of censure and criticism, so by casting his revisionary narrative in the form of a novel, which is largely unknown to traditional Islamic literature, Rushdie violated the poetic license granted to critic's of the Islamic establishment. Far from simply misinterpreting the Koran, Rushdie's sin, or hate crime, lies in placing the authority of the Koran within a historical and cultural perspective where it is subject to contestation or at least discussion of its premises and assumptions. It is not so much that the content of the Koran is directly disputed; rather, by revealing other possibilities within the framework of Koranic reading, Rushdie was accused of subverting its authenticity through the very act of cultural translation; he relocates the Koran's purposes and origins by reinscribing it in a novel that portrays post–World War II changes and migrations of peoples in the Islamic world.

The shocking Long Island Railroad massacre of December 7, 1994, attests to our vulnerability in the face of hatred and our predicaments in confronting it. In this instance, the victimizer and perpetrator of the crime had been shaped by a tumultuous personal history as well as social and historical events.

Many mass murderers and serial killers are defined and described in terms of psychopathic theories and personality disorders. In the case of Colin Ferguson, who committed the railway massacre, his acts of homicide may not be just a product of internal psychological forces but reflect a complex confluence of social and cultural realities that shaped his personality and temperament. Robert Kelly's essay examines the possibilities, meanings, and ramifications of *exile*—of being marginally detached, deprived, and isolated—and asks questions that complement the standard one of why it happened. Why, we might ask, don't such murderous acts occur more often? To what extent do modern conditions of immigration, race relations, and interethnic accommodations promote invidious distinctions and stresses that increasingly express themselves in hate crimes and acts of homicidal terror? If these questions are at the heart of our predicament, they are also at the heart of the solution.

DEFINING HATE CRIME

The essays reflect the scope of the hate crime phenomenon across national boundaries and historical periods. In the absence of detailed descriptive and analytical materials, it is doubtful that progress can be made scientifically in understanding the phenomenon or in developing techniques and responses to curtail and control it through law and law enforcement methodologies. However, it must be said that the purpose of control, which implies predictability and clear definitions, a prerequisite for empirical research, may be nothing less than wishful thinking given all the imponderables. The phrase itself, "hate crime," may be booby-trapped in that the very act of using the term constitutes tacit agreement about a whole range of motives that may not in fact stimulate offenders. Just using the term—a neutral enough designation in a criminal justice system where all agree about the defining properties of hate crimes—actually positions one in a vague area. In the arena of hate crimes, discerning the cluster of motives and sorting them out to determine the proximate causes of a crime are quite difficult and can result in baneful consequences.

In conceptualizing the problem of how to decide whether a hate crime has been committed, the qualifier *hate* conveys a particular sense about motivation—that behind a crime is an aversion for the victim or an attraction to a potential crime victim, precisely because of his or her perceived individual or social attributes. Street children can be destroyed not because of any particular dislike for them but because middle-class segments of society are appalled at their presence. Here an offender's motive for violence and murder may result from the tacit approval of an audience of "respectable" citizens. Attacking Jews, blacks, homosexuals, and politically proscribed groups may be driven by the key consideration that these people cannot defend themselves and are therefore vulnerable. Motives may be further complicated by offender ideas that include audience approval and the ratification of complex emotional needs quite apart from practical considerations, including whether potential victims are likely to be affluent.

Consequently, we have not tried to impose any conveniently coherent meaning and definition of hate crime on the contributors because the concept is fluid, internally conflicted, and overpowering. Every time it is used at this stage of its scientific and juridical status, we are under obligation to remember and rehearse the caveats about the concept's meanings and limitations. The phenomenon of hate crimes is not something that can be settled once and for all and then used and straightforwardly applied with a clear conscience. The concept has to come at the end, not at the beginning, of our discussions of it. Those are the conditions—the only ones we think that prevent the mischief of premature clarification—under which the term can productively continue to be used.

NOTES

1. Benedict Anderson (1983), *Imagined Communities: Reflections on the Origin and Spread of Nationalism* (London: New Left).

2. Allen Sapp, Richard N. Holden, and Michael E. Wiggins (1993), "Value and Belief Systems of Right Wing Extremists: Rationale and Motive for Bias-Motivated Crimes," in *Bias Crime: American Law Enforcement and Legal Responses,* 2d rev. ed., ed. Robert J. Kelly (Chicago: Office of International Criminal Justice, Univ. of Illinois at Chicago), 112–39.

3. David C. Rapaport (1990), "Sacred Terror: A Contemporary Example from Islam," in *Origins of Terrorism: Psychologies, Ideologies, Theologies, States of Mind,* ed. Walter Reich (New York: Cambridge Univ. Press), 151–79.

4. Mark Jurgensmeyer (1987), "The Logic of Religious Violence," *Journal of Strategic Studies* 10(4): 64–78.

5. Johannes G. Jansen (1986), *The Neglected Duty: The Creed of Sadat's Assassins and Islamic Resurgence in the Middle East* (New York: Macmillan).

6. Martin Kramer (1990), "The Moral Logic of Hizballah," in *Origins of Terrorism,* ed. Walter Reich, 123–46.

7. Edward Said (1994), *The Politics of Dispossession: The Struggle for Palestinian Self-Determination* (New York: Pantheon Books).

8. Noam Chomsky (1983), *The Fateful Triangle: Israel, the United States and the Palestinians* (London: Pluto), 3–6.

9. Robert Rieber and Robert J. Kelly (1991), "Substance and Shadow: Images of the Enemy," in *The Psychology of War and Peace,* ed. Robert Rieber (New York: Plenum Publishers), 92–119.

10. Irving Louis Horowitz (1993), *The Decomposition of Sociology* (New York: Oxford Univ. Press), 213.

11. Catherine MacKinnon (1993), *Only Words* (Cambridge: Harvard Univ. Press). In this connection, she writes that "group defamation is the verbal form inequity takes" (99).

12. First Amendment jurisprudence has always allowed that some speech is not protected and has included in that category libel, threats, and fraudulent advertising. Matsuda writes that "there is much speech that is close to action. Conspiratorial speech, inciting to riot speech, fraudulent speech, obscene phone calls, and defamatory speech" (Mari Matsuda et al. [1993], *Words That Wound: Critical Theory* [Madison: Univ. of Wisconsin Press], 32).

13. Matsuda and others employ powerful metaphors to explain how such words can be said to wound. Whereas the argument is that words can effect injuries that are not the same as physical injuries, the metaphors through which that injury is communicated tend to draw from scenes of physical injury, thus calling into question the distinction between physical and psychic harm. It may be that the kind of injury produced through language requires such a mixing of metaphors, but then it would be important to underscore the relation between psychic and somatic senses of injury conveyed through language. Matsuda (1993) refers to words that "hit the gut," "strike a blow," and "paralyze" (26–29).

14. Matsuda et al. (1993), 25.

15. "Whatever damage is done through such words is done not only through their context but through their content in the sense that if they did not contain what they contain, and convey the meanings and thoughts that they convey, they would not evidence or actualize the discrimination that they do" (MacKinnon [1993], 14); or, "cross burning is nothing but an act, yet it is pure expression, doing the harm it does solely through the message it conveys" (33).

16. Catherine MacKinnon (1983), "Feminism, Marxism, Method and the State: Towards Feminist Jurisprudence," *Signs* 8(4): 646.

17. Robert J. Kelly (1993), "The Rhetorical and Analytical Inventions of Self and Identity: Transformative Language and Stylistics in Feminist Ideology" (paper presented at the Centre National de la Recherche Scientifique Institut de Recherche sur les Societes Contemporaines, Paris, France, May 12).

18. Most people find the imposition and implementation of speech codes inherently offensive and more reprehensible if they seem unfair. The logic of speech codes presumably requires the disciplining of those who speak scornfully of whites, males, and even Nazis as well as the disciplining of those who ridicule blacks, women, and gays; for, after all, if the rule is that one should not discriminate, are not all acts of discrimination equal? No, actually. That is because (although lawyers will disagree) discrimination is not a problem in logic but in historical fact, which is the point of law professor Grey's argument in writing Stanford's speech code (which has been rejected by the courts). It sounds pretentious because its presentation fails to indicate that the code is flexible and could change over time. According to Grey, insults directed at traditionally persecuted or disadvantaged groups "draw their capacity to impose the characteristic civil rights injury to 'hearts and minds' from the fact that they turn the whole socially and historically incubated weight of . . . prejudices upon their victim. It is be-

cause, given our cultural history, no such general prejudices strike against the dominant groups that there exist no comparable terms of universally understood hatred and contempt applicable to whites, males, and heterosexuals as such" (Thomas Grey [1991], "Civil Rights vs. Civil Liberties: The Case of Discriminatory Verbal Harassment," *Social Philosophy and Policy* 8[2]: 81–107). To put it bluntly, the fact is that being called a "honkey" is not the same as being called a "nigger"; the epithets hurled at whites and heterosexuals do not have the same capacity to inflict psychological and material harm as insults hurled at blacks and gays.

1. Black Rage, Murder, Racism, and Madness: The Metamorphosis of Colin Ferguson

Robert J. Kelly

O n ninety-three counts of the indictment, the jury found Colin Ferguson guilty of mass murder and assault. Ferguson shot to death six and wounded nineteen people on a rush-hour commuter railroad traveling from New York City to an affluent, largely white suburb on Long Island. This case is particularly interesting and relevant to the discussion about hate crimes because it raises issues that transcend the neat categories of psychiatric and sociocriminological analysis. Was Ferguson just a terribly sick and deranged man who happened to be black (the label "African-American" does not apply to him)? Or did the racism he experienced, real or imagined—or some complex mix of fantasy and concrete experiences—precipitate his mad, indiscriminate violence?

Court-appointed psychiatrists found him legally sane. However, another psychiatrist, with no official connection to the trial, also examined the defendant at the request of the attorneys before the defendant dismissed them. Dr. Richard Dudley was a former commissioner in the New York City Department of Mental Health, and he had previously examined and counseled the survivors and families of the Howard Beach racial attack. His report on Ferguson was subsequently sealed by the Nassau County judge. Dr. Dudley, himself black, has written extensively on the relationship between a patient's psychiatric problems and his or her culture, so the details of his examination would doubtlessly provide invaluable information on Ferguson's turbulent life where the American dream had gone awry.

We can think of the Long Island Railroad murders as a species of hate crime where the offender is literally driven to acts of indiscriminate violence because, we may suppose, of entanglements and cultural conflicts on a personal level. Or Ferguson may have been driven to violence because he was somehow molded into hatred through relentless exposure to a xenophobic milieu saturated with negative stereotypes of racial, ethnic, religious, and sexually different "others." Hysterical impulses and abhorrent beliefs about blacks, women, gays, lesbians, and immigrants do not in themselves mitigate the outrage of the acts, nor is there much comfort for the survivors and suffering families of victims to learn that the perpetrator was provoked into rage and violence by racial torment. From the standpoint of the law, however, the monstrous event and anguish of the victims is actually marginal. In cases of homicide, motives that derive from bias and fear do not add more harm to the victim—only grief for the family and fear in the community. When the enormity of the crime is considered, the scope of additional harm caused by offender prejudice would seem relatively small; conversely, for less-serious crimes, the significance of bias might be greater.[1]

Considering Ferguson's statements during the court proceedings, documents presented by the prosecutor, and the defendant's own ramblings with the media—on the face of this evidence, it would seem that Ferguson was afflicted by a delusional disorder of the persecutory type.[2] The central theme of this behavioral syndrome involves the belief that the individual is the object and target of a conspiracy. The symptomology is complex, involving a sense of encounters and interactions with others that are filled with suspicions: There are the persistent and chronic anxieties of being spied on, followed by others, poisoned, drugged, maliciously maligned, harassed, and frustrated in pursuing goals. Small, incidental episodes are often exaggerated out of all proportion to their significance. The deterioration of rational judgment may deepen and trigger an obsessional preoccupation with redressing grievances and humiliations such that the delusional system turns on some perceived injustice that must be remedied by legal action. Should that fail, resentment and anger may mount, and violence occurs.

However a paranoid schizophrenic is not necessarily incoherent: the often tight, logical structure of the well-organized paranoid is a marvel to behold. Domarus delineated the logical structure of delusions, a logic he names "paleologic." In it, the natural syllogistic reasoning is topsy-turvy with a conclusion in search of evidence driven by an anguished quest for meaning by internal torments.[3]

In their clinical work with black patients, the psychiatrists Grier and Cobbs offer this disturbing observation: "Black people to a degree that approaches paranoia, must be ever alert to danger from their white fellow citizens. It is a cultural phenomenon peculiar to black Americans. And it is a posture so close to paranoid thinking that the mental disorder into which black people most frequently fall is paranoid psychosis. Can we say that white men have driven black men mad?"[4]

Ferguson's lawyers, William Kunstler and Ronald Kuby—whom he subsequently fired—intended to mount what they called a "black rage defense." The case was to be based on the Dudley psychiatric examination and the theory of black rage developed by Grier and Cobbs whereby their client would be characterized as a victim, driven insane by pervasive white racism, which culminated in violent acts of revenge.

The jury may have been open to the idea that Ferguson's revenge fantasies were aided and abetted by the mass media. In this respect, the acting out on the commuter train was a reenactment of a slasher film in which Ferguson is the star. His sense of persecution may have been eased by turning his victims into victimizers. In an interior drama with himself, Ferguson is both the victim and the hero-aggressor—powerless, but at the same time domineering, while battered by forces deeply embedded in the culture that are beyond his control. It is uncanny that the same rationale was explored by O. J. Simpson; he planned to represent himself as a victim of spousal abuse, even though he was charged with being the aggressor, the murderer.

In the railroad massacre case, the lawyers wanted to argue at trial that Colin Ferguson saw his oppressors in the faces of those weary, home-bound commuters he was accused of trapping and, with bursts of gunfire, inflicting death sentences on. Though the courtroom was haunted by the victims and the images of their ghastly death scenes, and though the black rage defense would have repulsed them, the jurors might not have found it so difficult to accept that a deeply disturbed individual could act in that frenzied way. But consistent with his personality disorder, Ferguson became distrustful of his white attorneys and refused to admit to the crime; rather, he claimed, incredulously, the real assassin was a "Caucasian" still at large. Throughout the trial, Ferguson declared in languid tones that he intended to vindicate himself.

Ferguson's legal ineptitude constantly got him into procedural troubles with the judge and also provoked public demands that the judge put an end to the trial. However, Ferguson's cross-examination of his own victims became an unprecedented event in American courtroom history and showed, if any demonstration was needed, just how ill this man was.

One witness in particular seemed to unnerve Ferguson and shake him momentarily loose from the grip of his delusions. During the cross-examination, Ferguson tried to confound the witness, who claimed in her deposition and trial testimony that she had closed her eyes and played dead. Ferguson asked how the witness could identify the shooter if her eyes were closed. (The repartee occurred within the contextual artifice of the court. Ferguson's roles as perpetrator on trial and defense attorney seeking to elicit evidence are thus confusingly collapsed, shielding him in a cloak of invisibility.) Ferguson's ploy did not work. The witness responded firmly and convincingly that her playing dead was a deception designed to save her life: having seen Ferguson shoot another person in the back of the head at point-blank range, and having herself been shot, there was nothing left to do after Ferguson and she, in the seconds that flashed by in the shooting scene, had locked eyes and the gun was leveled at her. Ferguson's parodic playing at lawyer was fully exposed. Thereafter, Ferguson lost his composure and stumbled over his words. His identification as the shooter was firm and incontestable.

Of course, Ferguson later described these accusations and the entire trial as an absurd, tawdry affair. The infrangible chaos of his mental regime and occluded emotional processes in his delusional world could not be made more plain than in the circumstances surrounding his interviews with the two court-appointed psychiatrists who had to determine his fitness to stand trial. Both reported that he was purposefully maligning to create an impression that he was not competent. What the white psychiatrists saw as egregious behavior was from Ferguson's standpoint simply his refusal to cooperate with them. By declaring him sane—which was not the finding of the black psychiatrist knowledgeable about Jamaican culture and customs—the court endorsed the public outrage about this "animal" (a term freely applied to Ferguson) who preyed on hapless victims on the crowded train.

Because Ferguson was declared sane, his attorneys were prevented from pleading him insane. In any case, an insanity plea might have led to

Ferguson being declared "cured" in a couple of years and that would only prolong and deepen the agonies of the survivors and victims' families and exacerbate racial tensions. Thus, the psychiatric decisions endorsed by the court were, to put it blandly, strategically expedient. To preserve the appearance of legality, the judge ruled that not only was Ferguson competent to answer the charges but that he could fire his attorneys—who had insisted all along that he was mentally ill and did not have control over his actions when he embarked on his murderous rampage.

The court, the prosecutors, and county officials were then faced with that terrible conundrum that polarized, racially brittle communities must always confront sooner or later: how to deal fairly with those it has brutalized and relegated to invisible status. Ferguson's actions and the reactions to it are emblematic of the racial problem—a cynosure of the brutal, sharpening distinctions between white and black. While the black community looked on, the spectacle unfolded. Those watching must have had the feeling that the tragic events and the pathetic individual tyrannized by his own emotional turbulence and fragmented thinking could not and would not be treated for what he was: a demented man trapped in his own furies, incapable of distinguishing right from wrong, who is dangerous and in need of confinement and treatment.

Throughout the country, white mass murderers are understood soberly, not sympathetically, and while their crimes are certainly not acceptable, they are handled within the parameters of the law regarding insanity. Surely had Ferguson been white, the tribulations would have been as heartrending and emotionally disastrous. Yet the other factor—the ultimate fear of angry blacks attacking whites—would have been absent. This would have prevented a legal proceeding from becoming a circus engulfed in ridicule and disingenuousness.

Colin Ferguson belongs to two marginalized communities: He is black; and he is a West Indian immigrant—which shapes his personality and may have magnified his delusional paranoia. Understanding these cultural facts is one of the challenges in understanding him. Ferguson's cultural and racial roots figure significantly in his reactions to the trial, in the media frenzy that overwhelmed it, and in the social dilemmas that confront West Indians and other black immigrants in the United States today.

News accounts and court records show that Ferguson was born in Kingston, Jamaica, into a middle-class family. His father was a pharmacist and well-known proprietor in a Kingston suburb some distance from the dreariness, squalor, and crime of the slums. Colin Ferguson attended a good high school in Jamaica, which functioned for most as a stepping stone to the University of the West Indies and a decent position in a profession, the higher civil service, or in teaching—the normal pathways available to the middle-class.

Ferguson's family life was gratifying and not one that left emotional deficits in the young man. However, the death of his father in a traffic accident in 1984 and the death of his mother some years later from cancer when he was already living in the United States seem to have taken their psychological toll. Other than these base facts, little is known about relatives, except that they are deeply embarrassed by the notoriety; Ferguson's brothers are understandably reluctant to come forward to refute much of the widely speculative media portrayals of his life and relationships with others. In short, the available evidence suggests nothing unusual or troubled about Ferguson's childhood.

His journey into madness began with a vacation trip to New York in the 1970s, which, at the time, made few impressions on the young man. Yet later, an economic crisis consumed Jamaica as a result of the 1973 Arab oil embargo; it produced a recession where living standards deteriorated drastically. The waves of political crises following in the aftermath of the economic downturn persuaded many middle-class Jamaicans like Ferguson that a lifestyle with prospects of mobility for the intelligent, industrious, and diligent could no longer be guaranteed. Faced with the possibilities of periodic economic collapse and social stagnation many Jamaicans—rich, poor, and middle-class—fled for Britain or the United States. At this point, the psychological discussion of the erosion of Ferguson's sanity ends and analysis of the social worlds in which he lived and moved begins.[5]

TWO IDENTITIES AND THE DOUBLE BIND

As with many West Indian immigrants, Ferguson was unaccustomed with the racism and the norms of racial etiquette in North America. And as he soon discovered, the menace of race became a serpent in the garden of his dreams, not easy to ignore or repudiate. The "Land of the Free" must have seemed like a monumentally self-serving fable to him after he arrived in the United States in 1982. Imagine someone who has digested the American ideology that the world lies open to them; who believes that the Horatio Alger myth is true, that the individual can invent him- or herself and reach fantastic goals through hard work. Imagine having accepted all that and then realizing that these hopes are mawkish, hollow, cruel, and deceptive. Ferguson's West Indian cultural orientation collided head-on with the realities of race in America, and together these "minor" episodes and incidents had a corrosive effect on his mental stability.

The great tragedy is that upon his arrival in the United States, Ferguson may have acted solely on the moral assumptions and values he had inherited from the community that produced him; contrast this with the reality that native-born African-Americans come to understand and cope with—that America is plagued by skin color. Though this is shocking and disaffecting for people born into it, to find oneself as an adult despised because of color must be contemptible. For someone whose sensibilities, as a matter of acculturation, do not countenance a hierarchy of status based on color, the tensions are bound to be unspeakably dangerous.

The great Caribbean scholar, historian, and radical political activist, C. L. R. James has argued that West Indians do not suffer from any form of angst; they have no deep-seated consciousness of failure, no fear of defeat. That is not their history.[6] The psychological obstacle of white America that African-Americans confront is not shared by West Indians, at least not initially. The claim may be exaggerated, but it retains a residue of validity about West Indian attitudes toward race and race relations in the United States that are sundered by separatism and segregation. Philip Kasinitz notes in his study of Caribbean blacks that the Pullman Company, a major railroad transportation company in the pre–World War II period would not hire West Indians because of their feisty attitudes and refusal to accept insults from passengers.[7]

From the events and the documents, it is clear that Ferguson could not handle this racial dance of sensibilities, especially when the cleavages of "us" and "them"—characteristic of the subterranean segregation behind the surface of things—traumatized him. His natural, culturally nurtured assertiveness constantly got him into trouble, and that confident boldness, sharpened by perceived insults and rejections, appears to have segued too easily into aggressiveness and finally into violence.

Ferguson's story begins in 1982, when he arrives in Los Angeles, California, into that raucous ethnic stew of whites, African-Americans, Latinos, and Asians. He takes a modest job in a liquor store and embarks on his cultural transformation by consciously changing the accents and speed of his speech, by trying to get along and not complaining. Over time, the racial tensions became palpable, and embittered by his experiences and frustrated when his hopes are stymied, he moves to New York City in 1985 into an even more racially embattled community. (In the mid-eighties, New York City was wracked by civil rights protests and marches organized around the issue of racial violence committed by police officers.)

Ferguson finds a job, still determined to make it on his own. While working in a paint store, he meets a woman and marries in 1986, and about the same time, he enrolls in Nassau Community College, a suburban school in Nassau County that lies east of New York City. School would be the stepping stone up the ladder of success. Still optimistic, Ferguson takes a bank teller's job, but neither this nor two other jobs in banks worked out.

According to newspaper accounts, the chronology gets blurry at this point. In 1987, his marriage fails, and with the breakup, he seems to have lost his moral compass and whatever psychological stability he possessed. His sense of the country—of Los Angeles and New York—had to be that of an outcast or at least a menaced interloper; his frustrations apparently affected his health. Yet he could not or would not face the humiliation of a return to Jamaica as a casualty, another defeated black immigrant shipwrecked in the states.

The marriage failure, the inability to hold a job, and the contentious experiences in school may have culminated in the flash point, the emotional catalyst deep in his psyche where Ferguson surrendered to the erupting passions for vengeance that had remained until then somehow masked and constrained. Those who knew him before 1994 say he was angry and beleaguered—but not terrifying. Ferguson doubtlessly thought of himself as in the process of "becoming" an American black man. Imprisoned by the delusion of his power, Ferguson is reminiscent of another West Indian, Marcus Garvey, who shared the dream of the Horatio Alger fable and clung to this fantasy even when he was hounded out of the country. Interviews with employers and with professors after Ferguson had been expelled from Adelphi University suggest that his anger was mixed with depression.

His story continues: Fearing ridicule, Ferguson becomes reclusive and survives by doing odd jobs in the West Indian section of East Flatbush in Brooklyn. In 1993, he returns to California to start again—in spite of the heartache and recriminations—at the Los Angeles liquor store where he got started. And it is at this time that Ferguson legally purchases a gun because liquor stores were so frequently robbed and clerks killed or injured. Back to New York after three months, Ferguson returns with the gun, and on December 7, 1994, boards the Long Island Railroad train.

The imagination is poorly equipped to accommodate what happened, but one can recognize the release of hatred. Beneath the microscope of police and prosecutors' investigations and the publicity given to the slaughter and the trial, all of it coalesces into an unforgivable violation spurred on by unmitigated anger and hatred.

WHITE RAGE

In retrospect, the collective sanity of whites depended upon Ferguson's mental competence even if that was a repellent charade. And what of the psychiatrists who declared him sane? Did they sense the blood lust in the community and act defensively seeking to appease the mob? The black rage defense, which would have cast Ferguson in the role of a modern-day Nat Turner, offered a plausible "double victimization" defense where the defendant himself is a victim of racism rather than just a racist murderer. But the court and the outraged community chose to see him as a wild man whose madness had no plausible context, and he unwittingly cooperated, preferring the role of the manqué Perry Mason—which was simply preposterous and disgraceful. Perhaps we shall never know why Ferguson remained obdurate, ignoring the advice of experienced attorneys, and instead chose to mount a spectacle where he made a fool of himself; perhaps this incapacity at self-appraisal is integral to his illness and denuded him of any self insight.

Attempting to understand what happened and why is difficult, but in trying to make some sense of it, the evidence and information available suggest that Ferguson was paranoid and delusional and that his murderous violence was indeed an irrational act. At the risk of speculating too ambitiously, I want to propose that the facts of Ferguson's life have significant sociological and psychological relevance in coming to terms with this tragedy.

STRANGER IN THE VILLAGE

Much of the evidence and chronological data about Ferguson are ambiguous, but notwithstanding the artificial precisions of the psychiatric nosological descriptions, the picture that emerges is of a man who craved success and whose temperament cast him alternately into moods of unflinching self-confidence and despair, causing both himself and those around him pain and chronic distress. One naturally wonders about the source and causes of his psychic warping. That may remain a permanent mystery that can only emerge from a thorough investigation of his early life and its contingencies. His employer in California talked about Ferguson's disdainful attitudes toward African-Americans, his use of the redolent stereotype of "Sambo"; the complaints and remarks about the laziness and fatalism of African-Americans, which were the operative metaphors of immature adolescents that Ferguson stumbled across growing up in Jamaica. The reconciliation would come later, when he could not remain untouched by the stigma of race, even with ethnic credentials that officially defined him as an immigrant.

The United States turned out to be an inhospitable environment. Typically, blacks from the West Indies who arrive with no personal social or political quarrels with the United States, who have been formed by the island culture or village community, and who bring their mercantile reputation with them, are likely to fare better than many African-Americans—at least for a brief and melancholy season, as Ferguson soon discovered. Ordinarily, the black immigrant does not initially question the country's different customs, considering that these have nothing to do with him. As Ferguson did when he arrived, the immigrant sticks to his kith and kin, works diligently, and educates himself, proving that the Yankee Puritan virtues are all that one needs to prosper in this brave new world.

At most, the euphoria lasts a generation and then one moves from the tenement closer to the madhouse or the grave. Ferguson did not indulge openly in the distasteful, patronizing airs of those who arrive and assure African-Americans that they, the West Indians, have never been slaves, that they can run their businesses profitably, save their money, and get ahead. Usually, the experience of being hurled into the fire ends up in bankruptcies and shattered dreams. For Ferguson, the business of racial tension was a real, palpable presence that caught him off guard. No doubt it frightened him and could not be confronted nakedly, so he launched reclamation projects to restore himself after the upheavals of lousy jobs, problems in school, and a stormy marriage. Interestingly, these plans did not include a return to Jamaica—his moral reference point;

perhaps that would have meant humiliation. In any case, whatever the status of his inner resources, material success was at the center of his identity, and because it was frustrated by losses, thwarted by professors and bureaucrats, the compulsion to succeed became so irresistible that it was transformed into a mania from which he could not escape; it became the impetus for breaking the boundaries of civility, right and wrong, life and death.

Another perspective, an extremely audacious one to be sure, elaborated in another context is that of Frantz Fanon and may have some usefulness here as a theoretical supplement and gloss. It treats violence as a "cleansing force," with therapeutic value for those who embrace it.[8] Fanon does not celebrate violence per se as the chief instrument for the resolution of conflicts or as a solution to the terror and betrayal the native experiences at the hands of his colonial oppressors. For Fanon, violence is the method by which the native overcomes the division between whites and natives; it enables the native to overcome his cognitive and emotional fragmentation by a desperate act of sheer will. The violence is actually a counter-response to the wholesale violence of the colonial regime, wherein a balance is achieved in a kind of extraordinary reciprocal homogeneity. The colonial settler makes even the dreams of liberty impossible for the native, and the native's task in this constricted, hostile environment is to imagine all possible methods for destroying the settler. The colonial theory of the absolute evil of the native produces in turn the native theory of the absolute evil of the colonizer. The antagonism thus engendered, if any probative evidence were needed, leads to a further, lethal conclusion.

Fanon puts this psychological emergence in biological imagery, and what happens is that the oppressed understand that their masters cannot give them freedom or equality—or in the imperialist context—independence; it must be taken, forced to yield by protracted struggle. Fanon calls this stage of resolute understanding the "alterity of rupture, of conflict, of battle."[9] I do not mean to use Fanon's work in a minatory way but as a dynamic psychological paradigm—informed by the categories of race, oppression, history, and the space of cultural realities—that helps us to understand how an individual might come to see violence as a means of imposing fear and anguish and, by externalizing his or her anger, relieve internal stress. Through his murderous acts, Ferguson may have reshaped himself psychologically, and through the tortuous logic of his own mind, somehow have vindicated himself.

Surely, it is one of the saddest moments to have witnessed the media coverage of the murders, the trial, and the publicity. One wonders what the black community makes of all of this, if anything. The violence on the train is one thing, but what of the trial with the accused, now the accursed, fumbling and confused? Is this another example of the white community's treachery and impudence? For black and white men and women, the high-minded platitudes about constitutional rights that allowed this inept and dangerous man to defend himself must seem hypocritical. It would be pretense to suppose that a neat, sociopsychological picture of the history of Ferguson's descent into madness can be constructed with biographical denouements, climaxes, and turning points in his life—that, in effect, an "archaeology" of the individual is possible and useful. None of that seems realistic. What we do know is that he isolated himself and believed in the possibilities for renewal drawn from his own autonomous and somewhat peevish self.

BORDERS AND BORDERLINES:
INSCRIBING IDENTITIES AND DESIGNATIONS

Much has been written about the demographic impact of expatriates, refugees, migrants, and minorities within the West and its great metropolitan centers. We are in the midst of new societies being formed in North America, Western Europe, parts of Latin America, and Southwest Asia, characterized by mass migrations and new interethnic and interracial relations. As a result, new hybrid and transitional identities are emerging. The bankrupt notion of the "melting pot" has been replaced by processes more germane to the times; most of the ingredients do melt, do acculturate over time, but some stubborn chunks are condemned merely to float. Thus, in the case of some newcomers, they do not assimilate totally but exist in the margins, between the needs of the host society and the deep culturally inscribed past of their origins. One might imagine countries such as the United States and increasingly vast settler communities in other parts of the world eventuating in the "minoritization" of the national society, filling it with people possessing diasporic identities and giving rise to fundamentalist psychologies on either side of the psychocultural abyss of separation and differentness.

For Ferguson, what began as a journey into success degenerated into an exile but not like that which the European ethnics in the great transatlantic migration experienced: modern migrant status no longer means being hopelessly separated from your place of origin. Would that surgically clean separation have been the case, then at least Ferguson would have the consolation of knowing that what he left behind was, in a sense, no longer thinkable or recoverable. The fact is that for many modern migrants, adjustments and accommodations are more difficult; they confer an exilic status in many instances. The difficulty consists not simply in being forced by one's own needs and desires to live away from home, but rather, given today's world, in living with the many reminders of who you are and what you are, that your home is, in fact, not so far away, and that the normal traffic of everyday contemporary life keeps you in constant but tantalizing and unfulfilled touch with the old place. The immigrant/exile therefore exists in a median state, neither completely at one with the new setting nor fully disencumbered of the old, beset with half-involvements and half-detachments, nostalgic and sentimental at one level, but causing anger or rejection on another. Being skilled at survival when one is doubly marginal by culture and race becomes imperative when the danger of rejection and hostility is always present.

Ferguson was never fully adjusted; he always seemed outside the familiar world inhabited by natives, tending to avoid and even dislike the trappings of the African-American cultural ethos. We see his restlessness, the movement back and forth from coast to coast, the attempts at school, at marriage, and home life all overwhelmed, confounded increasingly by the tense realities of race. Because of the exile, Ferguson saw things both in terms of what had been left behind and what was actually here and now; there existed a double perspective that never saw things in isolation.

For immigrants, every scene or situation in the new country necessarily draws on its counterpart in the old country—however ignominious and distasteful those experiences might have been. Events, persons, experiences are always counterpoised with one another, thereby making them both appear in a sometimes new and unpredictable light: from that juxtaposition one may get a better, perhaps even more universal idea of how to think about things, or the experience can be emotionally quaking, widening a deep psychic fracture that is not easily healed. In any case, once a person leaves home, life in the new world cannot simply be taken up. It is fraught with awkwardness, regrets as well as elations and satisfactions, envy and befuddlement.

For Colin Ferguson, being black and migrant and doubtlessly psychologically wounded, his experiences became deprivations—not new found freedoms, fulfillments, and liberations but barriers and constraints that ended in tragedy.

NOTES

1. Robert J. Kelly, ed. (1993), *Bias Crime: American Law Enforcement and Legal Responses*, 2d rev. ed. (Chicago: Office of International Criminal Justice, Univ. of Illinois at Chicago), 189–96.

2. *Diagnostic and Statistical Manual of Mental Disorders* (1994), 4th ed. (Washington, D.C.: American Psychiatric Association), 297–302.

3. E. von Domarus (1944), "The Specific Laws of Logic in Schizophrenia," in *Language and Thought in Schizophrenia: Collected Papers*, ed. J. S. Kasanin (Berkeley: Univ. of California Press), 303–9.

4. William H. Grier and Price M. Cobbs (1992), *Black Rage* (1968; reprint, New York: Basic Books), 178.

5. A vast literature on legal and psychiatric conceptions of insanity has emerged since the publication of Szasz's celebrated and rather contentious essay, "The Myth of Mental Illness"; see his *Law, Liberty and Psychiatry* (1963, New York: Macmillan), 131–59. Useful discussions of the history, evolution, and applications of the insanity defense may be found in Richard Moran (1981), *Knowing Right from Wrong: The Insanity Defense of Daniel McNaughton* (New York: Free Press), 171–92; Thomas Maeder (1985), *Crime and Madness: The Origins and Evolution of the Insanity Defense*, (New York: Harper & Row), 18–46; and Abraham S. Goldstein (1983), "Insanity," in *Encyclopedia of Crime and Justice*, vol. 2, ed. Sandford H. Kadish (New York: Free Press).

6. C. L. R. James (1985), *A History of Negro Revolt* (1938; reprint, London: Race Today Publications); C. L. R. James (1963), *The Black Jacobins: Toussaint L'Overture and the San Domingo Revolution* (1938; reprint, New York: Vintage Books). James's work is composed in a politically liberationist vein filled with important sociological agendas—namely, to detect through events the intertwining of social patterns, protagonists, and antagonists in the eighteenth-century black Caribbean insurrections that drew their energies and power from a native (or colonial) reality ignored or betrayed by Europe. The study of revolt, along with his *The Black Jacobins*, also published in 1938, is remarkably prescient: James forecasted an unbroken history of agonized and still profoundly unsettled Caribbean life. The works are premonitory in other ways, even though they attend to major historical events and figures. The analysis of the great black revolutionary, Toussaint L'Overture, brings out a theme that is somewhat apparent in Colin Ferguson's life: Toussaint rather naively embraced the great rhetorical discourses of the European Enlightenment, taking the pronouncements of Diderot, Voltaire, and Robespierre, at their word, while failing to see their specifically histori-

cal and class-based interests. Ferguson's latent flaw was to assume much the same, believing unconditionally in the American Dream.

7. Philip Kasinitz (1992), *Caribbean New York: Black Immigrants and the Politics of Race* (Ithaca, N.Y.: Cornell Univ. Press).

8. Frantz Fanon (1963), *The Wretched of the Earth* (New York: Grove Press).

9. Fanon (1963), 106.

2. The Neo-Nazis and Skinheads of Germany: Purveyors of Hate

Robert Harnishmacher and Robert J. Kelly

His [Hitler's] best epigram yesterday: "For our struggle God gave us his most abundant blessing. His most beautiful gift was the hate of our enemies whom we too hate with all our heart."
—*Joseph Goebbels,* Early Goebbels Diaries, *June 10, 1926*

In *Mein Kampf,* Adolf Hitler simply formulated charges against Jews as enemies of the world and stated the case for a military drive to the East to attain living space. The horrendous logic of his argument is useful to recall, because it illustrates the kind of thinking that lies beneath so much of the worldwide conflict stimulated by bigotry and ignorance.

The Jew, Hitler wrote in *Mein Kampf,* was merely impelled by the same motives as everyone else in the struggle for life; the only difference was his purpose: "His [the Jew's] ultimate goal is the denationalization, the promiscuous bastardization of other peoples, the lowering of the racial level of the highest peoples as well as the domination of his racial mishmash through the extirpation of the folkish intelligentsia and its replacement by the members of his own people."

This ultimate goal according to Hitler was what made the Jews the threat of mankind; because their ultimate aim was the conquest of the entire world, Hitler's battle against them was for the good not only of Germany but of the entire world.

By 1928, Hitler had finally come to the realization that his two most urgent convictions—danger from Jews and Germany's need for sufficient living space—were related. If the Reich failed to acquire essential living space, it would perish. If the Jewish menace were not stemmed, there could be no struggle for *Lebensraum*, "living space," and the nation would decay.

In all likelihood, Hitler had reached a point of no return with this essential formulation of his worldview and philosophy. Now a dual task lay before him: to conquer new living space in the East and to annihilate the Jews. What had seemed to be two separate, if parallel, courses converged into a single, frightful road.

Nazism and the Holocaust consumed more than fifty million people, including the genocide against Jews, and was no aberration. In the Soviet Union and the Peoples Republic of China, in the former colonial world crushed beneath the weight of imperialism, hatred consumed even more millions. Bias thrives on stereotypes, on shallow images of the "other" that portray individuals different than ourselves as strange, hideous, or dangerous. It is no wonder that in a world driven by the fury of political polemics and sophisticated propaganda that hate crimes should be so universal a phenomenon.

Since 1989, the former Communist German Democratic Republic has been integrated into the Federal Republic but resembles in many ways the Appalachian region of the United States. While the big political parties, the Christian Democrats and the Social Democrats, dominate the scene, it is the small, far-right parties that have taken root and are growing fast. Their message of nationalism, racism, and xenophobia set against a background of high unemployment, reduced wages, and inflation has a wide and growing appeal. In this new politically adolescent world of a united Germany, the Skinheads are the shock troops of the extreme right's march across Europe.

The hopes cherished by those who pulled down the Berlin Wall have been overwhelmed by events. Many East German youth are filled with contempt for their parents but look back on their grandparents—the survivors of a prouder, more stirring Germany pulsing under the shrill beat of Hitler—with nostalgia; and when the young, newly liberated East German youth met their counterparts from the West, who were also sick of their own society but for different reasons, tensions mounted. More and more, hatred of each other and foreign scapegoats seems to be the politics of a new Europe rising out of the collapse of the cold war.

In the case of Germany in particular, events rekindle a haunting question: Has the old German virus resurfaced? The parallels of modern hate crimes with the Nazi-era Kristallnacht frighten many Germans and others, especially Jews.

A leading German intellectual, Hans Magnus Enzenberger, paints a gloomy picture about the problems of ethnicity, immigration, violence, and hate groups affecting not only Germany but many other countries and regions.[1] According to Enzenberger, "Violence has freed itself from ideology," and from any higher purpose. Though it is widely believed that the neo-Nazi phenomenon emulates aspects of the Nazi era that helped to create *Gemeinschaft* (community) out of the economic chaos that ravaged post–World War I Germany, Enzenberger does not think the extreme nationalist right is interested in that kind of communal renewal and rapprochement with its eastern other half. What it has done is embrace the anti-Semitism and racial lunacy of the Nazi movement.

For Juergen Habermas, the disturbing events in Germany are caused by small groups of youthful offenders. He calls attention to the link between their acts of violence and a publicly sanctioned, xenophobic rhetoric disseminated by the Nazi movement. As Habermas emphasizes, the real problem is not just the youthful perpetrators of hate but the state and its criminal justice agencies, which through their passivity indirectly condone acts of violence against foreign minorities.[2]

In 1990, within the space of a year, Germany's political landscape changed more radically than it had over the past forty years. The image of the East German state vanished as suddenly as if it were a kind of Fata Morgana.

However, the accelerated social transformations now occurring in the unified Germany have a price of admission: a relatively higher level of base unemployment persists because segments of the population are too old or too poorly trained for an adequate or robust reaction to the considerable pressures for technological and economic adaptation. The impact of the crises on the institutional structure of German society affects life histories in significant ways: the "asylum debate," the status of immigrants, and the Skinhead phenomenon are expressions of the dislocations and transformations occurring throughout Germany.[3] The problems associated with massive dislocations of peoples are not limited to Germany:

with the collapse of the Soviet bloc and Warsaw Pact, immigrants have streamed into the peaceful and prosperous countries of Europe and North America from all regions of the world afflicted with civil war and poverty. There are potentially dangerous imbalances between the economically developed societies of northern and western Europe and those of southern Europe, along with those states who regained their national identities as a consequence of the collapse of the Soviet Union in the East who have long been excluded from world markets.

The problems associated with the new immigrants are just as difficult to manage as are the consequences for those countries hardest hit by immigration. Nations such as France and Germany, which in contrast to the United States, are not (at least in the twentieth century) countries of immigrants, have been most affected by the torrent of newcomers, refugees, displaced persons—those who want a better life for themselves and their families. Of course, both Germany and France recruited an immigrant labor force out of self-interest in the 1960s and 1970s; today the "guest workers," mainly from North Africa in France, and from Turkey and the former Yugoslavia in Germany, make up a considerable portion of the working population. They are overrepresented in the low-paying sectors of the economy, working in jobs that are avoided by the indigenous population; and they have an above-average rate of unemployment. Meanwhile, families have followed in a sort of "chain migration." The rapidity of the changes and the inundations of peoples from the liberated eastern provinces of Germany create a tense atmosphere where mutually opposed stereotypes of the "other" collide, resulting in increasing levels of violence. The fear of the foreigner and the easterner contribute to outbreaks of radical right-wing violence associated with the Skinheads and neo-Nazis.

The Skins and Nazis relentlessly agitate among young males in Germany, who have become increasingly sympathetic with the political philosophies and programs of right-wing parties. As in all of Europe, these changes in the politics of the young express a general level of resentment against the established political parties, which are themselves overwhelmed by the nature and scope of the problems. The youth gangs that are pressing the old Nazi symbols back into service are taken up by the international media and have succeeded to some degree in reawakening a familiar syndrome of prejudices in the broader population. The hatred of foreigners has frequently been translated into anti-Semitism as well as resentment against other ethnic minorities. Thus, it is not the Skinheads per se who are the only genuine threat so much as it is a cluster of circumstances and practices including the passivity of the police; prosecuting authorities who drag their feet in bringing perpetrators to justice; the courts—which hand out incomprehensible sentences; the military and militia units, who themselves attack asylum shelters; and the political parties that divert attention from the real problems of a badly engineered unification/assimilation process.

Coupled with the nuanced critiques of Habermas, Enzenberger sees the hypocrisies and contradictions of state policies as precipitating and breathing life into the radicals on both sides of questions concerning immigration, asylum, assimilation of eastern Germans, and control over violence-prone groups. Indeed, according to Enzenberger, Germany is a nation immersed in immigration, and more than most, it is the product of continual population shifts and changes to which Germans have adapted in the past. On the other hand, Enzenberger dislikes the moral posturing of those on the left who want Germany to solve the Third World's problems, and he questions whether it is realistic for Germany to become a truly "multicultural" society. His venom is reserved for the right-wing for whom he has no patience and whom he regards as the instigators of the incoherent and irrational violent rampages of the young.[4]

INSIDERS AND OUTSIDERS

Germany is particularly rich in youth gangs, all with their distinctive uniforms and politics; and uniforms hold a deep attraction: which gang one joins may be partly a matter of ideology, temperament, or taste in jackets, boots, music, symbols, and paraphernalia. Most gang members— right or left, "Skinheads" or "Autonomes" (members of a bleak, antifascist futurist movement that grew out of the late 1960s Italian youth scene sympathetic with the Red Brigade frenzy)[5]—come from the same class, lower-middle to lower. Their politics seem confused and incidental to their lifestyles, but this is not without significance on the national, European, or international scale—Skinhead and neo-Nazi groups have proliferated in the United States, Canada, and throughout northwestern Europe.[6] The main attraction is a sense of togetherness that gangs foster for their members and the lockstep conformity demanded of members. Singing, beer drinking, and assaulting foreigners intensifies this "we feeling" among Skins, while among antifascist groups, attacking Skins reinforces a sense of camaraderie and consciousness-of-kind. Skins disfigure

Berlin subway trains with slogans such as "Foreigners Out!" These compete with the antifascists' "Kill the Nazis!" But not all antifascists are peacefully inclined, nor are all Skinheads attracted to Nazi symbols.[7]

The "Autonomes" create squatter settlements in eastern Berlin where there are still abandoned properties; the artists and creative types among them paint and sculpt using street debris; the look and style is punk. To understand the Skinheads, one must look back to the 1960s when groups of young men first appeared wearing high-laced working boots, suspenders, plaid shirts, and hair cut close to the scalp. They were a spin-off of the British Mods, white, working-class kids in Britain who appropriated the styles of West Indian immigrants but did so with a clean-cut, working-class style.

While there are Skinheads across the continent of Europe and in North America, the main center of political activity is in Germany, where the Nazi Skins function as the knife's edge for the use of the far-right parties. According to some estimates, there are approximately 6,500 to 8,000 Skinheads in Germany, perhaps half of them "Oi," or Nazi boneheads, mostly young men from fourteen to twenty-five years old.[8] Other estimates suggest that 36,000 to possibly 60,000 youths belong to Nazi groups or are sympathetic with them.[9] Roughly, these groups break down into formations of right-wing extremists and right-wing Skinheads who see themselves as part of a neo-Nazi international movement that extends beyond Germany and Europe; and "Red Skins," nonfascists who oppose Nazi-oriented right-wing groups.[10]

Surveys of Skinheads (right-wing, neo-Nazi sympathizers) responsible for criminal acts show that in terms of age and sex, the majority are males between eighteen and thirty years of age, and contrary to expectations, they are mostly employed, with more than 70 percent in skilled and unskilled crafts and office jobs, with others (the majority) identified as students.[11] Their family lives may be indicative of their attitudes toward others and toward the use of violence. Police data along these parameters present a profile that includes an authoritarian family atmosphere where parents, though domineering and given to violence as a means of discipline, are aloof from their children. They are caught up in time-consuming jobs so that the interactional patterns between parents and children are not tender and supportive but very often hard and brutal.[12] As children, they become accustomed to violence as victims and utilize these experiences later in adolescence and young adulthood as victimizers.

Other explanatory perspectives include the "frustration aggression hypothesis." This is a mixture of instinct—and learning theory concepts—where the blocking of human desires causes aggression.[13] The social desires of love and acceptance are frustrated in broken families, leaving children with few ways of expressing their feelings. The "incomplete" youth is looking for a scapegoat, much like his or her parents do. Such a confused person may seek out weaker people and brutalize them.[14]

The collective sense of "us" (and "them") may be reclaimed and reinforced, not in the structurally flawed family setting, but in the distorted world of street gangs that are grounded in an ideology of racism. The motivational compulsions toward hate crime may be spontaneous, random, and episodically chaotic, but they may also be inspired by the cluster of beliefs and attitudes deeply embedded in a philosophy of violence and hatred. Eventually, the Skinhead gang becomes an adolescent's principal frame of reference, bound and woven together culturally and aesthetically by "Oi" music (the clandestine, outlawed emblematic symbol of the Skinhead neo-Nazi underground). The assimilation of Skinhead beliefs and points of view enables the fledging member to participate in acts of violence and understand these as instances of patriotism enveloped in the heroic ecstasy of Nazi philosophy. It appears that attacks and criticisms have not weakened the Skins and Nazis but have bound them closer together. As with many groups, external threats create greater internal cohesion and solidarity. Along with the signature music, distinctive clothes, physical appearance, dreaded political symbols of the Nazi past, and bonding rituals are the barbarous histories of the recent past that function as a set of rationalizations for the enmity of the Skins and Nazis toward their victims.[15]

CRUELTY AND SOLIDARITY: FABRICATED MEMORIES
OF THINGS PAST AND ANTIIMMIGRATION SENTIMENT

Two "revisionist" historians explaining how the Holocaust never happened get top billing in the ranks of the German extremist wing. The Holocaust is seen as a myth. Extremists do not believe there were mass exterminations of Jews, foreigners, communists, and homosexuals; on the other hand, the extremists support what amounts to "ethnic cleansing" policies. In the half-century since the Nazi regime was destroyed, Germany has not suddenly returned to a collective embrace of racism. Nevertheless, the public displays of intolerance by Skinheads and the mounting evidence of attacks, of hate crimes against foreigners, is cause for genuine alarm that a "Fourth Reich" may boom in Germany's distant future. There is, after all, something unnerving about the sight of German youths screaming, "Sieg Heil!" But even more unpleasant is the sight of complacent, ordinary people jeering as foreigners are driven from their homes and humiliated in the streets by thugs cavorting in a dreadful pantomime of Kristallnacht.

It must be said that brutality against foreigners is not just a German problem. Similar violence is happening across Europe: the politics of xenophobia is a pan-European phenomenon infecting France (Le Penism), Belgium (Vlaam Blok), Great Britain (the United Front), and Italy (Movimento Sociale and the Lombardy League, which helped elect a right-wing government).

In Germany, it seems that opposition to foreigners is haunted by Nazism, with Hitler's ghost hovering over immigration offices, political meetings, talk shows, parliamentary debates, editorials in the press, and Memorial Day speeches. Hitler and his legacy cannot be shaken off.

Grappling with the past and present runs through the intellectual legacy of German philosophy and political theory. The works of the constitutional jurist, Carl Schmitt, and for many, the philosophy of Martin Heidegger, resonate with the fear, if not subtle rhetoric, about alien contamination. Schmitt's and Heidegger's policies and attitudes toward democracy were congenial to the Germany of the 1930s and for significant segments of it today.[16] Echoes of the dangers of immigration and democracy, and the resistance to these, can be heard more and more throughout Germany and Europe.[17]

Many of the foreigners living in Germany, who are increasingly the prime targets of hate crimes, were invited there by the German government as far back as the 1950s from Italy, Spain, Greece, Turkey, Morocco, and Portugal. These "guest workers," as they were called, took jobs in all sectors of the economy during its recovery and growth. Today they are an integral part of the economy and make up a significant percentage of the population in communities like Frankfurt, Munich, Hamburg, Berlin, Cologne, Düsseldorf, and Stuttgart.

East Germany, when it was the German Democratic Republic, recruited thousands of foreign workers, mainly Vietnamese and Africans from politically aligned Marxist and Communist states. More recently, in the late 1980s when the reunification processes gathered momentum and east rejoined west, large numbers of refugees began streaming into Germany.

Germany's immigration laws are quite unlike those of the United States or other European nations. The German Constitution guarantees asylum to all who can prove that they are politically persecuted in their homelands. However, most of those who are not persecuted have no legal way to emigrate, so most foreigners who arrive have no real options but to claim that they are political refugees; otherwise, they are summarily turned away. The radical right tends to hysteria over the issues of immigration, asylum, and citizenship. The cry has been—even among mainstream Christian Democrats fearful of newcomers from the disintegrating nations of the former Warsaw Pact and Soviet Republics—that Germany is not a country of immigrants. But Germany has been a mixture of regions, ethnic groups, religions, nationalities.[18]

Many refugees go to Germany because of its liberal asylum policies. It has been the salvation for many whose lives in their homelands have been destroyed; the policy has also been the occasion for some of the worst antiforeign, antiimmigrant violence the country has seen since the end of World War II. Germany is in a demographic dilemma: The indigenous birthrate is low, so the country needs outsiders; and without immigration, the presently constituted German political economy could not work. The highly successful auto and shipbuilding industries would close were it not for immigrant labor.

Since the 1990s, Germany has been a residential sanctuary for almost one million refugees from all over Europe, Africa, and Eurasia, and the antiforeign sentiment has also been the ugliest. The pressures are immense: with 80 million people living in a country approximately the size of the state of Montana, feelings of inundation by refugees are magnified as is the blame for Germany's social ills laid at their doorstep. Since 1991, Skinheads and neo-Nazis have mounted more than 3,500 attacks on those perceived as foreigners. Most Germans condemn the violence of the young neo-Nazis, and the government has responded, erratically, unfortunately, but has, nonetheless, prosecuted offenders. At the same time, it has agreed to consider restrictions on its asylum policies because of the mounting public pressure and hysteria.

THE CONUNDRUMS OF LEGAL AND POLITICAL RIGHTS AND ALIEN HIERARCHIES

For reasons that go deep into twentieth-century history, discussions on how to deal with immigration and the hate crimes it triggers are complicated and contorted by references to mystical bloodlines, guilt, and unfortunate, though deliberate, allusions to the past. The conventional, "politically correct" moral posture, the one preached by almost all political parties is that foreigners should be welcomed because, given Germany's sordid past, there is much to make up for; Germany has a special responsibility toward refugees from all countries. This point of view reflects the generous asylum law of the German Constitution, which allows all victims of political persecution to apply for asylum in Germany and, uniquely, to appeal if the application is rejected. While the application is pending, asylum seekers are housed and taken care of by the regional governments. But, according to Ian Buruma:

> only 5 percent of the foreign asylum seekers are officially allowed to stay—and even then virtually none is granted citizenship. The others are seen as economic refugees—the lowest level in the alien hierarchy: greed knocking on the doors of a community of culture and blood. But again because of the guilty German past, few of them are actually forced to leave. As a result, more and more people pile up in large holding centers on the outskirts of inhospitable German towns. I drive past one of these every day in West Berlin: white wooden barracks with children of every hue peering through a fence, guarded by police patrols against neo-Nazis and Skins. Unemployed, cut off, and without rights, it is no wonder some of them turn to crime.[19]

There are already some five million Turkish, Greek, Croat, and Italian refugees, many of whom are awaiting to become German citizens, and up to a million "status Germans," mostly Volga Germans from the former Soviet Union, who are also waiting to get in. These matters raise a genuine identity problem as to who is and who is not a German citizen. By law, German citizenship is based on blood, instead of birth or residency. Unlike the United States, a child born in Germany of foreign parents does not count as a German. In fact, this is not so unusual in Europe: France has residency and birth requirements, while the Netherlands does not; but Germany like Israel, Taiwan, and Russia, also has a law of return. Any former citizen or descendant of a citizen of the Reich, as it existed before 1937, is entitled to German citizenship[20]—thus, the inequities and bizarre regulations. For instance, a Pole who speaks nothing but Polish but who can demonstrate that his grandfather served in a regular unit of the Wehrmacht in World War II, counts as a German. And it goes even further. Descendants of Germans outside the borders of 1937—the "Volga Germans" in Ukraine, Belarus, and Russia are considered "status Germans." They might very well feel German and speak an archaic dialect, and their ancestors may have migrated east centuries ago; but they would have been deemed a category of people suitable for "Germanization"—people, in effect, who are "biologically eligible" (to use a Nazi phrase of the time). They, too, are accepted as Germans and can apply for immediate citizenship. Many do. By 1990, nearly a half-million arrived in Germany, about twice the number of non-Germans who seek asylum.

The inadequacies of out-of-date immigration policies create awkward situations, as noted, where immigrants are isolated and become increasingly frustrated and insular. The politics of Muslim emigrés are a good example. Cut off from the country of their parents and treated as foreigners in the country of their birth, the young sometimes seek an identity in the religion that is then a means of defining and stigmatizing them. The consequences that result, including separatist agitation for schools, privileges in dress, language use, and religious practice in public life, emerge in the atmosphere of confrontation. Added to these are high rates of unemployment, the effects of economic recession on lifestyles and opportunities, and the inefficiencies of welfare bureaucracies that pile still more difficulties on existing problems.

CONDITIONS OF COUNTERTERROR AND DETERRENCE

The hate crimes of the neo-Nazis and Skinheads would appear to emerge out of the larger social and political conflicts occurring in Germany and to reflect as well, in however distorted a form, the political beliefs, aspirations, frustrations, and fears of larger segments of German society. We believe that any policy or strategy designed to curb or cope with the hate crime phenomenon in Germany might begin with a hypothesis that links the Skinheads and neo-Nazis to a community of support. And we think that the scientific examination of such relationships is essential to understanding the occurrence, persistence, and growth (and decline) of hate groups engaging in what is nothing less than internal, domestic terrorism. Such a perspective implies that the analyses of the ideologies and psychological traits of hate crime offenders and of the social dynamics of their gangs and groups is incomplete unless we understand their reciprocal relations with larger sympathizing publics.

Some of the proposals made by professional criminal justice specialists and social scientists about domestic terror and hate tend to be preoccupied with its causes and say little about the general circumstances responsible for its decline. Insofar as the question is addressed at all, it is assumed that movements such as the Skinheads and neo-Nazis decline as a result of some combination of security countermeasures and failure to achieve publicity or larger political objectives. We doubt that answers dependent heavily on criminal justice deterrence strategies are sufficient in themselves.

Backlash was evident in the German public's negative attitudes toward "revolutionary" acts by the Baader-Meinhof group and its successor, the Red Army Faction. But general public antagonism and its counterpart, support for strong countermeasures, did not prove fatal to these terrorist groups—evidently because a significant residue of sympathy for revolutionary action remained on the German left. In the case of the neo-Nazis and Skinheads, it is safe to assume that significant numbers of people are not outraged by Skinhead acts of hate and that their radical commitments and preferences for collective acts of violence occur in what amounts to a community of support for violent militancy.

The structure of the argument bears reiteration: in itself, revulsion against deadly violence—even when directed against stigmatized groups—is not a sufficient explanation for the decline of violence among the Skinheads and neo-Nazis. Secondly, deterrence policies by government and criminal justice agencies are likely to be effective to the extent that they reinforce, or are reinforced by, other changes in the bases of support and sympathy for hate crime violence among wider sectors of the population. Put another way, if the communities that tolerate or support Skinhead/neo-Nazi violence begin to reject it because of revulsion to violence and growing expectations of peaceful reform and change designed to rectify, resolve, and end problems that give rise to the violence, law enforcement deterrence will enhance and facilitate the process. On the other hand, if support for the cause and tactics of Skinhead violence that is targeted at specific groups remains substantial, the likely effects of tough anti-Skinhead policies and the apprehension of neo-Nazis engaged in hate crime will intensify resentments and strengthen support groups for hate violence.

Moreover, the price of high-tech, intensive security is high, imperfect, and transient. Risks can be reduced, but the security gains may be, at least, temporary for a number of reasons, not the least of which is that terrorists—and there is no reason to exclude the Skinheads and neo-Nazis from this classification—have demonstrated repeatedly that they will bide their time and initiate new campaigns when security and surveillance is relaxed. These dynamics, we suspect, are responsible for the periodic re-surgence of hate crime violence in different regions of Germany.

Some suggestive evidence about the effects of deterrence are provided by cases in the United States involving groups engaged in systematic domestic violence. The revolutionary terrorism in the 1970s of the Weather Underground was never effectively countered by the authorities. In 1974, the Weather Underground voluntarily suspended its campaign of violence without the arrests of its members. The most that can be said about deterrence in this case is that the Weathermen (a radical offshoot of the Students for Democratic Society) were afflicted by paranoia about being penetrated or detected by the FBI and police. Their leaders' obsession with security had corrosive effects on morale and inhibited revolutionary actions.

To summarize, policies designed to stymie the Skinheads and neo-Nazis, whether they emphasize traditional law enforcement techniques or, as in Italy, incentives to defect, are most effective when they coincide with larger shifts in the climate of public opinion away from support or tolerance of Skinhead causes and tactics. Law enforcement strategies may reinforce the erosion in support for hate crime mongers, but they cannot create it.

NOTES

1. Hans Magnus Enzenberger (1994), *From L. A. to Bosnia* (New York: New Press).

2. Juergen Habermas (1992), "Die zweite Lebenslüge der Bundesrepublik: Wir sind wieder 'normal' geworden," *Die Zeit*, Dec. 18, cited in Habermas (1994), *The Past As Future*, ed. and trans. Max Pensky (Lincoln: Univ. of Nebraska Press), 38.

3. In the wake of German unification, the issue of political asylum became, apart from economic issues, the most contentious problem on the federal level to emerge in the expanded Federal Republic. Tensions increased with the sharp rise in immigration from Eastern European countries as a result of the collapse of the Soviet bloc.

4. Enzenberger (1994); see his final essay, "The Great Migration."

5. Robert J. Kelly (1991), "Terrorism and Intrigue," *The Italian Journal* 5(1): 29–43.

6. Mark S. Hamm (1991–93), *American Skinheads: The Criminology and Control of Hate Crime* (Westport, Conn.: Praeger).

7. Alexis A. Aronowitz (1994), "Germany's Xenophobic Violence: Criminal

Justice and Social Responses," in *Hate Crimes: International Perspectives on Causes and Control,* ed. Mark S. Hamm (Cincinnati: Anderson), 84–119.

8. Verfassungsschutz Rheinland-Pfalz (1993) "Skinheads," *Magazin für die Polizei,* no. 8: 18–24.

9. Klaus Farin and Eberhard Seidel-Pielen (1993), *Skinheads* (Munich: C. H. Beck).

10. Innenministerium Nordrhein-Westfalen (1993), "Skinheads in Nordrhein-Westfalen," *Stern,* no. 36: 34.

11. Bundesministerium des Innern (1993), "Verfassungsschutz-Bericht 1992," *Stern,* no. 36: 82.

12. Hans Dieter Schwind (1993), *Kriminologie* 5, (Heidelberg: Auflage Heidelberg), 407.

13. Wolfgang Stoebe et al. (1990), *Sozialpsychologie—Eine Einführung* (Berlin: Karstadt-Hertie), 178.

14. Dr. Rinus van Warven (1993), "Gewalt und Rechtsextremismus aus philosophischer Sicht im Licht der aktuellen Probleme," *Magazin für die Polizei,* no. 210 (Oct.): 43, 45.

15. Marie C. Douglas (1992), "Ausländer 'Raus! Nazi 'Raus! An Observation of German Skins and Jugendbänden," *International Journal of Comparative and Applied Criminal Justice* 16(1): 441–72.

16. Carl Schmitt (1928), *Verfassungslehre* (Berlin: Duncker and Humblot), 228–46; Hans Sluga (1989), "Metadiscourse: German Philosophy and National Socialism," *Social Research* 56(4): 72–84.

17. Ridgeway and Muller assert that there is a transnational network linking Europe into a skein of fascists operatives: "There has long been an underground railroad on the far right in Europe, with the British Nazis, for example, sheltering Italian fascists; they hold conferences that bring the different groups together to network." See James Ridgeway and Beltina Muller (1991), "Wie Deutsch ist es?" *Village Voice,* Dec. 3, 34, 40.

18. Probably at no time were so many foreigners working in Germany as during the Third Reich—almost eight million in 1944—many of them *Untermenschen* (slave laborers) from the east.

19. Ian Buruma (1992), "Outsiders," *New York Review,* Apr. 9, 16–19.

20. Klaus J. Bade (1992), *Deutsche im Ausland, Fremde in Deutschland: Migration in Geschichte und Gegenwart* (Munich: C. H. Beck), 154–73.

3. The Ku Klux Klan: Recurring Hate in America

Robert J. Kelly

THE PRELUDE OF ORGANIZED HATE

Gunnar Myrdal wrote in *An American Dilemma* that "Americans of all national origins, classes, regions, creeds, and colors have something in common: a social ethos, a political creed. It is difficult to avoid the judgment that this 'American Creed' is the cement in the structure of this great and disparate nation."[1] Myrdal then chastised the American political community for failing to try to realize its ideals. The situation of African-Americans exposed the moral contradiction between the country's "American Creed," with its commitment to democratic ideals, tolerance, and egalitarianism, and its racist practices and policies. Myrdal believed that racism in the form of segregationist policies was embedded in regional groups and reflected local interest and antagonism. To him, the liberal ingredients of a greater national policy were universal, transcendent, and fundamental. Racism, anti-Semitism, and religious intolerance were merely aberrations that would eventually be resolved in favor of the American Creed, which expressed the authentic ideals of the American political culture and social community.

Myrdal was optimistic in his appraisal of the dialectical partnership between the uplifting and the craven aspects of the American moral landscape. The depth of the dilemma, however, was not fully appreciated. With one dimension identified of a complex political belief system that emphasized the cherished notions of democracy—government by consent of the governed, inalienable rights, and a structure of politics open to all—what was not fully acknowledged was that throughout American history, these democratic values lived side by side with another grim political tradition that included the genocidal suppression of Native-Americans and African-Americans.[2] According to Michael Hughey, the nativist, xenophobic style that incubated in the political culture had its origins in secularized versions of Puritanism, which also stimulated democratic, republican ideas.[3]

The darker side of the Puritan heritage, nurtured and interwoven into the civil society, restricted the rights and privileges of full participating citizenship to those groups that were qualified to exercise them. The dominant groups in American society—those who arrived first and defined the culture of the society—have preponderantly shaped the institutional legacy that would determine the criteria for political evolution. Consequently, the operations of democracy have been monopolized practically and symbolically by racial and religious elites, who have appropriated rights and privileges, while excluding and discriminating against racial, sexual, ethnic, and religious groups.[4] In these divergent orientations and styles, the political traditions, with their heretical elitism and systemic discrimination, have existed and have even merged into the operative conception of community. An important struggle in American society is, consequently, intrinsic to its core values. The social conflict that has raged is not simply one of purging social anomalies and pathological elements that infected our politics. It is a deep moral crusade in which values and their fugitive opposites coexist in a dynamic tension that threatens to burst the consensual détente prevailing throughout centuries. If one can imagine the ideological heart of American political culture, one would see that it contains elements at war with one another—inclusive and exclusive ideals, tolerance and rejection, and unrealistic and restrictive values. It includes an abiding collective sense of "we-ness" and "others-ness."

As the United States grew with surges of European immigrants, these and other groups of Asians and blacks began to press claims for political membership and their share of social resources. As American society drifted increasingly and inexorably into cultural, religious, and racial pluralism, major fractures in the political covenant emerged. Curiously, a "core" America in which everyone looked the same, spoke the same language, worshiped the same gods, and believed the same things never existed. In some sense, America is a mental construction neither of race, inherited class privilege, or ancestral territory. The creed, such as it is, was born with the arrival of jostling scores of ethnic immigrants who became American to the extent to which they accommodated one another. Such accommodations succeed unevenly and often fail; the melting pot we now know did not transform disparate peoples into a wholly new breed, "that race now called Americans."[5] Contrary to theorists and advocates of the melting pot, America is an act of imagination, the making of which never ends. When the collective enterprise of mutual respect and social community-building is broken, as often happens, the possibilities of the American Creed, as Myrdal optimistically describes it, disintegrate.

The factors that coalesce to form the xenophobic nativism that constitutes the sentimental structure of the Ku Klux Klan phenomena lay in the historical religious covenant of the early white Protestant groups. These groups formed the American political community during at least fifty years following the Revolutionary War.[6] As Hughey states, particular segments of the revolutionary strata, especially in the Northern and New England colonies, retained from their Puritan past a self-conception of themselves as an elected elite with a special destiny. They would create the institutional structure of the civil society and forge the rudiments of a new state. It was they who were entitled to define the terms of the political-social contract, regulate its operations, and establish the criteria for entry and membership.[7]

In effect, the culture and social blueprint of what it meant to be American was Anglo-centric in its origin and core values. The political exclusivity of the white Protestant heritage was not readily apparent in the aftermath of the Revolution and the formalization of the Constitution. The general economy of the country was predominantly agrarian; non-Protestants were few in number; and most of the black population remained enslaved. In secularized form, the religious orientation and theological paradigms of the Protestant community gradually expressed themselves as "Americanism." Against this ideological background, relationships between dominant and subordinate groups emerged through specific struggles over particular issues marked on all sides by concrete economic interests. Although the confrontations between elites and newcomers devolved around practical economic concerns, the infrastructure of ideas and traditions, possessed by both new and entrenched groups, informed their attempts to organize and make sense of their world.[8] The

"Americanization" movement—consisting of a conflated cluster of Anglo-cultural ideals and values that were taught in the schools, preached in church, and stated by courts in judicial terms—was seen as a bond linking all Americans, including beleaguered nonwhite minorities, European ethnics, and Asian immigrants. There were, however, conspicuous failures in the consensus that for some were crucial to political and social order.

The high noon of Anglo-centric culture occurred in the last decades of the nineteenth century. The submergence of separate ethnic identities, which may have seemed necessary for the harmonious interweaving of races and ethnic groups in the United States, was challenged in the great cities. Ethnic and racial minorities formed their enclaves and ghettos to live in their own way. Chinatowns, Little Italys, and Harlems reflected a hybridization of the Anglo-centrism of America with that of the culture of each minority's nation of origin. As the immigrant populations increased and the emancipated black population emigrated from the South into the industrial North and Midwest, ethnic and racial spokesmen appeared who were moved by a real concern for distinctive ethnic values and also by real, if unconscious, vested interests in the preservation of ethnic constituencies. The impression grew that the melting pot was nothing less than a social device to impose Anglo images and values upon hapless minorities and immigrants—an impression reinforced by the rise of the Americanization movement and nativist groups fearing the polyglot minorities. The nativist response is, consequently, an extreme reaction to the erosion of the Anglo-centric hegemony, which for many whites was the cohesive bond and consensual faith on which national unity rested.

Since the middle of the nineteenth century, the United States has witnessed several episodic waves of xenophobia. At various times, Catholics, Mormons, Freemasons, Jews, blacks, and Communists have been targets of groups, such as the Klan, seeking to defend "American" ideals and values. Fear of others and a compulsion to defend the faith comprise the paranoid style in American political traditions.[9] The Klan exploited mass anxieties throughout its history by charging targeted groups with social and political subversion. Despite the numerous differences of minorities, nativism viewed each as the antithesis of American ideals. Different groups were transformed into "un-American" groups.

After the Civil War and through the twentieth century, the nativists were further threatened by the biological differences and alleged deficiencies of blacks. Nativists began to redefine their defense of the American Creed as one that had to include racial responsibility.

KLAN GENESIS: THE AFTERMATH OF THE CIVIL WAR

The legacy of mythic prestige and privilege reinforced by a religious heritage that many sectors of Southern white society embraced left the South traumatized by the Civil War. Regional elites in the Confederacy were able to absorb the shocks of war and defeat, but the poor, rural tenant farmers and working-class secular populations were overwhelmed by the catastrophic effects of the war.

The enormous exertions and sacrifices required by the war, along with the blockades and the Union Army's "March to the Sea"—which ravaged the Southern countryside—left in their wake a disintegrated economy and social structure in towns and villages. Backs against the wall, exhausted and demoralized, many whites resorted to extreme measures against the most vulnerable targets of their anger—the helpless ex-slaves.

Union occupation forces exacerbated resistance and extremism. The carpetbaggers and Unionist bureaucrats came to display the characteristics of bureaucrats everywhere. Their vested interests set them increasingly apart from the indigenous populations they were there to aid.

Each repressive measure of the Reconstructionist provisional governments occupying states in the South further undermined the moral claims of the occupation. Not unexpectedly, social resistance emerged within the former rebel states.

From the ranks of the defeated and embittered arose voices that demanded redress and revenge for the insulted soldiers of the Confederacy. In the rebel states, many ruined people thirsted for vengeance. The early Klan did not know how to cure the evils of postwar depression, but it knew how to harangue and pound its fists. What was needed was the ventilation of ideas to create new life and energy. What occurred was a cry for retribution.

The insurgencies of hate are rarely isolated phenomena; organized hate groups reflect the diffuse sympathies, confused longings, and aspirations of large segments of society. Perhaps more than any other group in the United States, the Ku Klux Klan that rose in the post–Civil War South illustrates how hatred can be transformed, redefined, sustained, and mobilized around the energies of those whom society has failed in one way or another. During the past 125 years, the Klan has played an often significant part in the development and proliferation of the hate movement. Even more than its episodes of overt violence, the Klan illustrates the pivotal role of ideologies in forming a climate of opinion receptive to and supportive of politically motivated violence.[10] In its ideological aspects, the Klan may be America's oldest and most prominent terrorist organization.

| Like other terrorist organizations, the Klan has resorted to violence for a variety of reasons. It has often defined itself in the defense of privileges its members perceived to be threatened. Not rigidly committed to a specific historic cause but more flexible and skillful psychologically than most extremist hate groups, the Klan has deftly redefined both its mission and enemies to retain its viability and appeal.

The Ku Klux Klan spread throughout the South, and although Congress passed acts to safeguard the rights of blacks and put an end to the Klan, the *Enforcement Act of 1870* was ineffectual.[11] The Klan was not smashed; it transformed itself and assimilated itself into hundreds of local power structures. The Klan's purpose never really changed; its overriding aim was to resist and suppress, violently if necessary, any attempt by minorities to gain any political and economic power.[12]

Since the 1870s, the Klan's reign of terror in the South never diminished; its periodic resurgence and decline may speak more to its success than its failures. It often assumed power directly or indirectly, but it was not just marginal. It remained at the center of power.

The cycles of growth and decline mark periods of influence, repudiation, and success. When Klan members became government officials, the Klan's ideological principals of white supremacy gathered social strength and its ideas and social practices were incorporated into local and regional government policy. The image of an outlaw terrorist organization faded. A decline in Klan influence provoked the appearance of the outlandish rituals, costumes, and public displays of militant hatred, while its success as a powerful force in local government meant that its public spectacles of defiant intolerance diminished.

THE EVOLUTION OF THE KU KLUX KLAN

Formed around 1867 by Confederate veterans as a secret society determined to resist Northern Reconstructionist policies, the Klan sought to preserve white supremacy in the newly emancipated South.[13] As an irredentist movement, it vowed to restore the South's antebellum heritage, to resist Northern occupation, and to oppose the Reconstructionist's social, political, and economic reformations.[14]

Estimates of early Klan membership suggest that it was at first a comparatively small reactionary group.[15] The Klan's modest size may be explained by its extreme views that necessarily limited its appeal. It also failed to mobilize truly mass support, which requires time, skill, effort, and constant mobilization. No matter how widespread popular dissatisfaction may be, if a movement expects to survive and thrive, it must constantly recruit members. During its early existence, those sympathetic to the Klan may have feared open identification with a dissident organization. Lack of recruitment and of identification with it may have provoked the Klan into premature violence in order to portray itself as strong and popular.

Blacks symbolized to the South defeat and became the early victims of the movement. One purpose behind the humiliation of blacks was excitational; threats to black families, cross burnings, and other acts of intimidation were meant to inspire timid whites to further acts of vengeance. In exciting white violence, the Klan served as a social catalyst, not as a substitute for mass revolt.

In the 1870s, federal troops were withdrawn from the Southern states, and occupational governments were returned to local control. Although blacks were technically free, they profoundly altered the ways in which, first Southerners, and then people in the rest of the nation, began to make sense of the Civil War's consequences. Society and the dogmas of liberty were no longer comfortable abstractions but became for many a series of afflictions. The defeat of the South had created a mass psychological reaction that significantly depressed people; the impact of the cultural crisis there was far more violent than its transformation to a new social order. What happened in the South was more than the sum of the sufferings inflicted, the millions lost, the institutions irreparably shattered, and the people uprooted; it was an education by shock. Panic overshadowed events. This panic was often significantly disproportionate to the losses of those who were most afraid; despair became the tone and motif of the period. Both blacks and white, rich and poor were deprived of their security and left impotent in the face of the war's disasters.

In the South of 1865, everything seemed to have disintegrated at once. Southerners of all classes and both races at first had neither a sense of history nor the consolation of traditional values. They were, each in their own way, oppressed by forces that were incomprehensible and therefore all the more humiliating. They were oppressed by more than an economic collapse; their traditional social institutions, customs, and folkways failed them as the calamity of the war and its aftermath made themselves felt.[16]

The agony of losing a world, of losing one's moorings, can be personally terrifying. The crisis in the social order of the South occurred at an accelerated rate, causing a sudden rupture that was wrongly understood to be the fault of the former slaves. In fact, ex-slaves began to be blamed for the South's defeat in the war.

During the crisis, new signals emerged marking an instantaneous break with other lifestyles and other needs. People's lives derived substance from fear and a struggle for expression in a bleak social setting that became ahistorical and unconstitutional. Southern whites had once needed only to adapt their lives to the externals of society; after the war, many were directly menaced by society and physically victimized by it, much as black ex-slaves had experienced society for almost two centuries. The crisis was not a mere disenchantment capable of being endured and overcome; it was a profound paralysis. This despair was not merely poignant; the brutality of the white response became an expression of the need to survive. The Klan fed on the paranoid feelings of despair.

The social milieu of the Klan was a psychologically fractured postrevolutionary society. Individuals saw themselves moving through a succession of situations linked only by surface symbolic consistency. The movement and rhythms of life in the defeated white South lacked the familiar cohesiveness provided by the antebellum culture. In the absence of cultural attachments, social conflicts intensified. The enfranchisement of blacks and adverse aspects of a disintegrating traditional life led Southern whites to involvement in and support for extremist groups. The Klan seized opportunistically upon the pervasive rapport among the discontented as a basis for mobilization.[17] It infused some sense of solidarity and promulgated myths of racial unity, and through its criminal activities and attacks, it provided models of defiance and challenge to the intrusive Northern authorities, thereby breaking the inhibitions of reflexive obedience. A major Klan objective was to heighten the moral isolation of government by forcing it to act in a void that degraded its authority and tarnished its legitimacy. When federal troops were finally withdrawn in the 1870s, blacks remained free but intimidated by segregation laws that prevented their voting and that re-created the racial caste system.[18]

The overt racial rancor subsided momentarily until the great transatlantic immigrants reignited Klan fervor at the turn of the century. By the end of World War I, millions had flocked to America from eastern and southern Europe. Poles, Russians, Hungarians, Italians, Greeks, and Jews fled a war-torn Europe for real or imagined opportunities in the United States. The Klan's natural fear and contempt of strangers was strengthened by another exclusionary movement that developed in those regions of the United States most heavily affected by the waves of immigrant settlers needing jobs and housing.

Several nativist organizations each fixed upon some internal alien influence as a grave threat to national unity. Generally, all nativist regimes are defensive psychologically and chauvinistic politically. They lash out rhetorically and violently against a religious or racial peril and sometimes against a perceived revolutionary threat.[19] Nativists assume that foreigners are disloyal and inherently threatening to the nativists' way of life. Their deep, unexpressed, unconscious fear is of being dominated by others in much the same way that they wish to control and influence the lives of newcomers.

In the South, the strains of unregulated capitalism produced more insecurity than most people could tolerate. Moreover, previous idealistic beliefs yielded to a doctrine of racial determinism that both reflected and intensified the sense of insecurity. The new racist ideology concerning blacks, Jews, Catholics, eastern and southern Europeans, and Asians heightened feelings of vulnerability because it made cherished values and institutions dependent upon biological factors rather than upon their own intrinsic merits.

A sweeping ethnocentrism was also aroused in the first decades of the twentieth century by the sheer scale and ethnic variety of the immigration.[20] The problem was not just blacks any longer, the nativists believed; the great problem included outsiders of all kinds, alien in blood, faith, and heritage. The United States was becoming so heterogeneous that every social problem could be construed by xenophobes and ultranationalists in terms of ethnic subversion. The force of prejudice against blacks, Catholics, Jews, Chinese, Japanese, and southern Europeans was embodied by the Klan to symbolize the convergence of antiminority feelings and to provide an outlet for every racial, religious, and ethnic hatred.[21] The Klan offered a way to relieve the anxieties that had festered among the nation's white Protestant majority.

Unlike its earlier incarnation in the post–Civil War South, the revived Klan sought to purify America and restore the supremacy of the old stock. Its task was to cleanse the nation of its moral and racial pollution.[22]

KLAN RENAISSANCE AND DECLINE

In 1915, the original Klan had all but vanished in the South as Southern sectionalism disappeared in the swell of industrial growth and urbanization. The emerging new Klan possessed a demonology more inclusive than its predecessor; it stressed anti-Semitic themes, and its influence spread chiefly in rural towns and villages.

Jews were represented as part of an international plot to control America through big-city vices—bootlegging, gambling, and prostitution. Consistent with its original mission of maintaining white supremacy, the new Klan pursued its social objective of controlling blacks but added religion and nationalism to its causes and grievances. Unlike its former self, the Knights of the Klan were more restrictive in membership. The original Klan admitted white men of every background; the new Knights accepted only native-born, Protestant whites and stressed antiblack, anti-Semitic, and antiforeign attitudes with equal fervor.[23]

Between 1915 and 1920, the new Klan recruited approximately five thousand members.[24] Expansion was particularly brisk in 1920. Negative social and economic trends—depression, prohibition, immigration, isolationism, and disillusionment—fueled the Knights' plans. The Klan had no economic program except its enforcement of discrimination through force and intimidation. Hoping to influence votes for its political candidates, the Knights threatened businesses that catered to blacks, burned commercial enterprises, and marched in flamboyant parades.

White supremacy remained a defining characteristic as the Klan spread north and west, but it is not the only issue that preoccupied the Knights. The Klan also attacked whites sympathetic to blacks and embraced the anti-Catholic, anti-Semitic views within other nativist movements. Hate becomes more viable and perhaps more tolerable as it envelops more targets and becomes more familiar and guileless. Had the Klan remained a single-issue organization concerned only with white supremacy, its life expectancy would have been seriously abbreviated by its successes, by the often fickle changes in public opinion, and by the mass exodus of blacks from the South.[25]

The Knights' outcry of anti-Papist, anti-Catholic feeling was closely related to the growth of religious fundamentalism in America.[26] Given its religious convictions, the Klan served as an excellent barometer of the militant repudiation of a liberalized gospel and a secularized culture that began to make itself felt in the closing years of the Progressive Era.

As World War I exhausted itself in Europe, the political cynicism and spiritual fatigue of its aftermath fueled the Klan's deluded prophecies that America and Americanism were threatened by the Bolshevism, Papism, endless crime, political intrigue, and moral chaos sweeping through European countries ravaged by the fighting. The Klan's campaign of fear urged isolationism. Patriotism and Christianity became the principal values to the Knights of the KKK. Ironically, as a censor and moral organization, it was often impatient with legally constituted authority and violated the law opportunistically. Local statutes could not stand in the way of Klan, as they sought to punish those "deviants" who violated its sense of regeneration and the ancient standards of Americanism. Illegal boycotts, petty extortions, larceny, arson, and murder—more serious crimes than night riding and hell-raising—were all part of the Klan's vigilantism.

By 1921, the Klan claimed to be operating in forty-five states.[27] In 1924, membership reached three million. The Klan was, at the time, deeply embedded within American society; it was no longer a rural, sectional, marginal irritant. From the 1920s, it had situated itself in the burgeoning cities of the economically booming South, Midwest, and Southwest;[28] it agitated among those who feared urbanization, the influential growth of the trade unions in political affairs, and the proliferation of high-tech industries. Klan political leverage soon became significant among many white citizens in regions where economic growth was accelerating.

The zenith of the Knights' notoriety and influence occurred in 1924 at the Democratic convention, which was deeply divided over a resolution that denounced the Klan by name. William Jennings Bryan, a charismatic fundamentalist and self-styled knight-errant of the oppressed rural agrarian class, said: "We can exterminate Ku Kluxism better by recognizing their honesty and teaching them that they are wrong."[29] Bryan was unmercifully heckled from the gallery; the Democratic Party by 1924 was very closely identified with the trade unions, immigrants, and urban working classes. These groups contained many Jews, blacks, Catholics, and other minorities—victims of the Klan—too many to heed advice from an apologist for hate and violence.

The Klan declined in power during the tumultuous 1930s and early

1940s when immigration lessened and Catholics and Jews ascended to economic and political power. The nation became preoccupied by World War II.

THE CIVIL RIGHTS MOVEMENT

The 1954 Supreme Court decision against segregation in public education was a flash point for hate mongering in the United States. All the bitterness of the past seemed to resurface in the four years following the Court's momentous decision. Approximately 530 cases of racial violence attributed to the Klan or its sympathizers occurred in this period.[30]

Within five years after the *Brown v. the Board of Education* decision, the Klan's campaign of terror included six murders and more than forty felony assaults, bombings, and arsons at schools, churches, and homes.[31] As the Civil Rights movement gained impetus in the 1960s, the Klan's violence accelerated.[32]

The Klan's resurgence during the Civil Rights era was indirectly aided by the government's reaction to the leader of the Southern Christian Leadership Conference, Reverend Martin Luther King; Malcolm X, the charismatic Black Muslim activist associated with the Nation of Islam; and the Black Panther Party. The latter's programs for community control, coupled with its controversial attitudes toward armed defense, heightened racial tensions.[33] Malcolm X, in particular, sought to bring the issue of racism in the United States before the United Nations and had partially succeeded in embarrassing the American government before the world community.[34] In response, the FBI defined Malcolm X's organization, the Black Panthers, and the Southern Christian Leadership Conference as dangerous and subversive. A counterintelligence program to expose, disrupt, misdirect, and discredit these protest groups was initiated by the FBI director, J. Edgar Hoover.[35]

THE CONTEMPORARY KLAN AND ITS OFFSPRING

At least twenty-five different factions of the Klan have been identified across the United States.[36] Other kindred hate groups are involved with white supremacist organizations. Klanwatch estimates that as many as seventeen thousand individuals belong to groups like the Aryan Nations, the Order, the Posse Comitatus, and the Skinheads. The Anti-Defamation League, which monitors many anti-Semitic organizations, reports that three thousand Skinheads in thirty-four states have aligned themselves with various factions of the Klan and other racist groups.[37]

Linked with the Klan is the Christian Identity Movement, which promotes a theological rationale for racial and religious bigotry.[38] In its tortured interpretations of Old Testament texts, various leaders present exegetical analyses to demonstrate that Jews and nonwhite minorities will be destroyed in an apocalyptic race war from which only the "true Israelites"—white Anglo-Saxons—will survive. More ominous is their stark vision of white racial supremacy as nothing less than God's Law. Identity theology urges its followers to prepare a religious utopian commune—a holy land thought to be America—to be secured by force if necessary.

This movement operates with a petulant moral logic that conveys something of the disillusionment felt by entire segments of the white population bewildered by the massive demographic, social, and economic transformations occurring in the country and the significant changes in the legal culture. Crude as it may seem, Identity theology reflects panic caused by a belief in a racial struggle in which the unchosen are doomed. What may have begun as a groundswell of feebly organized social protest, and an amorphous rebellion against agro-corporations overtaking rural life, overnight grew in size—due to a new influx of competitive foreigners and the relentless affirmative action programs promoted by the Civil Rights movement. From alienation came aggressive political consciousness filled with resignation, hate, and aggressiveness.

The core of Identity theology is not an intellectual penetration of theological mysteries concerning the existence of God or the shape of the afterlife, but a thin religious interpretation of social and cultural questions. What is not discussed in any satisfactory detail in the literature is the potentially terroristic nature of the modern Klan and the religious movement linked to it. Identity theology has some interesting structural parallels with religiously based terrorist movements in the Middle East.

Everyone has noticed the phenomenon of what David Rapaport calls "sacred terror."[39] Guided by radical and often delusional interpretations of the Koran, members of Al Jihad spectacularly assassinated President Anwar Sadat of Egypt in 1981. The group's charismatic leader had written a pamphlet that explained Al Jihad's constitution and justification for its attacks. Similarly, the Hizballah of Lebanon evolved into a radical Shiite movement with violent militias that engaged in terror campaigns throughout the region.[40] Inspired by Shiite clerics, Hizballah, or the "Party of God," has struck repeatedly and lethally against its enemies, who include nonbelievers, foreigners, and apostates. The movement's declared ultimate aim is the creation of an Islamic state in Lebanon. Its mission is not just to improve the relative position of one of Lebanon's constituent communities vis-à-vis all others but to make of Lebanon an ideal Islamic polity and society. In Hizballah's vision, Islam will redeem Lebanon from the ravages of civil war and foreign intervention.

Members of the prominent *ulama*, a council of religious teachers and advisers, in Hizballah were trained in the Islamic theology of Ayatollah Khomeini, who stressed in his lectures on Islamic government and economics the need to develop alternatives to Western and Communist influences and to demand exclusive rights to political rule. The Shiite clerics absorbed a coherent criticism of Islamic decay and were equipped with a revolutionary program of change.

Shiite Islam is not unique in commanding the fanatical, suicidal devotion of its followers. At different periods in their histories, Judaism and Christianity have been able to mobilize unqualified devotion and commitment among their believers for armed struggle and the willing sacrifice of their lives for the cause.[41] Similarly, followers of the Christian Identity Movement are guided by their minister's interpretations of the Book of Revelations in the Old Testament. They are called upon, in many ways like their Shiite brethren in the Islamic armed militias, to cleanse their land of the children of evil—that is, Jews and nonwhites.

Social malignancies for which sharp lines are drawn between "us" and "them" lead to the plausibility of suppressing and even annihilating others. Those who draw such lines are motivated by a cultivated, nurtured dynamic of hate. *Hate* is a promiscuous word: it is more than intense dislike or animosity. It foreshadows and epitomizes what Lifton called a "psychic numbing" and a "psychism"[42]—the exaggerated reliance upon will and psychic power to achieve goals.[43] The imagery of Identity theology, which is consistent with Klan visions of a restored heroic social past, creates mythological futures to be achieved even if blood must be spilled. The "untainted" Book of Revelations is construed to justify the ideological future for revolutionary change—an Armageddon in which whites are destined to defend America and defeat those impure races and religions that embody evil.

Another way of looking at these ponderous theologies that have an intellectual grip on extremist fundamentalist sects is to see them in terms of the psychological bonuses they bestow on their followers. Believers are emotionally rescued from oblivion. The doctrinal interpretations of the

Old Testament in terms of an apocalyptic race war in which white Christians emerge triumphant and vindicated is gratifying for the believer. The victims, the white Christians, are destined to win and regain their land-given heritage of privilege and power.

An encounter with the perversions of Klan ideology and Identity theology induces a cessation of feeling and an emotional and intellectual anesthesia. The believer becomes immunized against the brutalizing effects these ideologies have on others. This paralysis of the mind and feeling is a defense against fear, but like all defenses, it can overstep itself. Becoming a victimizer means relinquishing the role of victim. Klan members, like Christian Identity Movement followers, establish their sense of omnipotent conquest by rendering the victim, the object of hate, subhuman. The Klan's mentality is buttressed by the social environments in which Klan members live and function.

SOCIOLOGICAL AND PSYCHOLOGICAL PERSPECTIVES
ON ORGANIZED HATE

A review of Klan genesis, violence, decline, resurgence, transformation, and resurrection is suggestive of relative deprivation theories of organized violence. In Ted Robert Gurr's studies of conflict and violence in eighty-six countries, the author's main argument is conveyed as follows:[44]

> Exposure to a new way of life or to ideologies depicting a golden millennium seldom themselves generate either dissatisfaction or new expectations. But to the extent that men are already disconnected and see opportunities given to them to attain these goals . . . they are strongly susceptible to ideological conversion. An especially violent, often revolutionary response is likely when men who have been persistently deprived of valued goods and conditions of life are led to believe that their government is about to remedy that deprivation, but then find the hopes false.

Once socioeconomic change is under way within any segment of a society, other processes become operative. If a number of groups experience material gains, the most rapidly gaining groups are likely to be chosen as the reference groups by which others set their expectations.[45]

Individual anger is attributable to discontinuities and disappointed expectations that leap easily from individual anger to group action. For Gurr and others who ascribe to "breakdown theories to violence," the Klan's collective sense of deprivation would be a major cause of its violent reactions to lost privileges and power. Based on its statements and documents, the Klan and other white extremists groups may act on a theory that individuals and communities have a prior collective right to the resources they helped produce and accumulate. Those resources include land, employment opportunities, and educational preference. In its view, the Klan struggled with others who grouped and acted around the theory that the welfare of a state and of its population should take priority over the welfare of any segment of it. Among these groups, many disagreements developed about the distribution of resources, and these disputes did not end when the great transatlantic migration declined.

Today, Los Angeles, Miami, Houston, San Diego, San Francisco, and many cities on the Pacific and Gulf rims of the country have joined New York, Chicago, and Boston as ethnic metropolises, as new versions of Ellis Island. The international migration into these cities is propelled by the same factors that pushed and drove earlier immigrants from their countries—ugly politics, intolerance, and poverty. Like Americans who experienced the shock of the European immigration, those in the locales where the new arrivals concentrate feel besieged and resentful. Previous restrictions on language, cultural expression, and opportunities have dissolved, and immigrants are no longer met with official hostility and suspicion. The lack of official hostility exacerbates tensions among Klan-like extremists who interpret humane policies toward minorities and foreigners as favoritism and preferential treatment.

The collective predisposition to hatred and violence would seem to be a by-product of struggles for power, and the pervasiveness of hate is largely dependent on the reaction of government to the Klan's claims. The Klan, among many groups, feels threatened and betrayed by minority advancement and the changing racial demographics of the country. It is not irrelevant that Klan groups and other right-wing extremists attract people on the margins of the society. Membership in many right-wing groups consists of ex-convicts and people whose only means of contending and competing socially is through violence.

Klan violence has been described as a form of terrorism. Terrorism is usually defined as a strategy of violence designed to promote desired outcomes by instilling fear in the general public.[46] While the Klan has not operated indiscriminately against the public, its actions are designed to instill fear in minority groups. Particularized threats are certainly intimidating to groups specifically targeted, but they may necessarily terrify the general public. Indeed, the localized nature of the Klan leaves ordinary citizens generally unaffected by the fear of potential victimization.

However, it may be difficult for individuals, who harbor strongly felt grievances against hated groups, to attack innocents indiscriminately. How individuals develop the capacity to sustain free-floating hatreds and act on them requires powerful psychological machinations.[47]

Klan ideology has varied as social environments have changed, but as the social realities are transformed by new political values, the question is: to what extent do corresponding reorientations occur in an individual's thinking and feeling? How does an individual manage to sustain hate and act upon it? What moral controls must be selectively deactivated to enable a person to engage in violent behavior? What part do ideology, propaganda, and the messages of movements like Identity theology play in loosening internal control mechanisms that weaken self-sanctions against brutality and violence?

A preliminary point about violence engendered by hate is that it exists in the plural; many groups are hated—not just one or another. English farm laborers of the early nineteenth century regarded violence against property as legitimate and moderate violence against persons as justifiable under certain circumstances, but they systematically refrained from killing in general. However, in conflicts between poachers and gamekeepers, fighting to kill was permissible.[48]

It seems useless, except as a legal excuse for repression or as a debating point about "never yielding to force," to treat various kinds and degrees of violence as essentially indistinguishable. Actions of the same degree of violence may differ sharply in their legitimacy or justification, at least in public opinion. The great Calabrian brigand Musolino, when asked to define *bad* or *evil*, said each meant "killing Christians without a very deep reason."[49]

The violence of hate groups, although governed by "rules" and limited to clearly articulated targets, may become uncontrollable and depersonalized when distinctions concerning actions are lost. Like the violence of terrorists, the violence of hatred may be seen as the weapon of the weak, but it will attract attention to the perpetrators' grievances. For the disoriented fringe, violence and cruelty—sometimes in the most socially ineffective forms—serve as the surrogates for private success and social power.

To engage in hate that materializes into violence, the individual must "morally disengage."[50] Hate and violence are usually impulsive but would seem to be far more dangerous and destructive when they are principled. Individuals may be subjected to psychological assaults that relax moral inhibitions and socialize the individual into new personal thinking that fosters cruelty, hatred, and violence against particular targets. How do individuals, who in everyday situations act decently to further their interests, nonetheless resort in still other circumstances to ways that are injurious to others?

The Klan may be seen as a socialization mechanism that enables members to absorb ideas that provide self-exonerations needed to erase prohibitions against violent behavior and hate. Albert Bandura's model of the sociopsychological process is instructive (see figure 1).

The Klan's history is filled with rationales that morally sanction hate crimes. Destructive conduct is made personally and socially acceptable for Klan members by portraying such behavior as in the service of socially desirable goals. Identity Movement ministers construe violence as conduct necessary for moral purposes in the fulfillment of God's will as revealed in their interpretations of the Old Testament. Individuals then may voluntarily act on a moral imperative in response to images of non-white, non-Christian hordes threatening the historic mission of white Christians.

Intensive exposure to Klan and Christian Identity Movement hate lit-

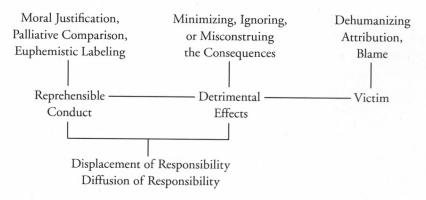

Fig. 1. Psychological mechanisms of moral disengagement. Based on Albert Bandura, "Mechanisms of Moral Disengagement," in *Origins of Terrorism: Psychologies, Ideologies, Theologies, States of Mind*, ed. Walter Reich (New York: Cambridge University Press, 1990), p. 162. Used with permission of the publisher.

erature has effects on attitudes and behavior. In group settings, individual behavior and judgments are strongly influenced by the powerful forces of group dynamics. Pressures are so magnified in the hate group that the group may become for the participant the only authentic and trustworthy source of information. In the face of external hostility and threat, the group becomes the only source of security. Consequently, individuals, who may deplore violence, can be transformed rapidly into individuals within 'a group who are filled with the intense emotions of hatred and with a shared sense of pride in violent behavior.

The conversion of socialized individuals into dedicated haters is not only achieved by altering their personalities, aggressive drives, or even moral standards. By cognitively restructuring the moral value of crimes committed against specific groups so that violence can be committed without censuring doubt, the task of making hate morally defensible is facilitated. What further augments restructuring is the political isolation of fringe groups. Because nonviolent options appear not to have worked effectively, militant action comes to be regarded as the only recourse to redress grievances.

The Klan has rarely engaged in mass killings. Its targets have been the weak, the hapless, and the unfortunate, chosen opportunistically. A few incidents of terror are usually sufficient to incite widespread public fear, because Klan acts have seemed so random and unpredictable. They create an atmosphere of continual vulnerability. The question—Who will be next?—haunts everyone. The risk of death or injury in a Klan hate attack is great, and minority individuals are understandably fearful of the terror of an attack.

The mass media can heighten the sense of fear and uncertainty. The Klan's long history, its distinctive costumes, and frightening imagery disturb people. The visual effects of white hoods and burning crosses are greatly intensified by the melodramatic power of television. In its history of intimidation, the Klan has astutely exploited the media and has generated a distorted sense of its power and influence.

Membership in Klan groups and exposure to their acculturation processes produce psychological defenses against abhorrent behavior. Much like accused Nazis who refused to acknowledge their responsibility for Jewish mass murder, Klan members can engage, among themselves, in self-deception about reprehensible activities through rhetoric that is palliative. The irresponsible act can be transformed magically from the repugnant to the plausible within the insulated world of a Klavern.

Numerous examples exist of language that disguises and therefore distorts heinous behavior. Military clichés describing "clean, surgical strikes" and "collateral damage" have been used to alter and sanitize vicious conduct. Language can change the nature of culpability and can disinhibit individuals by interpreting their behavior as less loathsome and dangerous than it really is. Klan literature describes its mission not as social genocide but as the maintenance of the supremacy of the white race. Whites are elevated above the common standard of human creation, and claims are made that the Creator has intended that "inferior" races of nonwhites and groups of Jews, Catholics, and Muslims be separated and dominated so that an Aryan, Christian nation will prevail.[51]

The Klan's organization into quasi-secretive Klaverns includes the language of hate, a generally confidential membership, the infamous white hoods and gowns, the dramatic cross burnings at night rallies, and the skillful denunciations of racial and religious groups. A sense of camaraderie is enhanced in such environments; paradoxically, members have a mutual feeling of being victimized, as they victimize and detest others.[52] Acts of violence or "armed resistance" in the euphemistic rhetoric of the Klan can be invoked to justify situational imperatives and tyrannical circumstances. "Jewish/Communist plots" in the government can drive the Klan to acts of violence and to organizing armed groups to expose Jewish leaders wielding power in the centers of government and business. Within the Klan environment, relabeling Jews and others as victimizers achieves credibility because of the Klan's closed, secretive nature.

Another function served by Klan organization is to diffuse and displace responsibility for hate-motivated criminal acts. By creating a hierarchy of Imperial Wizard, Grand Dragons, Klokards, and Kleagles and by creating a network of semiautonomous, local Klaverns, the Klan has devised a world of "alternative institutions" within the United States (see figure 2).

Klan rallies and ceremonies provide other ways to weaken conventional self-restraint. Because group actions can be largely ascribed to the behavior of other members, brutal behavior is more likely when one's sense of responsibility is obscured by collective actions. Individuals can subsequently deny personal accountability.

The nature of the Klan and its organization conspire to dehumanize both victims and victimizers. By divesting people of human qualities, savage conduct against them is possible. J. B. Stener, chairman of the National States Rights Party, is a former Klansman from Georgia whose

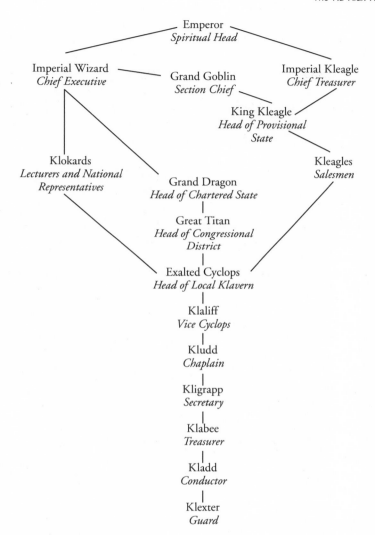

Fig. 2. Klan chain of command

anti-Semitism and antiblack political positions are well known. He indicated to a journalist during an interview about racial violence that "I
didn't advocate it, but if somebody else does it, I never criticize 'em. Niggers are animals. They're wild animals. Niggers are killing white people
from one end of the country to the other ever'day, so that if a white man

kills a nigger, why I say more power to him. It's like the killing of Martin Lucifer Coon [Rev. Martin Luther King, Jr.], I didn't shed any tears over it. I'd find life very dull if I didn't fight for the white race. I get pleasure out of it."[53]

Once dehumanized, as Stener's comments show, potential victims are no longer persons with feelings, hopes, and concerns but are subhuman objects. Stener portrays blacks as "animals" and "killers." Because subhumans are regarded as insensitive to killing, they deserve the killing they get.

Imputing blame to one's victims and antagonists is still another expedient that can serve self-exonerative purposes. One's own conduct can then be viewed as compelled by fortuitous factors as well as by the influences of personal predilections and social inducements. The nurturing of hatred and a capacity to do violence occur within an intensified communal milieu insulated from mainstream social life. As an organization, the Klan provides a setting that cultivates brutality and enables its members to act callously and to disregard anxiety about guilt toward their victims.

THE ARCHIPELAGO OF HATE

From its birth in Tennessee to the present, the Ku Klux Klan has rebuilt itself to focus on new targets of hate. However, its traditional victims have been and are American blacks.

The name *Ku Klux Klan* is from *Kulios*, a Greek word meaning "bonded circle." Because many original members were of Scottish-Irish descent, the word "Klan" was added.[54] Apparently, it was not born in hatred and bitterness but evolved rapidly into a intimidating force that became more than a collection of pranksters. Originally, Klaverns operated independently; as the movement expanded into countries and other states, organization was needed. In time, a hierarchical structure of offices, duties, roles, and statutes emerged. Passwords, oaths of secrecy, costumes, and elaborate rituals were devised. The infamous cross-burning ceremony was derived either from the film, *Birth of a Nation*, or from Sir Walter Scott's *The Lady of the Lake*. A "Kalendar" lists dates and events from the Klan's origins and its 1915 rebirth; it has become part of the Klan's institutional paraphernalia and tarnished history.

In the Klaverns, members learned the art and science of hate. Victims were classified according to race, religion, politics, ethnicity, and sexual orientation. In spite of night-riding forays, murder, and mass meetings, Klan Wizards, resplendent in purple and green silk gowns, would egregiously deny that they were racists. They claimed that Jews were excluded from memberships because they did not believe in Christianity; Catholics were initially banned from membership due to discretionary preferences—much as the Knights of Columbus chose not to admit Protestants. The Klan's public claims about race did not refer to a celebration of white supremacy or race hatred but involved race pride and the preservation of white civilization, as they indignantly and relentlessly claimed.

The Klan's popularity in the South was somewhat understandable because of the racial distrust and fear beneath life there. However, its strength was not confined to rural pockets in the South. In the 1920s, the Klan flourished everywhere—in the East, the Midwest, and in the Northwest.

The seemingly tremendous national growth of the Ku Klux Klan can be demythized because there is no such thing as the Klan. There are many Klans with variations on the original name—the United Klans of America, Knights of the Ku Klux Klan, the National Knights of the Ku Klux Klan, the Original Knights of the Ku Klux Klan, the Dixie Klans, and others.[55] Each local group seizes upon a problem that preoccupies that particular part of the country. In some places, it may be unemployment; in others, government incompetence, drug and alcohol problems, or crime. Local Kleagles or Klan organizers and recruiters may identify a local issue and exploit it. The sociology of blame, in which victims themselves are blamed, is too superficial to warrant detailed examination. However, the Klan was and is skillful at finding fertile fears and discontentedness for its emotional appeals.

Klan targets have been not only blacks competing with local working-class whites for jobs. In Oregon in 1921, the Prohibition laws were openly flouted. The Klan, having won the support of the Women's Christian Temperance Movement and several churches, organized a ʴaign against bootleggers, corrupt police, and foreigners operating   ʿimi-larly, it gained political power in Indiana in 1924 by cratic officeholders implicated in liquor and gamblir

The Klan speaks of its own history and destiny Eras." The first era lasted approximately a decad Civil War. The second "great" era occurred dur' D. W. Griffith's film, *Birth of a Nation*, was relea' the Klan had been in eclipse, Klansmen chose film as evidence of an awakening and growing interest in their racial ideology. During this period, a Klan organization, the Hooded Order, a previously Southern-based organization, spread into the North, East, and West. The ideas of the Hooded Order were rooted in the native backlash against the huge influx of Catholic immigrants and Jews from southern and eastern Europe who had settled in northern and midwestern cities. Klan membership increased dramatically; Klan influence in electoral politics was evident in 1925 when forty thousand members marched down Pennsylvania Avenue in a large parade in the heart of the nation's capital.

The third era of the Klan began in 1954 when the Civil Rights movement was forming. During the struggle for civil rights, the worst Klan atrocity occurred; in 1963, a bomb exploding in a Birmingham Baptist church killed four black children. Of all the hate crimes committed by the Klan, these murders were the most unforgivable, and as a result, the Klan lost membership and influence. As in other decades, the decline was inevitable, because the Klan had no solid base or positive program beyond hate, fear, and violence. The Klan depended solely on fanaticism and emotions that could not be sustained at a feverish pitch. Historically, however, the Klan never really faded into total obscurity. The Klan still lurks beneath the surface of American life. When issues are intensely felt and tap the deep wells of prejudice, the Klan reemerges to furiously ride the crests of hatred and brutality.

According to its sympathizers, the fourth era of Klan destiny began in the 1970s. The theme of the newly media-conscious Klan was, nevertheless, the same that had motivated ex-Confederate soldiers in Tennessee's first Klavern: resistance to change in the racial and religious composition of society. The Klan had always been resourceful in responding to new fears and anxieties in the population. In the 1970s, resistance strategies changed; not only did the Klan urge that blacks be kept in their place but also Jews, various minorities, non-Christians, gays, and women activists.

In this phase of its history, the organization splintered. Women and Catholics were being accepted for some memberships, and a new charismatic figure emerged in Louisiana whose career would shock and polarize the nation. David Duke, the new Wizard of the Louisiana Klan, preferred the title, "National Director"—a name that typified his skill in appearing reasonable to larger audiences, while maintaining his constitu-
in the South. Duke was the youngest Grand Wizard in Klan his-

tory. His appeal was based not only on his racist message; his glib style allowed his fans and the press to endow him with whatever qualities they chose. Duke's gubernatorial campaign showed the influence of Klan propaganda and the strength of vindictiveness in large parts of American society. In the Louisiana race, Duke might well have received more than 56 percent of the vote were it not for status anxieties among the upper middle class and the college-educated, his two weakest voting blocs. He resigned officially from the Klan in order to avoid being tainted by his affiliation.

Other new extremists, active in the hate politics associated with the Klan, are openly militant. Duke was prepared to pursue revolutionary policies on television talk shows; others are not so sanguine. Strategies of a fifth era imagine a future when the Klan goes underground and operates as a traditional terrorist organization. Louis Beam, a former Grand Dragon of the Texas Knights, led a terrorist campaign in Galveston, Texas, against Vietnamese immigrants in the shrimp industry. Bean eventually drifted north and became involved with other extremist groups, including the Order, perhaps the most violent of Klan splinter groups. The Order, an offshoot of Aryan Nations, trains and prepares for guerrilla war. It was founded in the Pacific Northwest in 1983 and has engaged in bank robberies and counterfeiting to finance its operation.[57]

In the 1990s, the Klan is again in a state of turmoil. The major formations of the 1970s—the United Klans of America, the Knights of the Ku Klux Klan, the Invisible Empire—are in disarray, which does not indicate that hate-inspired violence has subsided. Throughout its troubled history, the Klan demonstrated a remarkable will to survive: it has outlived pretenders and rivals. Because it thrives on prejudice and hate, skillfully adapts to each social era, and allies itself with any cause that will promote it, the Klan or Klans have been able to revive themselves. One must wonder after the beatings, stabbings, murders, the burning of blacks' homes, the desecration of synagogues, and the open contempt for gays and immigrants, how a country that historically has been a melting pot for diverse ethnic and social groups could ever come to nurture such frenzies of hate and violence.

SUMMARY AND CONCLUSIONS

In a sense, American innocence and regionalism ended with the Civil War; everyone had to face the political and moral contradictions that had festered since the beginnings of the Republic. In such a period, marked by a sense of insecurity and unrelieved crisis, a movement began that never really clung to its announced objectives of white redemption and salvation but that reflected a spiritual fatigue and fear of the world.

The prime symbol of torment that energized the Klan was race. The emancipated slave gave a vivid reminder of defeat and dissolution. To regain a bucolic, white past and to somehow reassert white authority, blacks had to be terrorized and humiliated. Although they lived for decades side by side with blacks, whites in the South never did "see" blacks. Because whites knew little about blacks, relationships between them were invested with strains of fear and uncertainty.

As the Kerner Commission grimly observed more than two decades ago, American society is so fractured—perhaps irreparably—along racial lines that there are two societies, one black and the other white, each wary of the other. Today, polarization seems very acute. It is as if two societies, identified by color and divided by a legacy of hypocrisy and suspicion, are poised for action, much like hill-dwellers facing each other across a valley. What they have in common is the mutual danger of falling from their respective cliffs. However, they cannot stop looking across the chasm without wondering what the others are doing and thinking.

Scattered across the United States are many areas of hate that are psychologically invisible and imperceptible and are inhabited by hooded Americans. These enclaves of angry, embittered people exist in small, clandestine groups in cities, towns, and villages throughout the country. Many have seen and heard something vague; others know nothing of the Klan. As time passes, many have been touched by the brotherhood of hatred and know its violence.

Given the anxieties among racial, religious, and ethnic groups, the United States faces another "American Dilemma." The Klan today represents not only a virulent hate group but perhaps signifies deeper, unresolved structural problems in American culture and political values.

The new dilemma is moral and sociological. Its essence is in the struggle between concepts of integration and pluralism. The question is conventionally posed as an issue of boundaries. Integrationists look toward the elimination of ethnic, racial, and religious distinctions. Pluralists believe in the maintenance of distinctions and integrity. The primary difference concerns the scale and character of the community each takes as a model. Integration is pledged to a community yet to be realized: the brotherhood of humankind. Pluralism is pledged to microcommunities of local groups, distinctive but cooperative.

From this fundamental difference—for which the Constitution itself never established any explicit guidelines for adjudicating—flow other differences concerning which perspective has a legitimate claim to be the true champion of democracy. However, democracy means different things to each group. Consistent with its universalist criteria, integrationists favor a majoritarian emphasis; they expect a simple majority to approximate the general will. Pluralism is a philosophy of minority rights, and it is likely to dispute the legitimacy of any simple majority.

Pluralists conceive of democratic politics as a process of building coalitions. In many respects, the Klan is a distortion of the tension to build coalitions within the political culture and signals the failure of integrationists or pluralists to articulate a clear vision of American politics. The nativist dimensions in Klan ideology and its quasi-religious irredentism suggest that it recognizes and fears the durability and power of ethnic and racial groups. No ethnic group, once established in the United States, has ever entirely disappeared; none seems about to do so. At the same time, the Klan mistakenly assumes, as pluralists do, a rigidity of ethnic, racial, and religious boundaries and a permanence of group commitment, which does not occur in American life. Evidence indicates that all American ethnic groups perpetuate themselves, but none survives intact. Their boundaries are undefined and changing. The unity that various groups attain is usually temporary and precarious—unstable unless confronted by a common enemy. Pluralism encourages the illusion, which Klan groups embrace, that ethnic, racial, and religious groups typically have a high degree of internal solidarity.

While the Klan rejects the value of ethnic identity among other groups, it cultivates separateness and racial-religious cohesion of its own. If the Klan promoted an assimilationist ideology, insisting upon an ethnic of self-transformation for all, it would not constitute a serious social threat. Instead, it would create an emotional cul-de-sac for admirers and activists by generating hatred for others and alienation from what it defines as its birthright.

The liabilities of each perspective are glaringly evident in Klan ideology. Assimilation into an American society that is multiethnic, multiracial, and multireligious is interpreted as disloyalty to the ancestral heritage. The Klan also adjures its followers to realize themselves through the group to which they belong and to forgo opportunity in the interest of separateness and cohesion. Demanding that others sacrifice their groups for the sake of individual assimilation into their version of the Anglo-centric culture, the Klan would put individual white Americans at the mercy of its ideology.

In the last decade, we have encountered diversity with a vengeance. It is too soon to say whether the return to ethnicity or multiculturalism is a temporary reaction or a mere interlude during the onrush of immigration. If sharpened and often abrasive minority group assertiveness is more than a passing phenomenon, Klan-like violence and hate is likely to continue.

The great tragedy of the Civil War—the collapse of an entire way of life—opened the road for the march of the Ku Klux Klan. The world of the antebellum South, which gave romantic impetus to the Klan, was once ruled by an elite class, aristocrats of privilege, and descendants of great wealth who held high office and authority. In the battles that raged across the Confederacy, men of high and low birth fought side by side; the depleted ranks of the aristocratic planters would eventually be filled by commoners left destitute and embittered by the war. From the ex-soldiers of the Confederacy and disenfranchised troops of the Confederate and Union armies, men emerged who would come to wield power and instill fear. Their legacy of hatred has transformed itself and continues to thrive.

Unlike National Socialism, which collapsed abruptly and absolutely after Hitler's death, the Klan has not collapsed like a bubble—due to changing national values and social attitudes. The Klan crusade continues. Certainly no other movement in the United States has disrupted so many lives or stirred so much hatred. The passage of more than 150 years has done little to alter the perspective of its true believers. What should be of concern are the general lessons that the Klan's success and failures might teach. What is to be learned from its periodic resurgence and spread, from its decline and contraction?

NOTES

1. Gunnar Myrdal (1944), *An American Dilemma: The Negro Problem and Modern Democracy* (New York: Harper & Brothers), 189.

2. Bernard Bailyn (1967), *The Ideological Origins of the America Revolution* (Cambridge: Harvard Univ. Press).

3. Michael W. Hughey (1992), "Americanism and Its Discontents: Nativism and Political Heresy in America," *International Journal of Politics, Culture and Society* 5(4): 533–53.

4. Ray Allan Billington (1973), *The Protestant Crusade, 1800–1860: A Study of the Origins of American Nativism* (Gloucester, Mass.: Peter Smith); John Higham (1978), *Strangers in the Land: Patterns of American Nativism 1860–1925* (New York: Atheneum).

5. J. Hector St. John de Crevecoeur (1806), *Letters from an American Farmer*, quoted in Arthur M. Schlesinger, Jr. (1992), *The Disuniting of America* (New York: Norton), 85.

6. William McLaughlin (1973), "The Role of Religion in the Revolution: Liberty of Conscience and Cultural Cohesion in the New Nation," in *Essays on the American Revolution*, ed. S. G. Kurtz and J. H. Hutsen (Chapel Hill: Univ. of North Carolina Press), 215–29.

7. Michael W. Hughey (1984), "The National Covenant: Protestantism and the Creation of the American State," *Culture and Society*, 1(1): 113–56.

8. Barrington Moore (1966), *Social Origins of Dictatorship and Democracy* (Boston: Beacon Press), chap. 3; Robert Merton (1965) *Social Theory and Social Structure*, rev. ed. (New York: Free Press), chap. 19.

9. Richard Hofstadter (1965), *The Paranoid Style in American Politics and Others Essays* (New York: Knopf).

10. Robert J. Kelly and Rufus Schatzberg (1992), "Galvanizing Indiscriminate Political Violence: Mind-Sets and Some Ideological Constructs in Terrorism," *International Journal of Comparative and Applied Criminal Justice* 16(3/4): 117–26.

11. See in particular 16 U.S. Stats 141 sec. 6 (Act of May 31, 1870).

12. Lawrence M. Friedman (1993), *Crime and Punishment in American History* (New York: Basic Books), chap. 8.

13. David M. Chalmers (1981), *Hooded Americanism: The History of the Ku Klux Klan* (New York: Franklin Watts).

14. William P. Randel (1965), *The Ku Klux Klan: A Century of Infamy* (New York: Chilton Books).

15. Ted Robert Gurr (1987), "Political Terrorism in the United States: Historical Antecedents and Contemporary Trends," in *The Politics of Terrorism*, 3d rev. ed., ed. Michael Soth (New York: Marcel Dekker), 549–78.

16. Vernon Louis Parrington (1958), *The Beginnings of Critical Realism in America: 1860–1920*, vol. 3 (New York: Harcourt, Brace and World); Stanley M. Elkins (1963), *Slavery: A Problem in American Institutional and Intellectual Life* (New York: Grosset & Dunlap).

17. Robert J. Kelly (1973), "New Political Crimes and the Emergence of Revolutionary Nationalist Ideologies," in *Deviance, Conflict and Criminality*, ed. C. McCaghy and R. S. Denisoff (Chicago: Rand McNally), 220–37.

18. Eugene Genovese (1974), *Roll Jordan, Roll: The World the Slaves Made* (New York: Vintage Books); Robert Blauner (1972), *Racial Oppression in America* (New York: Harper & Row).

19. John Higham (1975), *Send These to Me: Jews and Other Immigrants in Urban America* (New York: Atheneum).

20. Maldwyn Jones (1960), *American Immigration* (Chicago: Univ. of Chicago Press); Oscar Handlin (1951), *The Uprooted: The Epic Story of the Great Migrants That Made the American People* (Boston: Beacon Press).

21. Thomas Gossett (1965), *Race: The History of an Idea in America* (New York: Macmillan); Stephen Steinberg (1981), *The Ethnic Myth: Race, Ethnicity and Class in America* (Boston: Beacon Press).

22. Seymour M. Lipset and Earl Raab (1970), *The Politics of Unreason: Right-Wing Extremism in America* (New York: Free Press).

23. David Bennett (1988), *The Party of Fear: From Nativist Movements to the New Right in American History* (New York: Vintage Books).

24. John Higham (1988), *Strangers in the Land: Patterns of American Nativism, 1860–1925* (New Brunswick, N.J.: Rutgers Univ. Press).

25. Ellis Cose (1992), *A Nation of Strangers: Prejudice, Politics and the Popularity of America* (New York: Morrow).

26. Allen Sapp (1991), "Value and Belief Systems of Right-Wing Extremists: Rationale and Motivation for Bias-Motivated Crimes," in *Bias Crime: American Law Enforcement and Legal Responses*, ed. Robert J. Kelly (Chicago: Office of International Criminal Justice, Univ. of Chicago at Illinois), 98–117.

27. Higham (1988), 182.

28. Kenneth T. Jackson (1992), *The Ku Klux Klan in the City* (Chicago: Ivan Dee).

29. Richard Hofstadter (1984), *The American Political Tradition* (New York: Vintage Books), 203.

30. Chalmers (1981), 87.

31. Chalmers (1981), 91.

32. Klanwatch (1991), *The Ku Klux Klan: A History of Racism and Violence*, 4th ed. (Montgomery, Ala.: Southern Poverty Law Center), 40.

33. Philip S. Foner (1970), *The Black Panthers Speak* (Philadelphia: Lippincott).

34. J. H. Clark (1990), *Malcolm X: The Man and His Times* (New York: Africa World Press).

35. Robert G. Powers (1987), *Secrecy and Power: The Life of J. Edgar Hoover* (New York: Free Press).

36. Gad J. Bensinger (1991), "Hate Crimes: A New/Old Problem" (paper presented at the annual meeting of the American Society of Criminology, San Francisco, Calif., Nov. 21).

37. Anti-Defamation League (1990) *Neo-Nazi Skinheads: A 1990 Status Report* (New York: Anti-Defamation League).

38. Irvin Small and David Low (1987), "The Hate Movement Today: A Chronicle of Violence and Disarray," *Terrorism* 10: 345–64.

39. David C. Rapaport (1990), "Sacred Terror: A Contemporary Example for Islam," in *Origins of Terrorism: Psychologies, Ideologies, Theologies, State of Mind*, ed. Walter Reich (New York: Cambridge Univ. Press), 87.

40. Martin Kramer (1990), "The Moral Logic of Hizballah," in *Origins of Terrorism*, 141–59.

41. Leonard Zeskind (1986), *The Christian Identity Movement* (Atlanta: Center for Democratic Renewal); Bruce Hoffman (1987), "Right Wing Terror in the U.S." *Violence, Aggression, Terrorism* 1(1): 27–39; E. Sprinzak (1987), "From Messianic Pioneering to Vigilante Terrorism: The Case of the Gush Enumim," *Journal of Strategic Studies* 10(4): 383–402.

42. Robert J. Lifton (1971), *History and Human Survival* (New York: Vintage Books), 44.

43. Robert J. Lifton (1968), *Revolutionary Immorality: Mao Tse Tung and the Chinese Revolution* (New York: Vintage Books).

44. Ted Robert Gurr (1970), *Why Men Rebel* (Princeton: Princeton Univ. Press), 179.

45. Ted Robert Gurr and Raymond Duvall (1973), "Civil Conflict in the 1960s: A Reciprocal System with Parameter Estimates," (paper presented at the annual meeting of the International Studies Association, Mar. 12), 121.

46. M. C. Bassiouni (1981), "Terrorism, Law Enforcement and the Mass Media: Perspectives, Problems, Proposals," *Journal of Criminal Law and Criminology* 72: 151; Walter Lacqueur (1987), *The Age of Terrorism* (Boston: Little, Brown), x, chap. 4.

47. Albert Bandura (1986), *Social Foundations of Thought and Action: A Social Cognitive Theory* (Englewood Cliffs, N.J.: Prentice Hall), 95.

48. E. J. Hobsbawn (1975), *Revolutionaries: Contemporary Essays* (New York: New American Library), 210.

49. Charles Tilly et al. (1975), *The Rebellious Century: 1830–1930* (Cambridge: Harvard Univ. Press), 116.

50. Albert Bandura (1990), "Mechanisms of Moral Disengagement," in *Origins of Terrorism*, 161–91.

51. Randel (1965), 21; Richard G. Butler (undated), *The Aryan Warrior* (Hayden Lake, Idaho: Aryan Nation Press), 202.

52. Jerry Thompson (1982), *My Life in the Klan* (New York: Putnam).

53. Patsy Sims (1978), *The Klan* (New York: Stein and Day).

54. Wyn Craig Wade (1987), *The Fiery Cross: The Ku Klux Klan in America* (New York: Simon & Schuster).

55. Bill Stanton (1991), *Klanwatch: Bringing the Ku Klux Klan to Justice* (New York: Grove Weidenfeld).

56. Fred J. Cook (1989), *The Ku Klux Klan: America's Recurrent Nightmare* (Englewood Cliffs, N.J.: Messner).

57. Cook (1989), 37.

4. The Homeless Palestinians in Israel and the Arab World

Ghada Talhami

he history of the Palestinian people is a complicated subject, touching on Arab nationalism, British imperialism, international law, Zionist ideology, and Western guilt over the Holocaust. However, denial of the rights of the Palestinians to form a political community of their own and to enjoy security in their own homeland dates back to World War I. Furthermore, the major consequence of this denial, which determined the fate of the Palestinians during the twentieth century, was permanent homelessness. The Palestinians have either lived as a semicolonized people under British control, as annexed people under Jordanian rule, as an occupied population under the Israelis, or as stateless refugees under various Arab regimes. The first and most serious result of this statelessness has been national dismemberment, which by itself prevented and complicated what could have been an easy restoration of national sovereignty. Consequently, the perpetual state of Palestinian lack of sovereignty has existed for almost a hundred years.

The territory known as Palestine/Israel, which is claimed by Arabs and Jews alike, reflects the boundaries of biblical Palestine. The British were the first to rename this area Palestine following World War I. Previously, Palestine was under Ottoman rule and was administered as separate provinces. However, when parts of that country were administered from Damascus or Beirut, the Palestinian inhabitants enjoyed a culture and way of life that were somewhat distinct from the culture of neighboring Arab countries.

Britain and France concluded three secret agreements during World War I in an effort to divide the Arab territories of the Ottoman Empire between them. Britain, however, concluded conflicting agreements with both Arabs and Jews, promising each of them rights in Palestine. The Balfour Declaration allowed Jews to establish a homeland, not a state, in Palestine. At the same time, the Hussein-McMahon correspondence, promised Sherif Hussein of Mecca and the leader of the Arab revolt a united Arab kingdom, which would include Palestine. The understanding of the correspondence was fulfilled only partially in the creation of two smaller kingdoms, Iraq and Jordan, under the control of Hussein's two sons, Kings Faisal and Abdullah. The rest of the Arab territories were transformed into mandates administered by France and England according to the terms of the Sykes-Picot Agreement.

Palestine was assigned to Britain as a mandate, to be administered under the supervision of the League of Nations. Although Jews were given access to Palestine as immigrants, the local population was promised eventual independence under the terms of the league's mandate agreement. The Jewish population at the time was no more than 10 percent of the total population, but the rate of Jewish immigration to Palestine increased sharply, particularly following the Holocaust. Events in Nazi Germany created an international climate that was very sympathetic to the Zionist demand for a state in Palestine. The United Nations, therefore, quickly adopted the partition resolution of November 29, 1947, by which the Jewish population, by then one-third of the total population, received half of all of Palestine. The resolution precipitated the first Arab-Jewish war of 1948, resulting in the signing of armistice agreements between the new state of Israel and its Arab neighbors. No permanent peace agreements between these antagonists were signed until the Camp David Accords of 1978.

While Israel established itself on the western portion of British Palestine, Jordan annexed the eastern portion of the same territory. Between 1948 and 1967, eastern Palestine was known as the West Bank of the Hashemite Kingdom of Jordan. The Gaza Strip, however, was administered by Egypt without being permanently annexed to that country. Neither Egypt nor Jordan were ever accused by the Palestinians and international agencies of human rights abuse, of expulsion of the local population, of massive land confiscation, and of settling people in the midst of the Palestinian population. Israel was accused of such acts.

The June war of 1967 finally gave Israel control of all of the West Bank and Gaza, as well as Sinai and the Golan Heights. In December of 1987, a massive Palestinian uprising, known as the *intifada*, threatened to make the Israeli occupation too costly for the Israeli regime. The Palestine Liberation Organization's quick declaration of Palestinian statehood and its unilateral recognition of Israel finally deprived the intifada of its external sources of support. The Gulf war of 1990 eventually weakened the PLO sufficiently to lead to the Madrid peace talks and the Oslo Accords. By 1994, the PLO accepted control of two towns, Gaza and Jericho, in exchange for peace. For the majority of the Palestinians, however, the conditions that caused them to rebel were still unaltered, particularly the closeness of the Israeli settlers.

Palestinians under Israeli control or in the diaspora faced different problems, according to the date when they fell under Israeli rule. Since the creation of Israel in 1948, almost 20 percent of its population, or approximately 750,000 people, were Palestinian Arab. Following the 1967 Arab-Israeli war, the entire population of the West Bank and Gaza, including that of annexed Jerusalem, fell under Israeli rule. Almost 1.75 million Palestinians were added to the Israeli population. Palestinian refugees, who had fled or were driven from their homeland, in 1948 numbered more than half a million people. These people were technically classified as refugees by the United Nations' relief agencies. Since then, the numbers of the Palestinian refugee population have increased dramatically, and the total number of all Palestinians in the world and under occupation is estimated to be between 5 and 6 million people.

These people live as Jordanian citizens in Jordan and as stateless people in the refugee camps of Syria, Lebanon, and the Gaza region. Most Palestinians employed in the Arab Persian Gulf countries carry Jordanian passports. The status of Jordan's Palestinians, compared to Jordan's indigenous population, however, remains problematic. Jordan itself fought a civil war against its Palestinian population in 1970 and is often less than enthusiastic in defending the rights of its expatriated Palestinian population in other countries. More importantly, the Jordanians have never permitted the Palestinians living near the border to arm themselves while the West Bank was under Jordanian rule. Nor have the Jordanians prevented the Israeli official and unofficial abuse of its Palestinian captive population.

The growing importance of the Palestine Liberation Organization in 1964 succeeded in strengthening Palestinian national claims as well as Palestinian national identity. The PLO, however, found it difficult to extend actual protection to the occupied population. Until the intifada, which began in 1987, the PLO was headquartered outside of occupied Palestine and lacked a territorial base of operations. The intifada, amazingly, became a Palestinian war front inside Israeli-controlled areas. Consequently, the Arab-Israeli struggle moved within Israel's borders. The PLO became more successful in representing the Palestinian population and safeguarding their security in Lebanon. From 1970, when the PLO moved its base of operations from Jordan to Lebanon's Palestinian refugee camps, until 1982, when the PLO was expelled by the Israelis, the PLO served as a quasi-government in Lebanon's refugee camps. The camps became almost sovereign Palestinian entities, wholly outside the jurisdiction of the Lebanese state. As a result, the Palestinians became embroiled in Lebanon's fractious politics, making themselves increasingly vulnerable to Lebanese political violence.

The PLO's relationship to different sectors of the expatriated Palestinian population also varied according to the willingness of the host Arab governments to endorse the Palestinian national program. Wherever and whenever the host governments were determined to avoid any clash with the Israelis, the PLO and the Palestinian camp populations were kept under strict observation. However, avoiding conflicts with Israel never developed into a commitment by host governments to protect the Palestinian population. Often the Palestinian refugee population was perceived as being more politicized than the host population and as a threat to social peace. Governments kept Palestinian refugees under constant surveillance. Local populations frequently viewed the Palestinians as competitors for jobs and educational opportunities. Relations between the host Arab populations and the Palestinians thus became aggravated in times of severe economic or political crises, as the clashes between the Palestinians in Lebanon and the country's Shiite population during the mid-1980s illustrate. Although both populations had suffered equal degrees of civil discrimination and Israeli bombardment, increasing Israeli pressure in southern Lebanon pushed the Shiites to portray the Palestinians as victims.

The most serious exposure of Palestinians to hate crimes and violent acts of religious and racial hatred resulted from Israel's settlement policy.

Following the 1967 Arab-Israeli war and the fall of the West Bank and Gaza Strip, approximately 120,000 Israelis found themselves within Arab areas. The Israeli settlement policy included annexed Arab Jerusalem, where acts of violence and incitement began to occur. This settlement policy, an official instrument of the Israeli Labor government, placed very religious and zealous Israelis in close proximity to Arab centers of population. Friction was inevitable, not only because of the intruders' religious and political perceptions of the Palestinians but also because of the settlers' desire to own land.

Religious and nationalist Israeli settlers in the West Bank, Gaza, and Jerusalem repeatedly reminded their liberal Israeli critics of Israel's Zionist fever. The settlement movement claimed that Zionism itself—the ideology sanctioning the establishment of an exclusive Jewish state for all Jews—was based on the notion of limitless land acquisition. Sabri Jiryis detailed official Israeli methods of land usurpation, including the removal by the Israeli army of villagers from their ancestral village, presumably for security reasons, and then the dynamiting of their homes. The army sometimes simply expelled villagers from their homes and relocated them elsewhere. The Israelis also introduced legislation, stating that by 1950 any unoccupied or unclaimed Arab land would be declared absentee property and placed under the control of the "Guardian of Absentee Property." In an unprecedented action, this same law was extended to cover Islamic Charitable Trusts.[1]

The Israeli settlers, therefore, regarded Arab lands as open lands, which could be easily possessed with a slight manipulation of laws or of the resident population. Settling the Israeli Jewish population on Arab lands, which is prohibited under the 1947 Geneva Agreements, was begun by the secular Labor government for defensive purposes. The people who were willing to be settled on Arab land were Israelis who held excessive religious and national convictions. A well-known Israeli writer, Amos Elon, blamed secular Israeli cabinets for introducing Israeli zealots into the Arab areas. The first settlement in the Palestinian town of Hebron was constructed with the permission of Yigal Allon, the Israeli defense minister, who wished to demonstrate his intent to surround Arab areas with defensive settlements. Another secular cabinet minister, Ariel Sharon, was the first to give weapons to the settlers and help organize them in a regional defense unit. The settlers' racism toward the Arab population, according to Elon, was encouraged by such references to the

Arabs as "a cancer in the [nation's] body" and as "cockroaches in bottles" by Israeli general Rafael Eitan.[2]

The settlement of Arab lands, which the Israelis believe are open public lands, is essentially a continuation of fundamental Zionist policies. In the 1920s and 1930s, when the early Zionists were unable to acquire new land, they would purchase it from absentee Lebanese or church landlords. These lands were purchased by the Jewish National Fund, which declared that the land was the perpetual property of the Jewish people. Consequently, the history of the state of Israel is based on colonization.[3] Israeli determination to acquire land without its people can be traced to the U.N. Partition Plan of 1947. When the United Nations partitioned Palestine into Arab and Jewish states and the British declared their intentions to evacuate Palestine on May 15, 1948, the Israelis began developing "Plan D" (*Dalet* in the Hebrew alphabet). Because the land allotted to them included a small Jewish population and was not large enough to accommodate future Jewish settlement, the Zionists developed a final military plan to acquire as much territory as possible. They terrorized the civilian Palestinian population into fleeing their land by attacking Arab villages. The famous Deir Yassin massacre resulted from one such attack.[4]

The Jewish settlers, who were settled by a secular government into the occupied Arab territories of 1967, were religious nationalists highly suited for the expansionist purposes of Israel. Beneath their messianism— and their declarations that every stone and field in the Arab areas were the sacred and hallowed ground called Judea and Samaria—lay a mystification of force and the use of violence. Rabbi Zvi Yehuda Kook of the Merkaz Harav in Jerusalem was an ascetic man who resembled the Ayatollah Khomeini. Before his death in 1982, Kook trained a whole generation of "new Jewish men" who, armed with prayer books and Kalashnikov rifles, sanctioned the trampling of Arab watermelon fields in Samaria and uprooted Arab vineyards in Hebron.[5]

The settlers' ideology, according to Yori Heller, a leader of the Hashona'im branch of the Gush Emonim settler movement, is based on three tenets: to crown a king; to eliminate "'Amalek; and to build the Third Temple. Rebuilding the Third Temple, an objective shared by Israeli right-wing groups and religious organizations, entails destroying holy places belonging to Christians and Muslims. In 1967, large areas in the West Bank city of Hebron were occupied by approximately seventy-three armed religious Jews, led by Rabbi Moshe Levinger. They came to celebrate Passover and to renew their associations with the city of Abraham. They then refused to leave the mosque, and they built the settlement of Kiryat Arba."[6] In 1979, another group led by Levinger's wife moved into the city of Hebron itself.

The term *'Amalek* refers to an enemy of the tribes of Israel who, as the Old Testament states, oppose the entry of the Israelites into Palestine. "'Amalek is now used to describe all Palestinians, and it is said that the Old Testament justifies the total destruction of the 'Amalek. The Gush Emonim, furthermore, justify the use of force to restore Eretz Yisrael, the historical land of Israel, to Jewish control. Eretz Yisrael is defined biblically as Sinai, the Golan Heights, the West Bank, Gaza, all of Jordan, South Lebanon, and Jerusalem."[7]

The messianic implications of the religious settlers' thinking, according to Israeli professor Uriel Tal, creates a fear of genocide. The Gush Emonim also believe that Israelis today are living in the messianic era, in which Israel is being liberated from the satanic force, a mystical force described as evil and corrupt. The "Era of Holiness," in which all Israelis will be entering, will include all Zionist creation. For believers in Gosh Emonim, they must begin a genocidal campaign and assume a warlike and racist posture in order to destroy the alien 'Amalek in a sanctified land.[8]

When the Labor government was voted from office in May 1977, approximately thirty-seven settlements had been constructed on the West Bank, including four Gush Emonim settlements in the Nablus and Ramallah region, a dozen residential Jewish quarters in Arab Jerusalem, and other settlements in the Golan Heights, the Gaza Strip, and the Sinai peninsula.[9] The settlements occupy more than 50 percent of the land area of the West Bank. The number of settlers living in the occupied territories in 1991 was estimated to be between 98,500 to 120,000 settlers.[10]

SETTLEMENTS OF HATE AND VIOLENCE

The most common kind of settler violence against Palestinians is retaliatory. Each and every terrorist attack on Israelis has been avenged immediately against Palestinians. Such attacks are facilitated by the availability of weapons to the Israeli settlers. Because most settlers, like all Israeli males, are army reservists, they not only have access to weapons, they have been trained in their use. By contrast, Palestinians face police action if they are even caught possessing firearms. The occupied territories are also subject to two systems of law—laws for Israeli settlers and laws for Palestinian occupants.

The settlers' legal status improved significantly in 1979 when Military Order 783 incorporated the West Bank and Gaza settlements into councils similar to Israeli municipal and district councils. In 1981, Military Order 892 defined election procedures for the settlements' local councils and provided for the opening of municipal and rabbinical courts. In January 1984, the Knesset approved the extension of all the rights of citizenship to the settlements. Furthermore, when Israeli citizens committed acts of violence against Palestinians, the Israeli military commander of the occupied areas ruled that Israeli citizens could not be brought before a Palestinian judge. However, Palestinian offenders against Israeli settlers must be heard by an Israeli military judge.[11]

The two legal systems governing the affairs of Palestinians and Israelis certainly encourage settlers' retaliatory attacks. Following the knifing of a twenty-two-year-old Yeshiva student in Jerusalem on November 15, 1986, approximately seven hundred angry religious Jews rioted in Jerusalem. Windows were broken, and doors were smashed in the Arab quarter of the Old City. More than four hundred Israeli police and soldiers eventually ended the riots. Arab shop owners shuttered their stores, and many others were driven from the streets. Two Arabs were rescued by Israeli police from a bottle-throwing mob in an alley.[12]

A particularly bloody week of revenge by settlers developed in February of 1988, according to *Al-Fajr*, a Jerusalem weekly. The revenge was in response to stone-throwing Arab youths of the intifada. In response, many Arab villages and refugee camps were attacked. In the village of Ya'bad, groups of settlers attacked local residents, injured twenty-two, and smashed the windows of thirty Arab-owned cars. Attacking the village at midnight, the settlers fired guns and smashed windows. The settlers burned the village's water pump, and clashes with villagers continued until dawn. In addition,

> the village of Anabta in the West Bank was attacked in February. More than 750 settlers arrived in buses and vandalized homes and parked cars. At the time, the town was under curfew after two Arab youths had been killed by the army. The village of Abood, north of Jerusalem, was attacked by settlers in February. Arab women were dragged from their homes and ordered to remove roadblocks placed on village roads. Settlers also attacked the Azzeh refugee camp near Bethlehem during one night and clashed with the refugees for

several hours. Many car windows were smashed. In the Hebron area, home of one of the most militant settlements, settlers established twenty-four-hour patrols along the Bethlehem-Hebron road to search all travelers. Seven Israeli vehicles were used for this patrol. According to the settlers, the patrol would give Jewish travelers a sense of security and a feeling that the road was part of their own settlement.[13]

In March 1988, a twenty-six-year-old Israeli, Haim Shalo, foiled a knife attack by a young Arab boy near the town of Natanya in Israel. In retaliation, Jewish residents blocked Arab workers from entering the town, and four Arab youths were severely beaten by the Israeli crowd.[14] In the same month, the settlers of Hebron set fire to Palestinian cars in the village of Halhoul, in retaliation for the intifada's stone-throwing youth.[15] On July 7, 1989, an Arab grabbed the steering wheel of an Israeli bus and crashed the bus in a ravine. The bus had been traveling along the Tel Aviv–Jerusalem highway, and the crash caused the deaths of fourteen people and injured twenty-seven others. Soon after the crash, three Arabs were dragged from buses in Jerusalem by angry Israelis and beaten.[16]

Jewish settler violence against Palestinians can be categorized as crimes of racial hate or religious fanaticism. The most well-known and well-documented attacks have been directed at Muslim and Christian sites, especially in the Jerusalem area. These attacks began in April of 1982, when al-Aqsa Mosque, the third holiest place for Muslims and the area from which they believe Muhammad ascended to Heaven, suffered an arsonist's attack. On January 26, 1984, a guard foiled an attempt by two religious Jews to fire bomb the al-Aqsa and Dome of the Rock mosques. Israeli newspapers later reported that this attempt was backed by a group of nine religious Jews, some of whom may have been army reservists. Rabbi Meir Kahane, leader of the militant Kach movement, expressed his regret over the failure of this attempt. Muslims continue to complain of inadequate protection for the holy area of Jerusalem. Muslims also greatly fear that a large number of Israeli rightists and religious leaders wish to erect a holy temple on the grounds now occupied by al-Aqsa and Dome of the Rock mosques.[17]

When settlers in 1983 killed an eleven-year-old Palestinian girl in the city of Nablus on the West Bank, a religious text was used in their defense. The chief rabbi of the Sephardic Jewish community referred to a talmudic text, which justified killing an enemy if one can see from a child's eyes that he or she will grow up to be your enemy.[18] In December 1987, a seventeen-year-old Palestinian girl, Intissar al-Attar, was shot and killed by Israeli settlers in her school yard in the town of Deir al-Balah. This murder was attributed to a group of religious fanatics in Rabbi Kahane's movement. The killer was identified as Shimon Yefrah, teacher in the religious school of Shderot.[19] In March 1988, a petrol bomb was thrown at a school bus bringing Israeli children from nearby settlements to Arial on the West Bank.

The settlers began to argue for the removal of all Arabs on purely religious grounds. These settlers, who often organized raids on Palestinian villages, argued that the land of Abraham belonged to the Jewish people. They believed that all others should be removed by force.[20]

A shadowy, secret band of militant settlers had been attacking Arabs since the beginning of the intifada. The group calls itself *Sicarii*, the name of a group of Jewish zealots who lived during the first century A.D. and who specialized in stabbing people suspected of collaborating with the Romans. The Sicarii (Latin for "curved dagger") were part of the defense force of the ancient temple Masada, and they killed themselves, rather than submitting to the Romans. A member of Sicarii was responsible for firing an Uzi submachine gun at a group of Palestinian men standing outside Jerusalem's Jaffa Gate in April 1989. The Sicarii took responsibility for the attack, claiming that it was in retaliation for a stoning attack on Jews at the Wailing Wall during the previous week.[21] Israelis believe in and accept the heroism of the Masada defenders, and the contemporary Sicarii could easily claim a place in the popular Israeli imagination.

Encouragement of random public killings can also be attributed to the official Jewish religious designation of the Palestinians as the ancient enemies of the Israelites. Recent Jewish religious literature always refers to the Palestinians as the enemies of Israel, using the term,

'Amalek, to describe Israel's ancient enemies. Passages from the Bible are used to urge the total eradication of every Palestinian man, woman, and child. In a pamphlet, Rabbi Mayor Shmuel Derlich, religious counsel for the Israeli occupation forces in the West Bank, urged a brutal and bloody war against 'Amalek. When an Israeli journalist criticized the rabbi, the latter claimed that he was referring to the "German nation." However, the rabbi, who escaped any official sanctions, could not explain why he urged a war of extermination against 'Amalek. The biblical identification of Palestinians with 'Amalek and other religious zealots helps explain the religious fanaticism and violence against Palestinians.[22]

Much Israeli settler violence is caused by the desire to drive Palestinians from the land and to then occupy it. The determination by the settlers includes a campaign to transfer the Arab population to Jordan. Some political organizations representing the settlers, such as the Kach movement of Rabbi Meir Kahane, openly advocate the forcible removal of Palestinian Arabs to neighboring countries. These organizations consider all of the occupied territories that Israel won in war to be Israel's property by right of conquest. Emphasizing the slogan, "Palestine is Jordan," these organizations feel that any nation is justified in hastening the departure of the Arab population of the West Bank, Gaza, Judea, or Samaria.

Settlers' tactics to achieve the removal of all Palestinians sometimes entail the destruction of Palestinian groups and the ravaging of the environment. In April 1977, a large number of Israeli settlers burned orange groves belonging to farmers in a nearby Arab town in retaliation for an Arab attack on a pregnant Israeli woman in the occupied West Bank. That the attack targeted the land was a clear indication of the long-standing settler objective to clear the land of its inhabitants. In another attack, the settlers rampaged through the Arab village of Qalqilyeh and damaged twenty houses and sixteen cars, shouting commands to Arabs to leave the area.[23]

In attacks and counterattacks, it is often difficult to ascertain who initiated violence, because hostility quickly breeds hostility. Official investigations fail to immediately identify the real perpetrators of crimes. The failure of Israeli authorities to identify the guilty often results in counterviolence by the frustrated victims of violence.

On April 4, 1988, a clash between Arab villagers on the West Bank and a busload of Israeli teenagers resulted in the death of a Jewish teenager and two Palestinians. The Israeli army, which is in charge of security for the West Bank and Gaza, reported that the Israeli teenager, Tirza Porat of the settlement of Elon Moreh, was killed by a stone thrown by Palestinians. The army amended its report on April 6 and confirmed that the Israeli girl was killed by a Jewish guard's bullet. The altercation between Arab villagers and sixteen Israeli teenagers with their two armed escorts occurred during the settlers' outing on a nature hike through the Arab village of Beta. The village's inhabitants numbered approximately four thousand people. When the earlier report indicated that the girl suffered a head wound from a rock, right-wing settlers and their Knesset friends called for the leveling of Beta. After the army issued its second report, the settlers still considered the Arab villagers guilty and demolished thirteen homes in Beta.[24]

In response to the army's reports, religious nationalist settlers rallied in front of the office of Yitzhak Shamir, calling for the resignation of the chief of staff, General Dan Shomron. Knesset member Geula Cohen called for Shomron's resignation because he had suggested that the settlers went to Beta simply to provoke the villagers. In a cabinet discussion, Israeli minister Ariel Sharon demanded that the entire village be evacuated and that more settlements be built. Some newspaper accounts explained, however, that the Israeli guard responsible for Porat's death had also shot and killed a Palestinian man working in his field, as the bus carrying the youths entered the village. The death of the Palestinian brought crowds of screaming and stone-throwing Arabs to the bus to retaliate against the guard, Roman Aldubi, who was known for being a violent man of religious nationalist ideology. The army's report on the incident continued to draw attacks from the settlers.

No attack succeeds in deepening the hatred of Palestinians like those attacks on the sources of their livelihood and their agricultural way of life. In 1986, in the village of Medya, near the "green line" separating Israel from the occupied West Bank, the villagers were awakened by the sound of Israeli army vehicles surrounding the town at 3:00 a.m. The soldiers imposed a curfew on the village until 9:00 p.m. and proceeded to carve a road into the steep hillside to connect the village to a lower rough road below it. When the bulldozers and chainsaws stopped, an olive grove that had held three thousand trees appeared like an abandoned battlefield filled with corpses. Because the trees were essential to the livelihoods of Medya's population of 570 people, the villagers attempted to block the bulldozers with their own bodies. They were repulsed by tear gas and Uzis fired into the air, and those who resisted were arrested for the duration of the day and released in the evening.[25]

According to a later story in the *Jerusalem Post*, the trees were cut on a total area of 1,100 dunums, or acres. The operation was undertaken by the entire staff of the Israeli Land Administration Office, whose workers are members of the Nature Reserves Authority. The perpetrators numbered approximately one thousand individuals, including the soldiers who protected the operation. The Israeli Land Administration claimed that the operation was undertaken to prevent Palestinian encroachment on Israeli state lands. The villagers, it was claimed, planted the olive trees to stake claim to the land. The cut trees were said to be less than five years of age, although the diameter of most cut trunks was more than half a meter, meaning the trees were older. Israeli sources claimed that only one thousand trees were destroyed, while the villagers placed the number at four thousand. The Israelis further claimed that the land where the trees had grown was within the "no-man's land" between Israeli and Jordanian lines of the 1948 Arab-Jewish war. The villagers, however, emphasized the age of the tree stumps and also emphasized that the Israeli line was marked by a forest planted to the west of the village by the Jewish National Fund.[26]

The Medya incident illustrates settler and army collusion and Israel's undeclared policy of maximizing its land holdings wherever and whenever possible. The cooperation that the settlers often receive from the Israeli army also encourages settler attacks on villagers and the wanton destruction of Arab property. The tree cutting was perceived as a certain way to inflict psychological as well as economic damage on the helpless, unarmed Arab villagers.

In another kind of violence, settlers and other Israelis individuals often target Arab workers within Israel's boundaries. These attacks are clearly motivated by economic competition and feelings of racial antagonism. The settlements themselves represent stiff economic competition to the surrounding areas. In the Gaza Strip, eighteen Jewish settlements use almost 22,500 acres of land earmarked for the use of 2,150 settlers. The land-to-people ratio in the settlements represents about 10.4 acres per settler. In contrast, 37,319 Palestinian refugees have been resettled in government housing projects on 3,500 acres of land. The economic productivity of the settlements represent stiff competition with the agricultural productivity of the Arab refugees of Gaza. The unfair competition is due not only to the large land area reserved for settlers but also to the location of the settlements near the area's main aquifers. Settlers are permitted greater consumption of water resources than the nearby Palestinian population.[27]

The settlers' determination to prevent Arab workers employed in the settlements from undertaking any damaging activity sometimes takes on bizarre aspects of racist behavior. In June 1989, the Israeli attorney general, Yosef Harish, was compelled to investigate whether Mayor Ron Nachman, in the Ariel settlement north of Jerusalem, had incited racism by issuing badges stamped "foreign workers" to Palestinian laborers employed in the settlement. An Israeli and Arab storm of criticism forced Nachman to cancel his badges because the badges reminded the Israelis in particular of Nazi requirements that Jews were to wear the yellow Star of David. The mayor withdrew the badges in favor of new identity cards issued to the eight thousand Israeli settlers and four hundred Palestinian workers in Ariel.[28]

In November 1990, Jewish threats were directed at Israeli stores in Jerusalem that employed Arab workers. Jewish zealots burned shops and threatened merchants with violence, if they did not fire their Arab employees. Jewish shopkeepers were intimidated into displaying signs stating, "I don't employ Arabs." Other Israelis were shocked by such behavior reminiscent of the displays of signs denying the employment of Jewish workers by German storekeepers on the eve of the Holocaust. The Israeli campaign to fire Arabs was apparently led by followers of Rabbi Kahane and his Kach movement. The campaign began a few days after the shooting of Meir Kahane by an Arab-American in New York.[29]

Attacks on Arab workers and their right to employment in Israeli industry sometimes assumes legitimacy. The Israeli daily *Al-Hamishmar* recently reported a request by the secretary general of the official Israeli labor union, the Histadrut, to curtail the employment of Arab workers in Israel. Yisrael Kessar declared that the government, the Histadrut, and private businesses should establish a joint committee to oversee the employment of Arab workers from the occupied territories. The Israeli economy should attempt to reduce the number of Arab workers who are occasionally employed in order to safeguard the rights of Israeli workers. The number of Arab workers occasionally employed in Israeli industries decreased to approximately forty thousand in 1992.[30]

Attacks on Arab workers employed as daily-wage laborers sometimes degenerate into murder. In May 1990, seven Arab laborers from the Gaza Strip were shot and killed at Rishon Lezion in central Israel by an Israeli who asked to inspect their identity cards. Ten others waiting in line to be hired as casual laborers were also wounded. The Israeli attacker fled in the car of one of the laborers. Later arrested, the twenty-one-year-old attacker admitted using his brother's army weapon, an M-16 rifle, in the assault.[31]

In an investigative report on the conditions of Arabs employed in Israeli industries, a Jerusalem weekly stated that in the 1970s national and economic discrimination was the greatest problem facing Arab workers. Since the 1980s, however, these kinds of discrimination have been replaced by an increasing number of racially motivated attacks and by summary dismissals from employment. The demand for Arab labor from the West Bank and Gaza decreased sharply. The Israeli minister of labor in 1986, Moshe Kassab, reported to the Knesset that demand for Arab labor had dropped 27 percent from 1983 to 1986. The minister attributed the decline to Israel's continuing economic crisis and to the willingness of Israelis to take jobs that they had previously regarded as demeaning. The most frequently heard calls for the dismissal of Arab workers were usually accompanied by calls for the expulsion of Arabs from the land.

In addition, employers had often fired Arab workers just before they became eligible for unemployment compensation. Some employers also claimed that the Arab workers provoked attacks by Israelis, saying the Arabs instigated verbal assaults on Israeli workers. Because the Arab workers had been denied protection and membership in the Israeli labor federation, they could be dismissed from work without compensation. If the Arab workers were to strike, they might be dismissed easily and could not readily find employment again.[32]

The many racially motivated attacks by Israelis are the most random and violent incidents against Palestinians. *Al-Quds*, an Arab daily published in Jerusalem, reported on December 25, 1985, that two Israelis attacked Abdullah Khamis, a worker from Gaza, and seriously wounded him. *Al-Mithaq* reported on September 12, 1985, that border guards attacked an Arab worker while he was receiving treatment at a hospital. The Jerusalem Arab daily *Al-Sh'ab* reported on May 15, 1985, that widespread attacks against Arab workers occurred frequently in the Jerusalem area. The racial attacks were often directed by the Israeli police without any prior provocation. *Al-Quds* reported on April 9, 1986, that police awoke Arab workers at Eilat with beatings and kickings and arrested three of them. They were later released without being charged with any offense. The Arab-Israeli paper, *Al-Ittihad,* reported on October 8, 1985, that busloads of Arab workers from the West Bank and Gaza were often stopped by Israeli police and subjected to harassment and insults. The harassment included ordering the Arabs to perform clownish dances, to direct insults at each other, and to cause themselves delays that might result in dismissal by Israeli employers.[33]

Arab deaths or injuries are also frequently not investigated, and perpetrators are seldom caught or charged. The report in a Jerusalem weekly described unsolved murders of Arab workers in 1985 and 1986. Khalil A. Abd al-Majid from Gaza was found murdered in the Israeli town of Betyam; he was employed as a guard. Hassan al-Hattab from al-Shuja'iyyah was found murdered in his bedroom in Tel Aviv. Jamal Mahmoud Kheir al-Din from Jabalia, a refugee camp in the Gaza area, was found murdered in a factory at Houlon. Muhammed Younis al-Boulaqi from the al-Shati refugee camp in Gaza received a knife wound in his shoulder and a skull fracture after being attacked by unknown Israelis where he worked at Batyam.

Arab workers are easily dismissed from work because they are not entitled to any unemployment compensation. Labor union dues are deducted from all workers' wages because Israeli laws require deductions from anyone employed in Israel. The dues are sent to the Histadrut but not to Arab labor unions in the occupied territories. Arabs working in Israel do not qualify for any benefits from the Israeli federation of labor because they are not citizens. Demands to send these dues to Arab labor unions in the occupied territories have never been met.[34]

In August 1988, three Palestinian workers were set on fire as they slept in a shack near their place of employment at Or Yehuda in Israel. *Yediot Ahronot*, the Israeli daily, described the burning as the most shocking example of racial hatred and general indifference. A sixteen-year-old Israeli resident of Or Yehuda told an Israeli reporter that it did not matter if an Arab burns, because "it" is not a human being. The teenager added that he did not care if two thousand Arabs burned. A friend added that he would burn five thousand Arabs. The town of Or Yehuda, which lies at the edge of Tel Aviv, apparently was infused with anti-Arab sentiment. A thirty-year-old witness to the burning described it as "beautifully organized." He said that the incident only required throwing benzene on the shack, tossing a match, and then running away. The perpetrators were seventeen years old. One Arab victim did not die immediately but ran from the burning shack to a nearby road, but no one helped him. The *Yediot Ahronot* reporter was told repeatedly by people that they did not care if Arabs were burned because the area was part of the Israeli intifada. The reporter was also told of a similar burning of Arab workers in an industrial area nearby. It had not been reported because the workers survived. The reporter concluded his report with this irony: he quoted a man from Ramat Gan who said that he did not care if Arabs were placed in concentration camps.[35]

Another report in an Arabic daily of Jerusalem examined the conditions of employment of Arab workers in a work camp in Israel. The camp was some twenty kilometers southeast of the Israeli town of Natanya and served as a labor supply center for three Jewish settlements: Tel Mond, Meshmeret, and Herut. The Arab workers came mostly from Gaza and Rafah, which are perpetually congested and economically depressed, and from some towns of the occupied West Bank. The labor boss was an Israeli Arab from the nearby village of Tira. He recruited workers without informing them of what they might expect to earn as wages. Their wages apparently equaled ten dollars a day, from which sums for health insurance and food would be deducted. Living conditions were abysmal. Twenty people were crowded into one of many shacks. Some buildings used as hostels for the Arab workers had been stables recently converted to human needs. In other camps, the workers lived in old, derelict buses. When the workers arrived at the camp, they were told not to enter the settlement after dark. Every two or three days, a border guard patrol arrived to conduct searches of the workers and their shacks. They were looking for stolen oranges or other food.[36]

Difficulties exist in separating official government violence from extremist and individual violence of the fanatic settlers. Sometimes the army attacks Arab villagers and town dwellers to ease the antagonisms of nearby settlements. Sometimes the police and the army fail to curb settler violence and are nowhere to be found. On February 9, 1988, Israeli settlers launched a long attack on the West Bank village of Betunia. They raided houses and smashed doors and windows. They distributed threatening leaflets in Arabic, but the army never appeared. In the Old City of Jerusalem, armed Israeli settlers marched and fired their guns in the streets on the night of February 10, 1988. The Jerusalem police, however, failed to respond to appeals by the city's Arab population for protection. The Arab residents were forced to form their own defense teams. During the same period, daily settler attacks on Palestinian refugee camps in the villages and towns of the West Bank failed to convince the Israeli army, which is charged with the defense of the occupied territories, to intervene.

The Israeli army actually undertook joint raids with the settlers against the village of Salim in the Nablus area on February 5, 1988. The raids began as an attempt by villagers to place rocks and burning tires along the road to the settlement of Elon Moreh. Soldiers and settlers buried four youths alive and ordered an Israeli bulldozer driver to run over their bodies. He refused, and when the soldiers and settlers left, village women thinking that the youths were dead, hurriedly removed the wet earth from the barely breathing youths and took them to a hospital in Nablus.[37]

Dramatic violence by Israeli settlers occurred against the mayors of Nablus and Ramallah in 1980. Bombs were attached to the cars of the two mayors, Bassam Shaka' and Karim Khalaf, and resulted in the amputation of the former's legs and the latter's foot. The mayor of the West Bank town of Al-Bireh, Ibrahim Tawil, escaped injury during the same attack, but a Druze sapper, who attempted to defuse a bomb attached to Tawil's garage door, lost his eyesight. These attacks indicated the military and organizational sophistication of the settlers, most of whom acquire military experience while serving in the army. An inquiry into the settlers' violence, conducted by Knesset member, Dedi Zucker, was entitled, "Report on Human Rights in the Occupied Territories, 1979–1983." It indicated that the settlers see themselves as part of the Israeli security forces. Acting within the perimeters of their army reserve status, they imagine themselves as being another arm of the state, the main duties of which are to punish and impose rules of order. However, what has emboldened the settlers has been the evolution of a dual legal system in the West Bank and Gaza.[38]

Palestinians living in the occupied territories are subject to a set of intricate Ottoman, Jordanian, and British laws and more than a thousand orders of the Israeli military governor. The Israeli settlers enjoy the privileges of Israeli citizens despite their residency outside of Israel's recognized international boundaries. The legal status of the settlers began evolving with the 1979 Military Order 783. It incorporated all the West Bank and Gaza settlements into regional councils, based on Israeli municipal and district laws. The 1981 Military Order 892 established election procedures for local councils in the settlements and permitted the opening of municipal and rabbinical courts. In January 1989, the British emergency regulations, which had applied to all Arabs and Jews in the occupied territories, were amended to exclude Israeli settlers and settlements. Consequently, "all citizens to whom the Law of Return applies"—Jewish citizens residing in the West Bank and Gaza—were considered regular Israeli citizens. For Israeli settlers, army service, the payment of taxes, national insurance, and professional licenses were the same as those of all regular Israeli citizens. *Davar's* West Bank reporter, Danny Rubenstein, described the evolution of the legal system for settlements as "an orderly and legalized apartheid."[39]

An apartheid-like system, which treats the Arab and Jewish communities in the West Bank and Gaza as two separate but unequal communities, results in unclear investigative and prosecutorial procedures for the settlers. For instance, it is unclear whether the military or civilian police are expected to investigate complaints against the settlers. Because settlers' crimes occur in the occupied territory over which only the emergency British regulations and Israeli military orders have jurisdiction, one would expect that complaints would be dealt with severely. However, the perpetrators of these crimes are subject to Israeli laws, no matter where they reside. As a result, settlers enjoy an extraterritorial legal system and a frequent and inordinate political favoritism, especially when the settlers resist military and civilian investigations.[40]

REFUGEES IN LEBANON AND KUWAIT

Palestinian refugees have lived in sprawling refugee camps on the outskirts of major Lebanese cities since the 1984 Arab-Jewish war. Living a poor existence as a foreign proletariat, the Palestinians remained on the margins of Lebanon's political and economic life. In 1970, however, when the Palestine Liberation Organization suffered a defeat in the Jordanian civil war, it was forced to relocate its headquarters in Beirut. The PLO then began its well-known campaign to politicize and radicalize the refugees and to deploy its military units in southern Lebanon. The PLO also joined the fractional communal struggle in Lebanon on the side of the progressive and national front. Composed of the progressive wing of the Sunni community and the Druze of Mount Lebanon, the front sought to substitute Lebanon's constitution with a more equitable document reflecting the changed demographic balance among Lebanon's competing sectarian communities.[41]

Resistance offered by the ruling Maronite Christian community and their Muslim Sunni allies triggered Lebanon's second civil war in 1974 and in time led to the activation of the Shiite Lebanese of the south. The Lebanese civil war ended with the signing of the Ta'if Accord in 1990 but also resulted in the foreign occupation of parts of Lebanon by Syrian and Israeli troops. The Palestinians found themselves drawn into this dangerous occupation as political figures forced to defend their right to remain on Lebanese territory. For Palestinian refugees, disaster loomed as Israel mounted its invasion of Lebanon in 1982. The arrival of Israeli troops on the outskirts of Beirut and the ensuing siege of Beirut forced the evacuation of the PLO and most fighting Palestinians under the auspices of the U.S.-brokered Habib Agreement. The Palestinian military withdrawal left the Palestinian refugee camps unprotected. The assassination of Lebanon's president, Bashir Gemayel, and the Israeli takeover of Beirut in violation of the Habib Agreement precipitated a violent attack by dissident Lebanese Christians on the undefended Palestinian refugee camps of Sabra and Shatilla. The massacres at Sabra and Shatilla, which were observed by nearby Israeli troops, lasted approximately thirty-six hours. The Israeli cabinet of Menachem Begin knew about the massacres but failed to end them. Palestinian deaths ranged from a thousand to two thousand. The massacres entered the annals of Palestinian history as the most vicious in recent memory.[42]

The genocide at Sabra and Shatilla demonstrated the horrors of the Palestinian condition of homelessness and statelessness. The massacres were clearly the result of Palestinian engagement in Lebanese factional strife. Once the military troops of the PLO evacuated Beirut, the Palestinian civilian population lost not only its Palestinian defense units but any claim to protection by the Lebanese central government as a result of Arab League guarantees. The government of Amin Gemayel was generally representative of the Maronite Phalangists and was in no way beholden to the Arab League.

The absence of any political and juridical guarantees increased the horrors of the Palestinian refugees in Lebanon. By 1983, the Amin Gemayel government began to remove international supports for the Palestinian camps. A team of Italian doctors and nurses who kept the Palestinian hospital of Akka functioning was ordered to leave the country. These surgeons and orthopedic doctors who treated the poverty-stricken Palestinian and Lebanese war victims of West Beirut were told that their patients could not be removed. The government announced no need to replace the doctors, then yielded under tremendous pressure by the Italian ambassador and retained only two doctors on a temporary basis. Before the arrival of the Italians at the hospital, inadequately trained Lebanese personnel charged their hapless patients all kinds of fees. The Italian volunteers eliminated the livelihood of these Lebanese. The Lebanese governmental decisions were apparently motivated by a desire to convert the hospital into a hotel and to remove the Italians as eyewitnesses to the continued civilian harassment of the Palestinian refugees.[43]

In an interview, Walter Cavannari, the Italian doctor who led the orthopedic unit at the hospital at Akka, admitted that the mere mention of Palestinians in Beirut would lead to trouble. Most Lebanese authorities pretended that the Palestinians did not exist. Any foreigner who pleaded on the Palestinians' behalf was escorted to a plane and sent out of the country. Cavannari also described the Palestinian population of Beirut's camps, which by 1983 was composed mostly of women and children living in constant terror. His information came from some of his patients who ventured outside the camps and was also based on his own observations from the hospital. Most women and children remained in hiding, still suffering from the trauma of the massacres. Several acts of terrorism followed the massacres at Sabra and Shatilla. Most of the sporadic incidents of vengeance were undertaken by Phalangists or the Christian military. Cavannari confirmed that before the arrival of the Italian medical team at Akka Hospital, several kidnappings, killings, and rapes had occurred against members of the Palestinian staff. The Italians had arrived at Akka Hospital more than a month after the massacres of Sabra and Shatilla. Cavannari added that the Palestinians' greatest fears of kidnapping and disappearance kept most refugees confined to their camps.[44]

By 1984, the very survival of Palestinians in Lebanon was challenged. In an article dated 1984, a Palestinian reporter accused the Lebanese authorities of planning a campaign of racial cleansing against Palestinians. Although the Habib Agreement provided guarantees against the expulsion of Palestinians, Lebanese authorities and various Lebanese factions continued to terrorize the camps. Rather than protect the defenseless refugees, the Lebanese government used the constant attacks against the Palestinian camps as a justification for relocating them away from Beirut's airport. The Lebanese government was suspected of coordinating its campaign of racial cleansing against its original Palestinian population of approximately 400,000, by permitting increasing harassment by the Phalangists, the Christian militia, and other dissident factions. The Lebanese government simply indefinitely delayed renewals of Palestinian identity cards, registrations of birth documents, and travel permits.[45]

Hate crimes against the Palestinian community of Kuwait were preceded by years of dismissals from employment and a general desire to evict and expel large numbers of Palestinians. Although they had been residents of Kuwait since the destruction of Arab Palestine in 1948, Palestinians were still considered legal aliens, given two-year residency permits. The Palestinians faced unemployment and dismissal whenever the economy in the Persian Gulf deteriorated or suffered sudden reversals. In 1986, an economic depression affecting the Gulf region occurred after the Iran-Iraq war. Because Israel requires the annual renewal of identification papers as a condition of readmitting Palestinians to the West Bank and Gaza, those who left Israel before 1967 and the establishment of Israeli controls have been unable to return to their homeland. Their only option was to return to Jordan because their Jordanian passports permitted residency in that economically depressed country. By 1985, as many as fifty thousand Palestinian workers had left Kuwait as a result of the deterioration of oil prices and the elimination of government projects. By 1986, an additional thirty thousand Palestinian workers were expected to leave Kuwait. The Kuwaiti government then began to reduce the mandatory retirement age of Palestinian workers to fifty-five years of age and to cancel benefits to foreign workers. The government openly advocated a policy of "Kuwaitization" of all jobs and quickly replaced Palestinian workers with Kuwaitis. Native citizens and companies that had been required to cosponsor Palestinian workers and businesspeople began to refuse to extend sponsorship to Palestinians or to find them residency. Government schools began to close their doors to foreign children. The government also began to prevent twenty-one-year-old Palestinian children from rejoining their families after the completion of study periods abroad. The restriction applied to Palestinian children who were born in Kuwait. Unless these youths obtained a work permit, they were not allowed into the country again.[46]

Most Palestinian workers inhabit two poor and densely populated neighborhoods in Kuwait City, known as Hawalli and Nugra. Local Kuwaitis refer to the neighborhood derisively as Sabra and Shatilla. It has been rumored for years that the Kuwaiti government intended to demolish these two neighborhoods in order to end the dense congregation of Palestinians. Since 1982, Kuwait and a number of other Gulf regional states began to reject Palestinian applications for permits for new residences. Only Kuwait's mostly Persian Shiite population rivaled the Palestinians in stirring the political suspicions of the Kuwaiti government and population.[47]

The Palestinian population of Kuwait finally became the target of a campaign of official and unofficial terror by the restored Kuwaiti regime after the defeat of Iraq in the 1991 Gulf war. To Kuwaitis, the Palestinians' crime was their remaining on their jobs after the Iraqi invasion and after Yassar Arafat's refusal to sanction U.S. military intervention on behalf of Kuwait. Some Palestinians had collaborated with Kuwaitis; but despite reports of systematic Iraqi looting of Palestinian stores and attempts to impress Palestinians into military service, Kuwaiti attacks became vicious. The government's denial of kidnappings and disappearances of Palestinians finally ended on May 26, 1991. Kuwait's crown prince Shaikh Sa'ad al-Abdallah officially admitted on television that attacks upon Palestinians had to stop. The entire population was living in fear of the crime wave sweeping the country because many Kuwaitis were armed and attacks on Palestinians were frequent occurrences. Kuwaiti militias, which included members of the royal family, were terrorizing non-Kuwaiti Arab residents, particularly Palestinians.[48]

Although many Palestinians and Iraqis were acquitted in state trials in 1991, they were expelled from Kuwait. In July 1991, the government was still trying to disarm the Kuwaitis, who daily attacked the non-Kuwaiti Arab population. The State Security Court continued to hear the serious cases of alleged collaboration between alien Arabs and the Iraqis, thereby further fueling public sentiment against the Palestinians. A Saudi newspaper based in London conducted a survey among Kuwaitis, most of whom held the Palestinians in such loathing as to be in favor of recognizing Israel.[49] Emigration of Palestinians from Kuwait, whether voluntarily before the Iraqi invasion or through expulsion following the war, reduced the size of the Palestinian population to 100,000. As late as August 1992, the Committee to Defend Human Rights in the Arab World sent urgent appeals to the Arab League of States and to the Arab ambassadors in Paris to end mock trials against Palestinians in Kuwait and to stop all killings, torture, and confiscation of Palestinian territory.

THE HEBRON MASSACRE AND FUTURE PROSPECTS

The attack on Muslim worshipers at the Ibrahimi Mosque in Hebron on the morning of February 25, 1994, was a major incident in the ongoing struggle between Israeli settlers and the Palestinian population. Baruch Goldstein, a Brooklyn-born physician and resident of the nearby settlement of Kiryat Arba, appears to have acted with premeditation. He arrived early in the morning at the Jewish section of the mosque, which had been seized by Jewish worshipers following the 1967 war. After passing the few Israeli soldiers posted outside the mosque, he shot and murdered, according to a government commission, 29 individuals and wounded 125 others by firing 108 bullets in ninety seconds. After being set upon and killed by the rest of the Arab worshipers, he was declared a martyr by the local rabbis of Kiryat Arba.

Some have speculated that Goldstein was unhinged by memories of the Holocaust. Others claimed that he underwent a drastic transformation as a result of experiencing the daily bloodshed and violence of the West Bank. Contrary to what was claimed by the Israeli media, Goldstein was not an adherent of extremist ideologies but was a follower of the mainstream Gush Emonim movement. Israel Shahak, a prominent Israeli writer and human rights supporter, explained that the act of killing Arabs may have been religiously sanctioned in order to hasten the return of the Messiah. Gush Emonim, wrote Shahak, assumes that the coming of the Messiah is inevitable once Jews triumph over Gentiles. According to other writers like Ian Lustick and Yehoshafat Harkabi, Gush Emonim preaches that Jews are unique as a result of a covenant with God made at Mount Sinai. Because of their uniqueness, Jews cannot be expected to obey other people's codes of justice.[50]

The Palestinian population has suffered worldwide persecutions and discrimination as a result of the creation of Israel in its territory in 1948. The Palestinian predicament is created by their dispersal and homelessness, which denies them legal residence in most countries, and which erodes their credentials as a people. The diaspora experience of the Palestinians has been as cruel as that of European Jews—because it placed them both at the mercy of host governments. The Palestinians' long-standing national goal of the right to a state of their own is to them their only guarantee of safety and existence. Placed at the mercy of hostile governments, vengeful militias, and angry citizens, Palestinians have clashed with host governments and civilian populations whenever and wherever they have become politically active. Attacks on Palestinian communities have been motivated by fears for the personal security of local host populations. They have feared accelerated attacks by external forces like the Israeli armed forces as a result of Palestinian military activity. Some of these attacks were motivated in Kuwait by economic competition and the need to nationalize civil service jobs.

Israeli attacks on Palestinians are the most serious in Israeli-held territories because they have multiple causes, which have succeeded in forcing Palestinians to emigrate. Israeli attacks are undertaken either by the religious settler movement in occupied territories or by Israeli youths and workers in Israel. Desire for land acquisition, feelings of sheer vengeance, fear of economic competitiveness, and the need to convince the Israeli government not to relinquish the occupied territories all cause Israeli attacks against Palestinians. Historical hatreds may only cease when the Palestinians' historic struggle, their legitimacy, and their need for their own state are recognized.

Hate crimes against Palestinians are facilitated by the collusion of the Israeli government. Collusion within Israel is caused by the reservist status of settlers, which encourage them to act as a defending force expecting assistance from the regular Israeli armed forces. The disparity between the legal and civic status of the occupied Palestinian population and the Israeli settlers often causes the Israeli military government to favor the settlers. Collusion is also often the result of adhesion to an undeclared policy of population removal and Israeli expansion. While appearing to uphold law and order in the occupied territories, the Israeli military government acts to defend and protect the settlers. The settlers are sometimes temporarily restrained, but the Israeli government has yet to prevent their attacks against Palestinians.

The governments in Lebanon and Kuwait have silently cooperated with their citizens' attacks on Palestinians because of their undeclared objective to expel Palestinians. In Kuwait, the government's objective has been pursued quietly prior to the Iraqi invasion. Only the removal of Palestinians was capable of facilitating the goal of "Kuwaitization" of the civil service. In Lebanon, the unenunciated goal of the Maronite government to evict the Palestinian population and eliminate their potential role as participants in the Lebanese political system encouraged collusion with attackers.

It is generally difficult to distinguish individual and unofficial hate crimes from authorized genocidal campaigns by governments. Without the involvement of troops against Palestinians, hate crimes are difficult to categorize. Who were the perpetrators of the Sabra and Shatilla massacres? Were they individual attackers or members of Sa'ad Haddad's southern Lebanese militia dressed in civilian clothes? Were they Lebanese civilians trying to realize the wishes of the brother of the recently assassinated prime minister in Lebanon?

Hate crimes against Palestinians in Israel and in the Arab world are, consequently, generally motivated by political rather than economic factors. Anti-Arab racism contributes to Israeli crimes of hate but not in other Arab countries. The fragile civic standing of the citizens in other Arab nations contributes greatly to the violation of the human rights of Palestinians. The connection between the local population's civic rights and the guest population's human rights has already been made by the Kuwaiti opposition movement. Perhaps the only hope for the remaining Palestinian population of Kuwait and the Persian Gulf area is the improvement of general democracy. In time, an orderly, legal, and humanitarian approach can be made to the guest population. Israeli cessation of acts of vengeance and racially motivated violence against the Palestinians may develop only as a result of improvements in the total political picture. Only a peaceful and equitable solution to the Arab-Israeli conflict would bring justice and safety to the Palestinian population within Israel's borders.

NOTES

1. Sabri Jiryis (1967), *Al-Arab fi Israel* (The Arab in Israel) (Beirut: Palestine Research Center), 117–64.
2. Amos Elon (1984), "The Secular Messianists," *Ha'aretz*, June 1, quoted in *Palestine Perspectives*, Aug.–Sept., 2.
3. Michael Adams (undated), *Signposts to Destruction: Israeli Settlements in the Occupied Territories* (London: Council for Advancement of Arab-British Understanding), 4–5.
4. James J. Zombie (1981), *Palestinians: The Invisible Victims* (Washington, D.C.: American-Arab Anti-Discrimination Committee) 22–23.
5. Elon (1984), 2.
6. Yori Heller (1992), "Settler Strategy Patterns," *Jerusalem Press Service*, Jan., p. 11.
7. Shukri Abed (1984), "The Ideology of Settler Terrorism," *Palestine Perspectives*, Aug.–Sept., 3–4.
8. Advisory Committee on Human Rights (1985), *Israeli Violence in the Occupied Territories, 1980–1984* (Chicago: Palestine Human Rights Campaign), 112–13.
9. Advisory Committee (1985), 2.
10. Emma Murphy (1992), "Settling the Territories: The Cost to Israel," *Middle East International*, May 29, 19.
11. Advisory Committee (1985), 8–9.
12. "Israeli Mob Seeks Vengeance" (1986), *Chicago Tribune*, Nov. 24, p. 5.
13. "Settlers' Retaliation Increases in Areas" (1988), *Al-Fajr*, Feb. 7, 3.
14. Uli Schmetzer (1988), "Palestinian Sabotage Inside Border Makes Israel Edgy," *Chicago Tribune*, Mar. 4, p. 9.
15. Alan Cowell (1988), "In Hills above the Jordan River, Hatred Is Rising Between Jews and Arabs," *New York Times*, Mar. 16, p. 6.
16. Stephen Franklin (1989), "Fourteen Killed When Arab Forces Israeli Bus into Ravine," *Chicago Tribune*, July 7, p. 4.
17. "Muhawalat i tida athimeh dhid al-masjad al-Aqsa," (An Attempted Attack on the Aqsa Mosque) (1984), *Al-Bayader al-Siyasi* 3(87): 17–20.
18. Abed (1984), 3.
19. "The Killing of Intisar Al-Attar" (1987), *Al-Fajr*, Dec. 27, 11.
20. Uli Schmetzer (1988), "Israeli Settlers Lose Trust, Not Will," *Chicago Tribune*, Mar. 2, pp. 1–2.

21. Carol Rosenberg (1989), "Israelis Hunt Shadowy Group," *Chicago Tribune*, Apr. 12, pp. 1, 14.

22. "Israel Army Rabbi Incites Against 'Amalek" (1986), *Al-Fajr*, May 9, 4.

23. A. E. Ilan (1988), "Israeli Army Admits Escort Shot Teenager," *Chicago Tribune*, Apr. 28, p. 6.

24. John Kifner (1988), "Israeli Settlers Turn Against Army," *New York Times*, Apr. 11, p. 6.

25. Frank Collins (1986), "The Destruction of 3,000 Olive Trees: An Ecological Massacre," *Al-Fajr*, July 18, 8.

26. Collins (1986), 8–9.

27. "Gaza" (1986), *Al-Fajr*, June 20, 15.

28. Alan Cowell (1989), "An Israeli Mayor Is under Scrutiny for Racism," *New York Times*, June 6, p. 5.

29. "Jewish Stores Harassed over Arab Workers" (1990), *Chicago Tribune*, Nov. 27, p. 3.

30. "Lajnat IiIishraf ala thuruf istikhdam umal al-manateq al-mustachdamin fi Israel" (A Committee to Oversee Working Conditions of the Labor from the Territories Who Are Employed in Israel) (1992), *Jerusalem Press Service*, May 18, p. 5.

31. "Seven Arab Labourers Slain, Jewish Suspect Held" (1990) *Jerusalem Post*, May 26, pp. 1–2.

32. Adel Wazwaz (1986), "Nathrah ala waqi al-umna al-Arab fi Israel" (A Look into the Reality of Arab Workers in Israel) *Al-Awdah*, 4(91): 26.

33. Wazwaz (1986), 27.

34. Wazwaz (1986), 27.

35. "Burning Hate" (1988), *Palestine Perspectives*, Sept.–Oct., 3.

36. Salman Natour (1983), "A Work Camp for Palestinians in Israel," *Al-Fajr*, Jan. 7, 10, 14.

37. "Settlers Take over Where Army Stops: Four Youths Buried Alive" (1988), *Al-Fajr*, Feb. 14, 3; and "Buried Alive" (1988) *Palestine Perspectives*, Mar.–Apr., 7.

38. Advisory Committee (1985), 7–8.

39. Advisory Committee (1985), 8–9.

40. Advisory Committee (1985), 9.

41. Walid Khalidi (1979), *Conflict and Violence in Lebanon: Confrontation in the Middle East* (Cambridge: Harvard Univ. Press), 27–30.

42. George Ball (1984), *Error and Betrayal in Lebanon* (Washington, D.C.: Foundation for Middle East Peace). The Habib Agreement was negotiated by Philip Habib, special envoy of President Reagan. On the background of the Sabra and Shatilla massacres, see Tony Clifton and Catherine Leroy (1989), *God Cried* (London: Quartet Books); and Claude Morris and John C. Mathew, eds. (1983), *Eyewitness Lebanon: Evidence of Ninety-One International Correspondents* (London: Morris International), 220–29.

43. Livia Rockach (1983), "Italian Medics Expelled from Beirut Camp Hospital," *Al-Fajr*, Jan. 7, 16.

44. Rockach (1983), 16.

45. M. Ibrahim (1984), "Maseer al-Filastiyin fi Lebanon: wathiqat al-safar wa shabah al-tarheel" (The Future of the Palestinians in Lebanon: Travel Documents and the Threat of Deportation) *Filastin al-Thawrah*, Jan. 14, 19.

46. Khali Touma (1986), "Gulf Begins Closing Doors on Palestinian Workers," *Al-Fajr*, June 2, 8.

47. Nadim Jaber (1987), "The Gulf States and the Palestinians: A Changing Relationship?" *Middle East International*, Apr. 17, 13–15.

48. Nadim Jaber (1991), "Deteriorating Image," *Middle East International*, May 31, 1991, 12–13.

49. Nadim Jaber (1991), "Burnishing the Image," *Middle East International*, June 12, 9–10.

50. Israel Shahak (1994), "The Ideology Behind the Hebron Massacre," *Middle East International*, Mar. 18, 16–17.

5. Hate Crimes in India: A Historical Perspective

Asad ur Rahman

T he diversity of races, religions, and languages in India is the source of its rich culture and civilization. It reflects the country's long history through the many invasions, which brought a variety of races together to form the wealth of India's present cumulative heritage. At the same time, unfortunately, some of the worst crimes of hatred, on a large scale, are caused by the conflict of interest among the groups that belong to the diverse races, cultures, religions, and languages in the county. The problems in India that lead to hate crimes are, one might say, embedded in its history. It is not true, as some have been saying rather arrogantly in recent years, that one cannot learn anything from history. In fact, to a great extent, our present is conditioned by our past, and our future is hostage to it as well. Socioeconomic factors play their part in the development of a nation, but hatred between groups defies the effects of changing socioeconomic conditions and is bred by historical grievance, real or imaginary, which is passed down from generation to generation for hundreds, even thousands, of years. It is, therefore, necessary to examine India's present-day problems in a historical perspective.

The deep-rooted hatred of one community against another leads members of opposing communities to perpetrate heinous crimes on each other. These old animosities are not confined to religious communities—Hindu, Muslim, Sikh, and Christian—but also involve communities distinguished by their language, race, or tribe. In the eastern state of Assam, Bengali-speaking people, who had lived there for generations, became the victims of the wrath of the Assamese people, who considered the Bengalis "outsiders" and exploiters. In western India, Marhati-speaking people attacked and killed Gujarati-speaking people for similar reasons. In tribal conflicts, whole villages have been burnt down, women raped, and men killed. Intercaste conflicts, especially between upper caste Hindus and the lowest caste of untouchables, flare up often and lead to similar crimes.

The conflict between upper-caste (or high-caste) Hindus and the untouchables is the most intractable and goes back some 3,500 years. The untouchables are the descendants of the race that produced a highly developed urban civilization in India, which flourished from about 2500 B.C. to about 1500 B.C. It is believed that these people were short-statured and dark-complexioned. Around 1700 B.C., the Aryan people invaded India in wave after wave. They conquered the indigenous people and made them slaves. The Aryans were fair-complexioned, tall, and sharp-featured. They called the subjugated people "the Dark Ones," or slaves (Dasyus). The process of subjugation was probably completed by about 1500 B.C. The Aryans gained control of most of north India and pushed natives further east and south. The Dasyus were treated like slaves with no rights and no position in society at all. They were not allowed to live in the cities where they came to do the most menial kinds of work, like cleaning latrines, and had to leave by sundown to go to their slumlike dwellings beyond the bounds of the cities. In the villages too, they lived on the outskirts and were not allowed to use the village wells or other common amenities. In modern India, this pattern of life persists, and their lot is a wretched one. They are known in Hindu society as "untouchables" or "Dalits."

After India gained independence in 1947, the constitution of the country guaranteed them equality with the rest of the citizens, but in reality, the practice of some 2,500 years tenaciously persists. They are still considered "untouchable," although Gandhi gave them a more dignified name—Harijan, which means "God's children." Hatred toward them as inferior and dirty beings, not quite human, is deeply rooted in Indian culture. Many reformers—like Mahavira, the founder of Jainism, and Buddha in ancient times; Kabir, Nanak, Ramdas, and the Sufis (Muslim mystic saints) in medieval times; and in modern times, Raja Ram Mohan Roy and Mahatma Gandhi—tried to do away with the curse of casteism, this cruel exploitation and persecution of the helpless untouchables. But all these great men failed after some initial success, and the problem persists.

The Indian government has passed laws prohibiting discrimination against the untouchables and also has laws guaranteeing them a certain percentage of positions in government services as well as a percentage of admissions to educational institutions. These and other such affirmative actions have, in fact, helped some members of this community to improve their lives and raise their standard of living. Some hope lies in the fact that, in the cities, caste distinctions are slowly eroding because of the compulsions of modern urban life. A few years ago, a government commission on the plight of the untouchables recommended that a larger percentage of positions should be reserved, in addition to the existing 27 percent, for the untouchables, on the basis of their numerical share of the total population.

This report, the Mandal Commission report, long buried by the governments for reasons of political expediency, was resurrected in 1991 by the prime minister, V. P. Singh, with the intention of putting it into effect. The upper-caste Hindus immediately raised their voices in angry protest, and a furious public battle ensued against the report and also against the prime minister. The protests, which soon became part of a country-wide movement, were led by the Hindu rightist parties, like the Bharatiya Janata Party (BJP), the Hindu Vishwa Parishad (VHP), and various other such organizations created by the "mother" organization, the Rashtriya Sewam Sevak Sangh (RSSS). The result was the outbreak of rioting in towns and villages, arson, killing, and the disruption of public life, and Singh's government had to resign.

Brahmins and other upper-caste Hindus feared that their power and the control they exercised over the civic and economic life of the country would be seriously threatened if the recommendations of the Mandal Commission report were actually put into effect. Some Indian analysts attribute the heightening of the campaign against the preservation for the Babari Masjid (Babur's Mosque) in Ayodha as a shrewd tactic adopted by these rightist parties to force the prime minister out of office and, thus, to divert the attention of the public from the Mandal Commission report to another issue. As a consequence, the report remains dormant, even though the prime minister, Narasimha Rao, said on the eve of the by-elections in northern India that it is his government's intention to implement its recommendations. The country, meanwhile, is occupied with what is called the Hindu-Muslim problem, and the fear of the rising power of reactionary parties, even of the demise of Indian democracy, and of the advent of Hindu fascist power.

Hatred of the untouchables and hate crime against them continue in the length and breadth of the country, especially in the villages and remote towns, but they hardly get reported to the police or the news media. Since crimes against untouchables occur in the course of everyday life—they range from insults to beatings, rapes, killings, and, occasionally, the burning of their miserable thatched huts—they do not make the headlines in national newspapers. Some incidents do get reported to the police and to the news media sporadically, and amongst them is the case of an untouchable constable, a policeman in uniform, who took shelter in the porch of an upper-caste Hindu temple during a severe storm. He was dragged out and beaten to death for defiling their temple by his presence. Recorded and well-documented cases of this kind are now becoming available to the public, or rather to the conscientious information-seeker. A recent letter in *India Abroad* from H. L. Virdee and Dr. Ambedkar adds a graphic and horrifying account to this one recent example:

> The BJP and the other forces of Hindutva do not seek to make India a Hindu nation for all. What they are seeking to do is create a "Brahminocracy," where all others will remain subservient to the so-called "high castes." Here are some instances of the way they have threatened the lower castes or untouchables, whom they consider inferior to them. On June 6, 1992, in the villages of Kumher and Bhatpur in Rajasthan over 160 people, young and old were burned alive. [Four hundred] head of cattle and 500 horses were torched and more than 50 girls and women were gang-raped by upper-caste Jats. On June 11, 1992 in the presence of police officers, MLAs and MPs of the BJP and Congress Parties, an untouchable youth was butchered and his blood ceremoniously smeared on the foreheads of those who took part in the killing. The first to do so was the BJP MLA. This happened at the Chaumanda Devi Temple, Rajasthan. In Chundur village, Andhra Pradesh, 25 untouchables were murdered by high caste Hindus in collaboration with the local police and administration. The question is what is the Indian government doing to prevent this from recurring and bring justice to the bereaved families? The BJP-VHP-RSSS publicly state that "we are all Hindus" and there is "equality" among Hindus. Obviously some are more equal than others in the hierarchy of Hindutva.[1]

Dr. Ambedkar, an eminent jurist who was educated at Columbia University (one of this oppressed class who got a chance for a higher education, thanks to the liberality of an upper-caste Hindu maharaja), tried to persuade his fellow untouchables to convert to Buddhism to escape from the trap of belonging to a religion that reduces them to this abject status. A large number did, but not enough to make a significant difference in the situation.

But horrifying as this as situation is for the untouchables, who are victims of hate crimes of various sorts almost on a daily basis, they do not have to face large-scale, well-planned, and well-organized programs such as those that the Muslims of India have faced in recent years, or as the Sikhs did in Delhi in 1984.

The hatred of the Muslims by upper-caste Hindus has some historical basis, and some of it is the result of popular prejudice or imaginary grievances. It is a historical fact that Muhmud, Sultan of Ghazna (in present-day Afghanistan), attacked India repeatedly toward the end of the tenth and early eleventh centuries. In the course of these plundering raids, he destroyed many Hindu temples, including the famous Somnath Temple in the western part of India. He looted the wealthy temples, desecrated idols, and returned to his native land with the booty. Further Muslim incursions followed after his death. In A.D. 1206, Qutbuddin Aibak occupied part of northern India and made Delhi his capital. Successive Muslim dynasties expanded their territories by conquering adjoining Hindu kingdoms. These wars of territorial expansion, as usual, caused loss of life and damage to property, but they were not religious wars. It should be remembered that India had gone through the same process in ancient times during the invasions by the Aryans (the ancestors of present-day upper-caste Hindus), the Greeks under Alexander the Great, the Scythians, the White Huns, and many other peoples. In medieval times, apart from the wars between Muslim and Hindu kings, internecine warfare among Muslim rulers in the north, and among Hindu rulers in the south, added to the suffering of the people of both religions. Finally, Babur, the Turko-Mongol ruler of Afghanistan, invaded India in A.D. 1526 and defeated and killed the Muslim ruler of Delhi, Ibrahim Lodi, in battle and became the first king of the dynasty of "the Great Moghuls," as some historians have called it. Both the kings, the victorious and the vanquished, were Muslims. So were their armies. So also were the soldiers who died on the battlefield. It is obvious that Babur's invasion of India was not motivated by religious zeal. It was simply a territorial invasion.

It is ironic, therefore, that this dynasty has been the target of the fanatic Hindu parties in recent years, because it was one of the most liberal of dynasties that ruled the country. Babur was no fanatic like Muhmud of Ghazna, nor was his son, Humayun, a scholar and a mild-tempered, though inept king, whose reign ended when he slipped and fell from the steps of his library to his death. Babur's grandson was the famous Akbar the Great (died A.D. 1605), who incorporated elements of Islam and Hinduism into a composite faith that he called Din-e-llahi (religion of God) and tried to bring all his subjects into its fold. He married a Hindu queen, and his court celebrated Hindu religious festivals like Dussehra and Divali, along with Muslim festivals. He also gave important administrative posts to Hindu noblemen. Others he made generals who commanded his armies, and his successors maintained these traditions. Aurangzeb, the last of "the Great Moghuls," was a bigot in many ways, and he imposed *jizya*, the hated poll tax; but he had the highest number of Hindu noblemen and generals in his army.

Today, extremist Hindu political leaders and parties seek to create an impression that during six centuries of Muslim rule, the two communities, Hindu and Muslim, were always at each other's throats, with hatred in their eyes. The fact is that from the thirteenth century until the end of the eighteenth, the two communities lived amicably together, with their own educational institutions, and according to their own religious laws, as they governed their personal lives. The Muslim rulers did not try to impose their laws on the Hindus in these important spheres of life.

In the course of time, a rich, composite culture evolved, and a new common language called Urdu grew out of the normal intercourse of the two communities. The rich heritage of the poetry, music, and painting of the period, admired and loved even today by the educated Hindu and Muslim alike, was the symbol of this intertwining of multifold traditions from the two cultures. The same was true for architecture, and in all the arts, Muslim and Hindu thought and expression created a synthesis of aesthetic principles and practice.

In mystical religious concepts and practices, the Hindu Bhakti movement and the Muslim Sufi orders came so close to each other that their message can be said to be one and the same. The Hindu Bhakti poet-saints and the Muslim mystics (Sufis) touched the souls of the people of all religions with their message of universal love and universal brotherhood. They specifically called for doing away with the differences of creed, caste, and status in society. They strongly advocated that people remove those preconceived ideas about differences that keep people apart, particularly those created by Brahmins (Hindu priests) and mullahs

(Muslim theologians). They taught that it was through the love of fellow men and the love of God that one could seek union with the Creator.

The Muslims had adapted to their new environs quickly, and the large number of native converts to Islam helped the process of assimilation of the newcomers. The extent of Muslim adaptation to Hindu social customs, especially in Bengal (including present-day Bangladesh) and southern India, is such that it is difficult for an outsider to distinguish one from the other. The two streams joined together and were in the process of forming a mighty river when the British and other European colonial powers appeared on the coast of India. The British overwhelmed their other European rivals, the Portuguese, the Dutch, and the French, and, in 1757, defeated a young Indian king, Siraj-ud-Dawla of Bengal, who had put up a fight against the foreigners. Within one hundred years, after defeating several Indian kings, both Hindu and Muslim, the British became the supreme power in the subcontinent. They ruled in the name of the nominal Moghul king, who was virtually their pensioner.

The Indians soon came to resent the treatment they received at the hands of the white man, and the list of their grievances mounted. The result, in 1857, was what the British called "the Great Mutiny," and the Indians call the first year of independence. The significant feature of this short-lived rebellion was the joint effort that Hindus and Muslims made against their common enemy, at all levels of the polity, from the humble foot soldiers to the most eminent noblemen of both communities. The revolt was ruthlessly crushed, and a ferocious vengeance was visited on the Indians by the British. The Indians lost this war; but what is more significant is that they lost hope about any improvement in their condition and their confidence in their culture was shaken. The damage to the Indian psyche was great. From the moment Queen Victoria was declared empress of India, and the British parliament took over direct rule of the country through the crown's viceroy, in 1858, Indians had to rediscover and redefine themselves.

Some Hindu leaders tried to revitalize their people by reaching back to the ancient religion of the Vedas and a romantic view of the distant Aryan past. Some tried to reform their religion to rid it of practices like the worship of images and the caste system, which they perceived to be undesirable. The obvious example of this revivalist-reform movement is the Arya Samaj, founded by Dayanand Saraswati in 1875 with its headquarters in the Punjab. Another such movement was founded by Ramakrishna (1836–1888), a devotee of the goddess Kali, near Calcutta. His movement was a reaction against the teachings of the Brahmo Samaj movement and Western rationalism. His disciple, Vivekananda (1836–1902), presented a liberalized version of Ramakrishna's teachings to Europe and America.

Other Hindu leaders took the path of reform in a more liberal and universal direction. Raja Ram Mohan Roy, a great Hindu intellectual is the outstanding example of such reformers. A high-caste Brahmin, he was educated in both Hindu and Muslim traditions. He knew Sanskrit, Arabic, and Persian, and learned English, Hebrew, and Greek to read the Bible and the classical texts in those languages. Ram Mohan Roy founded the Brahmo Samaj (Society of God) movement, which was influenced by Christianity and Western rationalism. He devoted his life to the reform of Hindu society and, as Beatrice Pitney Lamb recounts, "The Brahmo Samaj was the seedbed of a movement that continued throughout the nineteenth century to press for reforms in harmony with social ideas learned from the west."[2]

The political vision of liberal leaders like Surendernath Bannerja, Gokhale, Gandhi, and Nehru was molded, in part, by the spirit of the Brahmo Samaj. The liberal religious movements focused on the spiritual and the social needs of the individual, while the revivalist ones were exclusive and essentially intolerant, and soon developed a militant tone and a political thrust. One of the reasons for this kind of response was the fear that Westernization and the inroads made by Christian missionaries would overwhelm their Hindu heritage. Lala Laipat Rai of Punjab and Bal Gangadhar Tilak of Bombay, both inactive in the national movement, had a vision of an independent India that was essentially Hindu. Their fierce nationalism moved in the direction of militancy and force. They sought a pure Arya Varata (land of the Aryans), purged of what they considered to be foreign infusions like the Muslims and the Christians. The Hindu Mahasabha represented this point of view. The Mahasabha was succeeded by the Jana Sangh in the forties, and by the Bharatiya Santa Party in recent years.

The Muslims, on the other hand, felt dazed after the 1857 rebellion was crushed. They found themselves essentially backward in education and in government employment, with no political support or focus. The gradual political reforms of the British government, giving Indians some degree of elected representation in local government bodies, made them realize their numerical inferiority and their political weakness in the arena of democratic politics.

Sir Syed Ahmed Khan, who tried to reform Muslim middle- and upper-class society through propagating the idea of the necessity for Western-style education and scientific knowledge, saw this rudderless community as clinging to its decadent social attitudes. He founded the Aligarh Muslim College and the Scientific Society in 1875 to redress this situation. He hoped to infuse a modern, rational outlook amongst Muslims through this educational institution as well as through many other of his reformist efforts. But he focused mainly on his own religious community, although many of his statements in speeches and his writings do show that he looked on India as the country of both major communities. His view of the effects of the simple-majority elections, which were being introduced by the British government toward the end of the nineteenth century, was that the conflict between the communities was not based on religious differences but on the competition for employment opportunities and elected office. He wrote to a British official, Mr. Shakespeare, "Now I am convinced that both these communities will not join wholeheartedly in anything. . . . On account of the so-called educated people, hostility between communities will increase immensely in the future. He who lives will see."[3] The problem of communalism, he foresaw, was the product of the attitudes of the educated middle class, and not of the illiterate masses. Asghar Ali Engineer in his article, "Hindu-Muslim Relations Before and After 1947," says that, in a speech, Syed Ahmed Khan expressed his fears that "the larger community would totally over-ride the interests of the smaller community and the measures [proposed elections to local civic bodies] might make the differences of race and creed more violent than ever."[4]

There were several other Muslim reformist movements as well that were "national," as opposed to "communal," in their outlook. One such movement was that of the great Muslim theological college, founded by Maulana Mohammad Qasim, at Deodand in Uttar Pradesh. Like him, his disciples and followers refused to accept British rule in India intellectually or make compromises with the British government as Syed Ahmed Khan had done. They believed very strongly that India was their home and they were as much Indian as their compatriots. They firmly and consistently opposed British rule and what they considered the unhealthy influences Westernization brought about by means of an "English education." They were conservative in the religious and social spheres, but staunchly nationalist in politics. In fact, Maulana Mahmud-ul-Hasan, the Shaikh-ul-Hind, was exiled to Malta and jailed by the British government, and his colleagues, Maulana Obaidullah Sindhi, Maulana Mansoor Ansari, and Maulana Uzair Gul, were also exiled for their revolutionary anti-British activities. In the twentieth century, the scholars of the Deodand College have been active in the political struggle for independence and have supported the Indian National Congress in the common cause. They formed the political party called Jamiat-ul-Ulema-e-Hind (the Party of Muslim Scholars) and mobilized support for the Congress among the Muslim masses. Maulana Husain Ahmad Madani, Maulana Mohammad Tayyab, and Maulana Hifzur Rahman have served as its leaders.

At the advent of the twentieth century, Hindu revivalism, which began in the previous century, extended its power and influence. Consequently, Hindu-Muslim riots, which had raised their ugly head after the establishment of British supremacy in India in 1858, occurred more frequently. The Congress Party, with its broad-based liberal and democratic philosophy, had established its position as the main political party of Indians striving to gain a greater share of political power in the country. The partition of the huge province of Bengal in 1905 by Lord Curzon, the viceroy, caused a furor in the country. When the Congress Party launched a massive agitation against it, the Hindu revivalist leaders took up the cause zealously.

The partition of the province—which then comprised the states of Bengal, Bihar, and Orissa, and Bangladesh—was an administrative action and should not have inspired the amount of political opposition that it did. As it turned out, the leaders of the antipartition campaign questioned the government's rationale for the action and claimed that the administration was bent upon dividing the nation. It must be remembered in this connection that the newly created province of East Bengal was to be only another province, like so many in the country, not an independent county or even an autonomous state within the country. What the campaigners did not say was that the eastern part of Bengal was probably the most backward and poverty-stricken part of the country and that the vast majority of its inhabitants were Muslim Liberal Party members. Moderate Congress Party leaders, like Surendernath Bannerja, opposed the partition for secular political reasons. The revivalist, upper-caste Hindu leaders opposed it because they did not wish to allow a political and administrative arrangement that was likely to provide a better chance of improving the lot of the backward and poor untouchables and Muslims, who were at a disadvantage in education and far behind the upper-caste Hindus in the number of administrative positions they held. E. A. Gait, the census superintendent, in a report on the 1901 census of Bengal, written four years after the partition, said: "The most noticeable feature of this return is the very small share of high appointments which falls to the Muhammadans and the practical monopoly of all such appointments held by Hindus, members of the Brahmin, Baidya, and Kayasth castes. The Hindus are less than twice as numerous as the followers of the Prophet."[5]

It was not just the Muslims who were taken aback by the antipartition agitation, but the untouchables, the Namasudra also, who were the largest of all Hindu castes in eastern Bengal. "The Namasudra," writes Sumit Sarkar, "did not join this movement despite an invitation from the best sons of India." He quotes a senior British civil servant, B.C. Allen, who writes in *The Gazetteer of Dacca District*: "Till recent years, they [the Namasudra] have been regarded with great contempt by the higher Hindu castes, and as a result they resolutely declined to take any share in the agitation against the portion of Bengal. Having been treated as pariahs and outcasts, they refused to listen to the invitation of the higher caste Hindus to join a movement directed against the established Government."[6]

The Hindu untouchables, as well as the Muslims, it is clear, were opposed to the agitation against the partition of Bengal.

In 1906, the Muslims formed the Muslim League to safeguard their interests in Dacca (now Dhaka) under the leadership of the Agha Khan. It was a move in reaction to the intensity of the national parties, like the Congress Party, and especially to the extremists in the Hindu leadership involved in the agitation. The seed of a separatist tendency among the Muslim middle class was thus sown. At this time, the Muslim League was a marginal group of landowners and upper-middle-class people who sought through the support of the government to seek redress of their grievances. As it happened, the partition of East Bengal was annulled in 1911, but the damages to the cohesion of the major communities was done, even though there was not a complete breach of confidence.

The *Government of India Act of 1909* gave Indians some measure of elected representation in local bodies but with the provision that each community would vote only for the candidates of its own people. It was meant to safeguard the interests of those minorities who could not otherwise have representation and was an affirmative action. In December 1916, Congress Party leaders signed a pact with the Muslims in Lucknow, accepting this arrangement of separate electorates. This pact, known as the Lucknow Pact, was negotiated by an earnest Congress leader who was also a leader of the Muslims, Mohammed Ali Jinnah. (Thirty-one years later he became the head of the state of Pakistan.) As Percival Spear explains in *A History of India*: "Separate electorates were one of the bones of connection between Hindus and Muslims. Muslims contended that with property franchise a joint electorate would mean swamping of Muslims by Hindus in a great majority of cases because of Muslim poverty. They, therefore, demanded separate constituencies containing only Muslim voters."[7]

This arrangement continued in the enlarged 1919 act, which gave Indians almost full power in provincial assemblies and in the Central Legislature Assembly. The 1935 act provided for a federal constitution with unrestricted adult franchise, something the 1919 Act did not provide. After the first general elections were held in 1937, the Congress Party formed governments in most of the major provinces.

The political atmosphere was charged by the Anti–Bengal Partition movement, and after its annulment, the national movement became wider and more intense. The relations between the communities, meanwhile, became more and more complex. The Congress Party supported the British government in World War I in the hope that this would hasten the process leading to full internal independence. The Muslims, however, became more apprehensive about their future. They feared they would not be heard by the unsympathetic majority community, which held the political power. They thought there would not even be a British government in the future to arbitrate disputes, and they would be left without succor. This feeling of helplessness is the lot of all minorities everywhere. The backwardness of the Muslims and the escalating round of communal riots made matters worse. After World War I, Mohandas Karamchand Gandhi emerged as the leading figure in Indian politics. He became the undisputed leader of the Congress Party. His philosophy of *ahimsa* (nonviolence), and his famous policy of *satyagraha* (nonviolent struggle), helped to calm intercommunal relations at this time and kindled a new hope for harmony between the various religious groups.

Gandhi had started the Non-Cooperation movement in 1921 to put pressure on the British government to move more quickly toward giving political power to Indians. At about the same time, the Muslims, perturbed by the harsh treatment of the defeated nation of Turkey (which had sided with the Germans in the war), started the Khilafat movement against the British. It was an effort to preserve the Califate of the Sultan of Turkey. Gandhi invited the leader of Khilafat (Califate) movement to join his Non-Cooperation movement. Accepting his offer, the members of the Khilafat movement joined Gandhi and supported his movement wholeheartedly.

For a while, these two movements became one powerful movement against the British government, which, for the first time since the rebellion of 1857, felt the full force of the political action of all Indians joined together against it. During this period a great feeling of brotherhood and comradeship developed between the two communities. Gandhi was honored by Muslims everywhere. Muslims even invited him to give a speech in the famous Jama Masjid (the Grand Mosque) in Delhi. The leaders of the Khilafat movement, men like Maulana Mohammad Ali, Shaukat Ali, and many others, were also Congress Party leaders at the time. The Aligarh Muslim College founded by Syed Ahmed Khan, which had been essentially pro-British, was now charged with a nationalist fervor. The British professors were forced to leave by the anti-British student movement. In the spirit of the Non-Cooperation movement, teachers and students abjured their college and started a counter institution, the Jamie Millia Islamia (the National Islamic College) in the same place. Gandhi was one of its patrons. Later the Jamie Millia Islamia moved to Delhi, and Dr. Zakir Husain became its chancellor (Shaikh-ul-Jamie).

By the mid-1920s, the Congress Party had become a truly national party. Its leadership included eminent Muslims like Maulana Abul Kalam Azad, who was twice its president; Dr. Mukhtar Ahmad Ansari, president of the Congress Party in the 1930s; Hakim Ajmal Khan; Khan Abdul Ghaffar Khan; and many others. In fact, there were prominent Muslim leaders in the Congress Party at all of its organizational levels—provincial, city, and district. When the British government arrested Congress Party leaders, something which happened repeatedly, the Hindu and the Muslim members of the party went to jail together and shared the jail cells and the hardships equally. Jawahar Lal Nehru and Maulana Abul Kalam Azad were together in one jail, and C. Rajagopalachari and Shafiq ur Rahman Kidwai in another.

However, Hindu chauvinism brought about by leaders like Tilak, Lala Laipat Rai, Dayanand, and others was growing and becoming powerful in the 1920s as well. V. D. Savarkar, the fiery ideologue of the Hindu Mahasabha, was evolving a militant Hindu ideology that was adopted by the Rashtriya Sevam Sewak Sangh (the RSSS). Savarkar's pamphlet, *Who is a Hindu?* (written in 1923) contains the formulations of this militant Hindu nationalism. The Hindu Mahasabha at its annual session in 1923, in Benares (now Varanashi), passed a resolution calling for the establishment of Hindu defense squads, and two years later, K. B. Hedgewar founded the RSSS at Nagpur, which provided the secretive organization that was to disseminate the propaganda to further the cause of the ideology. A paramilitary force of volunteers was created too, to give it the actual muscle power that was used so effectively both before and after independence.

After Gandhi suddenly and unilaterally stopped the Non-Cooperation movement, the Congress Party lost momentum and direction. In addition, the Khilafat movement was abolished by Kemal Ataturk, its Turkish leader. Reactionaries of all shades soon filled the political vacuum by communalizing every issue and causing widespread rioting from one end of the country to the other. A recent essay on the subject notes, "There were no less than ninety-one communal outbreaks between 1923 and 1927."[8] These riots were the result of the activities of communal parties of both communities. The Arya Samaj under Shardhanand launched a hectic campaign of *shaddhi* (purification), which was an effort at reconversion to Hinduism of the poorer classes who had become Muslims generations earlier. The other part of the campaign was *sangathan* (organization). The Muslims responded with *tabligh* (propaganda) and *tanzim* (organization). The Shaddhi campaign was much more militant than that of the Muslims because, in the purification campaign, it inflamed feelings and charged the atmosphere with communal hatred. Consequently, riots became more frequent and more vicious.

Once again, the Muslims began to feel victimized and started to lose faith in the Congress Party leadership after the Nehru committee's rejection of what they considered to be reasonable demands for safeguards. These demands were presented in 1927 by some Muslim leaders through Mohammed Ali Jinnah (later the founder of Pakistan) to the Congress Party leadership. In exchange for the safeguards, the Muslims were prepared to give up separate electorates and work with the party for the independence of the country. The two significant demands of the Muslims were that in Punjab and Bengal (Muslim-majority provinces) seats in the legislature should be allocated in accordance with the ratio of the population of the communities; and that Muslims should be given 30 percent of the seats at the center as a safeguard for their interests, even though their countywide population was less than 30 percent. A committee under the chairmanship of Pandit Nehru (the future prime minister's father) was entrusted with the task of reviewing the demands and providing the response to them. The committee decided that the party should not accede to the more important demands, and a unique opportunity for political unity among the major communities was lost. The result was disillusionment with the Congress Party and deep frustration in the Muslim community, following so soon after the period of impressive unity and mutual cooperation. Muslim opinion now swung toward communal parties, especially the Muslim League.

Besides the Muslim League, there were several smaller Muslim organizations, like the Majlis-e-Ahrar, whose orientation was narrow. This group supported the Congress Party and opposed the league in national politics. Then there was the Khaksar (humble workers) movement. Its leader was Allama Mashriqi, an eccentric, but potentially dangerous personality. His *khaksars* were clad in military uniforms, complete with army boots, but instead of *lathis* (long staves) or guns, they carried spades as symbols of their commitment to community service. They held "drill meetings" and marches, and in the late 1930s, their maneuvers bore an ominous resemblance to the fascist marches in Europe. However, they did not turn toward violence, and later their leader opposed the league for his own reasons. The movement remained marginal and did not survive after independence. On the other hand, the Muslim League was a party of landowners and affluent lawyers from its early days. It had no mass support among Muslims till after the rejection of Muslim demands by the Nehru committee in 1927. Actually, in the 1937 elections based on adult franchise, it lost heavily in all the Muslim majority provinces and regions. It is extremely significant that the Muslim League lost to noncommunal parties in all the provinces that later constituted Pakistan.

In the North-West Frontier Province, the Muslim League lost to the Red Shirt Party of the "frontier Gandhi," Khan Abdul Ghaffar Khan. This party was so closely related to the Congress Party that it was considered part of the party. The league lost to the Unionist Party of Sir Sikander Hayat Khan in the Punjab, which is now the bulk and the heart of Pakistan. In Sind, it was the party of G. M. Syed that was the rival of the league, and in Bengal, it was the Krishak Proja Party of A. K. Fazlul Haque that easily defeated the league. Even in Western Uttar Pradesh, where the Muslims had a large population, though not a majority, especially in the towns and cities, the league won only one seat out of twenty-three Muslim constituencies. It was only in areas where the Muslims were a very small minority that the league managed to win a majority of the Muslim seats.

After the elections, the Congress Party formed governments in all major provinces. In the first months after the ministries took office, there was an atmosphere of heady elation as people got a whiff of the sweet breath of freedom. It did not last long, however, because even under the Indian administration the riots did not cease to occur, as many had hoped. And riots could not be blamed on the perfidy of the British any more. The Muslim League exaggerated and exploited the growing feeling amongst the Muslims that they were the victims of discrimination. In a cumulative way, a sense of alienation grew amongst them, and the insensitivity of the Congress Party administrations in the provinces, especially in Uttar Pradesh and Bihar, to the needs of the minorities, seriously undermined their confidence in the party leadership.

It is an amazing fact that, in the 1937 elections, the vast majority of Muslims was actually opposed to the Muslim League and its separatist ideology. This fact is usually ignored by both the Muslim and the Hindu communalists because it does not suit their theories of separatism. which are similar in spirit. It is interesting that a reversal of this situation came about within a mere eight years, in the 1945 elections—the first general election after World War II—when the Muslim League won convincingly and its demand for Pakistan, a separate homeland for Muslims, was endorsed by a majority of Muslims.

When the Congress Party ministries resigned in 1939, at the onset of World War II, the political arena lay open to the Muslim League and the Hindu communal parties, and they made excellent use of the opportunity. The league in 1940 passed a resolution calling for the creation of a separate country for Muslims in the areas of the country in which they were in a majority. This move signaled a very significant shift in the maneuvers of the two groups, and everyone waited for the war to end and political negotiations to begin for the granting of independence.

The Congress Party leaders were released from jail when the war ended, and new elections were held in 1945. This time, the Muslim League made a clean sweep of almost all the Muslim seats, even in those Muslim majority areas where it had made such a poor showing only eight years earlier. After hectic negotiations between the party, the league, and the British government, it was agreed by all three to create a new country for Muslims, and on August 14, 1947, Pakistan came into existence. India became independent the next day, on August 15, 1947.

The year before, in 1946, large-scale and planned riots had broken out in Calcutta and had spread to adjoining Bihar and further north, to the Punjab. The Calcutta riots were initially instigated by Muslims, and the retaliatory riots that followed in Bihar and northern India were inspired by the Hindu leaders. Thus, India and Pakistan were born, in 1947, when riots were ranging in many parts of the subcontinent. The fury of the riots turned into wholesale massacres in the new countries. The massive transfer of populations took place in the following months, with Hindus seeking refuge in India, and Muslims in Pakistan. Delhi, too, was torn by riots and was burning when Gandhi hurried back to it from Noakhali in East Bengal in early September 1947. With his immense prestige and moral force, he helped to calm the situation. He stayed on in Delhi and held meetings everyday at which hymns from Hindu, Muslim, Christian and other religions were recited. At one such meeting, on January 30, 1948, less than five months after independence, a former RSSS man, Nathuram Vinayak Godse, fired several bullets from his revolver and killed the great man, the father of the nation.

This dastardly act was the culmination of the campaign of hate carried on by the Hindu parties, especially the RSSS. The RSSS, predictably, denied any complicity in the murder and still does so. It claimed to be only a cultural organization, not a political one, and that is what it continues to maintain. The hate crimes instigated and committed by it were against Muslims, but the bullet that killed the great man also made his philosophy of tolerance and nonviolence its target. The RSSS preached hatred of Muslims and Christians as foreign invaders, forgetting that the Aryans themselves were also invaders. This insidious propaganda made out that Gandhi's philosophy of tolerance, nonviolence, and communal harmony was making Hindus weak. Hindus, they exhorted, had to become strong and militant to save themselves from imminent extinction. "Hinduism in danger" was the theme of extremist Hindu leaders as early as the 1880s. Tilak, Lala Laipat Rai, and Dayanand had sounded this alarm. The next generation of such leaders, V. D. Savarkar, B. S. Moonje, and K. B. Hedgewar, who founded the RSSS in 1925, expanded the theme and added the element of marital clout. The Hindu Mahasabha had already called for Hindu self-defense squads in 1923 at its Benares session. One such training and indoctrination session is described in the following excerpt:

Between April and June 1927, the R.S.S. held a training camp. . . . There was training in the use of *lathi* (staff), sword, javelin and dagger—weapons it may be noted, which could be helpful in a select brawl with unarmed fellow Asians, but were of little use in fighting British soldiers or policemen. The boys played indigenous games [e.g. *kabbadi*] . . . and heard lectures on Hindu nationalism, the disloyalty of non-Hindus, the futility of Gandhian methods and the past heroism of the Hindus. The constantly reiterated message was that the Hindus were suffering because they had become unorganized, liberal, generous and peaceable. They needed to become militant and powerful and for that an organization like the R.S.S. was essential. The R.S.S. . . . played the major role in a communal riot in Nagpur in September 1927.[9]

The organization of the RSSS and its training camps grew in strength and spread to the whole county. It *shakhas* (branches) in towns and cities supplemented the training camps by daily martial exercises, along with exhortations to hatred and violence. The Hindu Mahasabha became its political wing and changed its name to Jan Sangh. This was changed again, in recent years, to Bharatiya Janata Party (BJP). The Hindu Vishwa Parishad (VHP), an organization meant to promote Hindu religious interest, and the Bajrang Dal (BD), a Hindu Youth organization, were added to what is known as the "family" of RSSS organizations. All these organizations have been especially active in the 1990s. Their combined forces organized the campaign for the demolition of the Babari Masjid (Babur's Mosque) and achieved that goal on December 6, 1992, to secular India's shame.

The success of chauvinist and fascist parties depends on the creation of a climate of fear, suspicion, and hatred. Fear is instilled into the minds and hearts of otherwise decent, peaceful people by creating a monster of an enemy, who then appears to be an imminent threat to the society and its very existence. Suspicion and hatred are instilled by painting the enemy as treacherous and degraded. Propaganda repeated every so often, with half-truths, distortions of facts, historical or otherwise, and blatant lies are the means of achieving these goals. Fascists in Europe employed it so successfully in the 1930s. Hitler and his Nazi propagandists continuously harped on the treachery of the Jews, their immense wealth, and their conspiracies. The success of the propaganda made average, decent citizens believe its falsehoods and so become complicit in the barbarities inflicted on the Jews, including the horrifying deaths in the gas chambers. Jews were the main target of the Nazis, but gypsies, socialists, communists, Catholics, and intellectuals of all kinds suffered the same fate as well. The hatred of Jews was the means used to make the people acquiesce in the usurpation of democratic power and so give their consent to authoritarian rule by the Nazis, and to the atrocities committed by them. Fascists have to have this consensual climate to perpetrate their hate crime on their chosen victims.

This consensual climate in India was created by the RSSS and its likeminded parties beginning in the 1920s, as has been mentioned earlier. Yet another factor in this issue must also to be recognized—that of the communal-minded leaders within the Congress Party. They were sometimes referred to as the right wing of the party and were symbolized by the formidable Sardar Vallabbhai, Nehru's deputy prime minister. The Indian Congress Party right-wingers were individuals who exerted their pressures in the decision-making process, and sometimes they did function as a group. The history of this element is varied and is of importance in the growth of communalism in national politics. Lal Bahadur Shastri, who was Nehru's successor as prime minister, encouraged the RSSS, perhaps unwittingly, by giving it a significant role in civil defense during the 1965 war with Pakistan, thus conferring legitimacy on it. Indira Gandhi in her second tenure as prime minister, it is said, decided to use "the Hindu card" on the advice of her close advisers in 1980. One cannot be sure of this view, but the fact is that her policies in the 1980s decidedly show a shift to the right, toward communal politics.

The June 1984 assault on the holiest shrine of the Sikhs, the Golden Temple in Amristar, with army tanks, is the most obvious example of this policy. This military operation, code-named "Blue Star," in which a place of worship was invaded and seriously damaged by deliberate and planned action, was a blow to the unity and fraternal relations that had existed until then between the Hindus and the Sikhs. This desecration was a more serious blow to the secular, democratic foundation of the country. It was immediately recognized amongst all thinking and peace-loving people in India, and indeed the rest of the world, as a very immoral act for a government and a party that had always declared equality and respect for all religions. No government, least of all a democratic government, should have crossed the line that Mrs. Gandhi's did.

In October of the same year, the newspapers of the world blazoned the horrifying news that Mrs. Gandhi had been assassinated, shot and killed by two of her own Sikh bodyguards. Immediately a pogrom against the

Sikhs was mounted by the Hindus in Delhi and its vicinity in which more than a thousand Sikhs were killed and much damage was done to their property. Among the several reasons that are given for the movement for Khalistan (land of Sikhs), it is clear that the desecration of the Golden Temple and the massacre of the Sikhs certainly played an important part.

During the 1980s, the corruption in the government and the communalization of the police and other security forces was such that the general public lost confidence in them, especially the Muslims and Sikhs who were the victims of their extralegal actions. Politicians of most parties, including the Congress Party, appealed to the base instincts of their constituents. They sacrificed the principles of democracy and secularism to get elected to office—ironically, to be chosen by a democratic process—by appealing to the religious caste or subcaste loyalties and chauvinism of the voters. This immoral technique for winning election is called "Vorebank politics." This practice too has strengthened communalism in politics and in the society.

Communalism is also helped and encouraged by the inaction of Congress Party leaders like former prime minister Narasimha Rao, who took no effective measures to stop the demolition of the Babari Masjid; or the chief minister of Maharashtra, Naik, who took no serious action before, during, or after the terrible riots in Bombay in early 1993 after the Babari Masjid episode. The following excerpt is from *Frontline*, India's national magazine:

> The destruction of the Babari Masjid by *Hindutva* vandals provoked the most terrible communal riots in the history of Bombay. Muslim masses were the primary targets of this violence, and the Shiv Sena was the main organizer and spearhead of the riots that tore the city apart. During the riots the Governments of Maharashtra (state) and India became, in substance, non-governments; they served the cause of rampaging Hindu communalism by standing and waiting and by following a scandalous policy of appeasement of the Shiv Sena and its infamous leader, Bat Thackeray.[10]

Such political weakness (some call it administrative lethargy) and immoral expediency is tantamount to complicity in the crimes of hatred perpetrated by the RSSS and its counterpart in Bombay, the Shiv Sena, and other such parties. Professor Sumit Sarkar in an article in the prestigious *Economic and Political Weekly* writes, "With the 6th of December [demolition of the Babari Mosque] and its aftermath [large-scale riots all over the country], elements frighteningly evocative of its totality of horror stab our streets, obtain connivance and implicit sustenance from within the highest corridors of power."[11]

Comparing the present political situation in India to that which existed in Nazi Germany, Sarkar goes on to say in the same article: "There is much surely, that is ominously reminiscent here [of Nazi Germany]. A mosque is systematically reduced to rubble over five long hours in total violation of a direct Supreme Court order and repeated assurances given by the leading opposition party [BJP] and its allies, and the central government does not lift its little finger. Countywide riots follow, marked by blatant partiality, with the guardians of the law not unoften turning rioters themselves."

There is another kind of governmental inaction that includes crimes of hate, including mass killings, rape, and arson. It is that the central (federal) or state governments have not, after the riots, prosecuted the criminals who committed murder, rape, and arson; and appropriate punishment has not been meted out to them, in accordance with the criminal law of the country. There have been hundreds, possibly thousands, of riots since independence in which thousands upon thousands have died in the last forty years. But no one has been hanged for murder, and no one faced the full brunt of the law for rape or arson. This kind of nonresponse has emboldened the criminals, the parties that organize riots, and the policemen who abet, and sometimes participate, in the crime themselves, as was reported in most of the world's newspapers after the recent Bombay riots. (See, for instance, *Time* magazine, January 25, 1993, page 42.) The result of all these forms of governmental dereliction of duty in not upholding and enforcing the law of the country is that the victims of these incessant riots and tyrannies, the minorities and the poor of both communities, especially the women, continue to suffer trauma and agony, with no hope or means of succor. A growing desperation seems to have taken hold of their minds.

The desperation and hopelessness have led some wrongheaded young men to try to counter the organized terrorism of the majority community by a terrorism of their own. In South India, the formation of a Muslim RSSS has been reported. There have been reports of police having been fired at, and also of attempts by members of the minority committee to collect arms and ammunition. The bomb explosions in Bombay,

Calcutta, and Madras are suspected to have been the work of Muslims. That is what government officials have broadly said, and the leaders of the Hindu chauvinist parties, like L. K. Advini of the B.J.P., have strongly asserted these to have been the work of Muslims and Pakistani agents. The truth about these incidents may or may not become known, but these developments are suicidal for Muslims, and dangerous for the country. Once driven to desperation, men sometimes do the most irrational and self-destructive things.

Minority communities, like the Muslims and Sikhs, appear to have lost faith in the leadership of the country. The Sikhs mounted a campaign in the form of a secessionist movement for a separate Sikh state, independent of India, in the aftermath of the Indian government's attack on their Golden Temple. It has cost the lives of hundreds of Hindus and Sikhs. The government was able to suppress this insurrection only after several years of military and police campaigns and by political maneuvering. The well-organized and extremely well-funded parties like the RSSS and its affiliates, the BJP, the VHP, and others are determined to exploit "the ancient rivalries" and prejudices to achieve their ideological aims and political goals; they aim to establish a "pure" Hindu India by means of large-scale riots and through atrocities like murder, rape, and arson. The chauvinistic and jingoistic policies of these parties are demonstrably fascistic in nature. Proponents want India to be armed with nuclear weapons. They want to suppress all minorities and to relegate them to a subservient position, just as the upper-caste Hindus (Aryans) have done for more than 2,500 years to the majority non-Aryan untouchables. In the first half of 1993, it looked as if these parties would take over the country by creating civil unrest and sectarian strife, by generating such passions of hatred and hostility toward minority communities, and by intimidating the secular and liberal forces (that were in utter disarray) through elections, which they have called for repeatedly. However, in November and December 1993, in the by-election in four major states, the right-wingers have suffered significant losses. This development gives some relief to the liberal-minded people in the country and some breathing space to the prime minister, Narasimha Rao. But it does not mean that the danger of the world's largest democracy sliding into the abyss of fascism and totalitarian sectarianism is over. All it means is that now there is an opportunity for the secular parties to pick up the courage and to muster the will to fight narrow-minded bigotry and Hindu fundamentalist demagoguery. It is the fight from which they began to retreat when Nehru died in 1964, and even more abjectly so when his daughter, Indira Gandhi began the second phase of her long rule (around 1980).

Nehru himself once said that it was not communalism of the Muslims that would destroy the secular character of India, only Hindu communalism can do that. Yet, Muslim communalism, as well as Sikh communalism, it must be recognized, have strengthened the hands of Hindu chauvinists. Secular parties and individuals have to fight the communalism of every community—be it Muslim, Sikh, or Hindu—to save the country's democratic and secular character and to avert the threat of disintegration. M. Basheer Husain has summed up the argument extremely well in his recent article in *The Hindustan Times* and one has to admit that not much more need be added to it:

> If secularism is on the retreat in the country, the entire blame should rest with the Government. Secularism is a bond that unites different religious communities. In fact, it is the foundation on which our democratic polity is based. It rests on the twin pillars of equality before the law and equal protection of law. If the secular vision of India is fading, it is because the rulers of our society have not strengthened the foundation of these pillars. On the other hand they have allowed the communal forces to chip away the pillars on which secularism rests.[12]

NOTES

1. H. L. Virdee and Dr. Ambedkar (1992), letter to the editor, *India Abroad* (New York) 12(5): 15–16.

2. Beatrice Pitney (1968), *India: A World in Transition* (New York: Norton).

3. Asghar Ali Engineer (1990), "Hindu-Muslim Relations Before and After 1947," in *Anatomy of a Confrontation*, ed. Sargepalli Gopal (New Delhi: Newberry), 184.

4. Engineer (1990), 184.

5. E. A. Gait (1993), quoted in A. K. Biswas, *Mainstream* (Delhi), July 17, 58.

6. Sumit Sarkar (1990), *Modern India 1885–1947* (New York: Macmillan), quoted in A. K. Biswas, *Mainstream* (Delhi), July 17, 58.

7. Percival Spear (1978), *A History of India*, vol. 2 (London: Longman), 184.

8. *Khaki Shorts and Saffron Flags* (1993), ed. Tapan Basu (London: Orient Longman), 10.

9. *Khaki Shorts* (1993), 18.

10. V. K. Ramachandran (1993), "Immolation of Morgue by Hindu Fanatics," *Frontline*, Feb. 12.

11. Sumit Sarkar (1992), "Contagious Destruction of Babari Mosque," *Economic and Political Weekly* (New Delhi), Jan. 30, 163.

12. M. Basheer Husain (1993), "Affront to Secularism," *Hindustan Times* (New Delhi), Nov. 25, 9–10.

6. Social Cleansing in Colombia: The War on Street Children

Suzanne Wilson and Julia Greider-Durango

I believe in God, the Holy Virgin and all that kind of thing. I know the Holy Bible says it's a sin to kill, but that's if you kill other Christians. Here it's animals, not Christians, that we're killing.
—*Alonso Salazar,* Born to Die in Medellín

Between February 1 and May 14, 1991, police found the bodies of 187 young people in Bogotá, Colombia, many of whom had been murdered by vigilantes like Don Rafael.[1] The killings were a form of hate crime known as *limpieza social,* or social cleansing, the methodical killing of *desechables,* disposable people. Like other kinds of hate crime, social cleansings specifically target groups who are marginalized, stigmatized, and labeled as undesirable by Colombian society or a segment of it. Victims of social cleansings include prostitutes, homosexuals, the mentally ill, street children, and other outcasts of society.[2]

As in other regions of the world, hate crime toward undesirable groups is not a new phenomenon in Colombia or Latin America. However, in the last thirty years, hate crimes in the region have taken a form reminiscent of recent ethnic cleansings in Eastern Europe—the widespread and deliberate killings of designated minorities. Under military dictatorships in Argentina, Chile, Uruguay, and El Salvador, *desechables* have been systematically harassed and killed. Social cleansings, however, are not restricted to military governments. Recently, the growing number of street children killed in Guatemala and Brazil under the current democratic governments has directed international attention to the problem. In Brazil, the number of children murdered for involvement in petty crime averaged one a day in 1989, and more than three thousand street children have been killed there since the mid-1980s.[3]

Studies have found social cleansings in Colombia to be systematic, methodical, organized, and concentrated in urban areas.[4] Although the number of deaths by social cleansing is invariably underreported, the figures are startling and indicate a rapid increase of these crimes during the past few years.[5] The Centro de Investigación y Educación Popular (CINEP), a well-known research institute in Bogotá, documented 1,801 deaths by social cleansing between 1988 and 1992, with an average of 26.5 per month between 1988 and 1991, and 44 per month in 1992.[6] Between January and September of 1993, one person was murdered every other day in a social cleansing; of those, sixty-two were classified as "delinquents" or minors.[7]

Every week Colombian social workers report finding the bodies of street children who have been shot, burned, suffocated, or beaten to death. The hatred and violence waged against these children has increased dramatically in the past decade as death squads and vigilantes "clean up" the streets of Colombia by eliminating the *desechables*. Not only are street children the targeted victims of social cleansings, but they are also likely to be at the scene of social cleansings against other targeted groups such as prostitutes. They are, therefore, placed in double jeopardy.

THE SOCIAL AND POLITICAL CONTEXT

Key to understanding Colombian "democracy" and politics is the history of its two major political parties. Shortly after the Colombian wars of independence from 1810 to 1816, the nation's elite founded two major political parties—the Liberals and Conservatives—which have continued to dominate Colombian politics. Despite clear control by the elite, these political parties generated intense partisanship during the nineteenth and twentieth centuries. This political dominance and partisanship of the elite have been accompanied by several periods of political violence, the most famous of which is *La Violencia.*

In the late 1940s and 1950s, the nation was engaged in a brutal and devastating civil war—known as *La Violencia*—which left two important legacies: a tradition of hired killers and paramilitary groups and the persecution of poor and socially stigmatized groups under the guise of wider political violence. La Violencia also introduced the widespread presence of street children in Colombia due to the death, displacement, and urban migration of thousands of Colombians during and after the siege.[8] Industrialization and a lack of adequate land reform measures during the 1950s to 1970s led to continued urbanization, which reinforced and increased the number of street children.

Unlike many Latin American countries, Colombia did not experience a military dictatorship during the 1960s and 1970s. In an attempt to end La Violencia, the elite supported a military government during the 1950s in Colombia. That government was replaced by the National Front in 1958 in a bipartisan agreement that divided political offices equally between the two parties, although officeholders were chosen electorally. Because of the elite's domination of the two parties, Jonathan Hartlyn notes, "most analysts have viewed Colombia since 1958 as a qualified democracy."[9]

In the late 1970s and early 1980s, a new period of political violence besieged Colombia. The violence was not rooted in partisanship but rather was characterized by the ascent of the cocaine trade, the growth of guerrilla groups operating throughout the country, and the accompanying expansion of the armed forces. Political violence in the 1980s and 1990s has created a renewed growth of paramilitary groups and hired assassins, often working in conjunction with the military and drug traffickers. Since 1986, over twenty thousand Colombians have been killed due to political causes.[10] Between January and September of 1993, political violence and human rights abuses claimed a total of 2,891 victims, approximately 320 people per month.[11]

In addition to political violence, Colombia has experienced an increase in other forms of violence and crime. Conditions accelerating the violence include a government overwhelmed by drug trafficking and political turmoil, the proliferation of private bodyguards and police, and a climate of impunity toward criminals. As a result, organized death squads and vigilantes increasingly resort to La Violencia's tradition of taking justice into their own hands. A 1988 government commission appointed to study violence in Colombia concluded that "private justice substitutes for legal powers in a zeal to defend a specific order."[12] The Colombian environment has not only failed to punish criminals for violent acts but has implicitly encouraged their abuses, including the social cleansing of street children.[13]

COLOMBIA'S STREET CHILDREN

Although Colombia's homeless children may be found in almost every town and region in Colombia, most of these children live on the streets of Bogotá. Of the 6 million inhabitants of Bogotá, estimates of the number of street children, or *gamíns*, range from 1,200 to 12,000, although many researchers consider the actual number to be larger.[14] The *gamíns* of Bogotá are primarily boys between the ages of six and seventeen who live on the streets twenty-four hours a day and have no permanent home.[15] They may have families but receive little or no economic support from family members. Many *gamíns* are children trying to make life better for themselves and their families by "striking out on their own" to become independently responsible for their own well-being.

Typically, a young boy from the slums will be sent by a parent or caretaker to beg on the streets to contribute to the family income. Once a boy is on the streets during the day, he will often meet older siblings or friends who have become *gamíns*. He gradually spends more time on the streets with the *gamíns* and less time at home. Because the poverty and despair in a household often lead to child abuse and neglect, he may find that street life gives him more freedom than he has at home. In addition, any money the boy collects while begging or stealing no longer must be given to a parent or caretaker; money he obtains may be kept and spent as he likes.

During the day, most *gamíns* are quite visible on the busy streets of downtown Bogotá. *Gamíns* often organize themselves into working groups, or *galladas*, to clean cars, sell lottery tickets, beg for change, and inevitably, to steal. At night, they sleep under bridges, in doorways, in cardboard boxes, under sheets of plastic, and in the city's sewage system. They seek refuge in any place that provides shelter from Bogotá's cold and rainy climate, and more importantly, which provides them protection from police, vigilantes, and others who might hurt them.

For the *gamíns*, survival on the streets is an unrelenting test of will and ingenuity. Within their *galladas*, the children usually determine a division of labor according to each child's abilities. In the evening, the children regroup to share money, food, and other resources they have obtained during the day. Finding food is usually not a problem for the *galladas*. The children commonly bargain with shopkeepers; in exchange for the day's leftover food, the children promise not to rob the store or harass the store's customers. Stealing food is fairly easy in the open markets, but as a last resort, the children may search through garbage cans for something edible.

The children do earn money by "working" and can be very creative in providing services to the public. Very often *gamíns* will board a bus to sing a song, recite a poem, or tell a joke. The children will then ask each passenger for money before exiting and boarding another bus. The children also sell lottery tickets, contraband cigarettes, flowers, candies, and other sundries to pedestrians and motorists. Because Bogotá's heavy traffic keeps vehicles stalled at busy street intersections, *gamíns* often take the opportunity to wash the windows or headlights of the cars in return for coins.

Street children obtain most of their money by stealing—an activity at which they are quite adept. Pickpocketing and purse snatching are most common, although *gamíns* will also steal goods from stores and markets and car parts from parking lots. They can easily sell stolen items in the *ollas*, or sectors of the underworld where prostitution, drug trafficking, and the buying and selling of stolen goods are the main activities. The *gamíns* are seldom caught. Police statistics for 1987 concluded that 90 percent of all street robberies perpetrated by *gamíns* were never registered because of the long, bureaucratic process involved in filing a complaint, particularly when it involves petty theft.[16]

The *gamíns* are forced to live their lives as if they were adults. The privileges and necessities of infancy are suspended as these boys take responsibility for their own survival. In Bogotá, the high rate of violence makes survival difficult for anyone. A street boy's life in the city is filled with dangerous and life-threatening conditions. By the age of ten, most street children have been exposed to drugs and alcohol, gang fights, heterosexual and homosexual encounters, illnesses and infectious diseases, abuse, and rape.[17] Carlos Palacios, a former Colombian street child said, "To live on the street is like living in the jungle. The strongest survive."

The weakest die. That is how it happened in my group, and it is still happening, and especially now when there are those in Colombia who are exterminating them."[18]

THE WAR ON STREET CHILDREN

While most Colombian citizens consider the street children to be no more than an unfortunate and minor nuisance, significant segments of Colombian society fear and despise the *gamíns*. Extremist and conservative factions believe the street children to be "dirty," sinful, and deserving of their impoverishment. They identify the street children with other morally unacceptable groups like homosexuals and prostitutes, and they believe that the children are receiving punishment from God for their "un-Christian" ways.[19] Moral stances fuel the fear and hatred that allow people to applaud and condone social cleansing as necessary for the good of society.

Although the right-wing ideology of cleansing society is at the core of hate crime in Colombia, the collective attitudes of apathy and tolerance found in Colombian society reinforce the stigmatization of street children and silently allow the social cleansings to take place.[20] Because of their economic status, many middle- and upper-class Colombians are prejudiced against the poor, including street children, and they often attribute their poverty to laziness.[21] Although most middle- and upper-class Colombians in Bogotá live in the isolated north side of the city and are unlikely to encounter street children daily, they often see the children on their way to work or while shopping. In markets and buses, middle-class *señoras* are commonly heard expressing their fear and disgust of "those terrible *gamíns*." One young mother, upon hearing about a massacre of street children in Bogotá, said, "Well, there have been plenty of times when I've felt like killing some of those dirty kids myself."

Shopkeepers, bus drivers, and other city workers also consider the children to be no more than thieves and delinquents. A well-known Colombian scholar and priest was sitting in a taxi in downtown Bogotá when a street child approached the window to ask for some coins. The annoyed taxi driver, after shouting at the child, said to the priest, "The government should just kill all of those *gamíns*." When the priest asked the taxi driver if he truly believed in killing the children, the taxi driver replied, "Well, maybe we could send them to the jungle to see if they survive."[22] Many small businesspeople, especially shopkeepers, share the disgust of the street children because the *gamíns* threaten their businesses by stealing and harassing customers.

Some Colombians within the lower classes also perceive *gamíns* as "undesirable elements" within their communities. In some of the poorest urban neighborhoods, civic action organizations and community groups have blamed street children for bringing vice into the community. To compound the problem, a number of violent gangs have formed in poor neighborhoods, generally comprised of armed teenagers and young men. Community residents often perceive the younger street children as guilty by association, although most *gamíns* are not involved in violent crimes.

To create and promote an image of Bogotá as a modern, clean, and safe city, the Colombian media has largely ignored the problems of street children. However, the occasional coverage given to the children often fuels negative attitudes by portraying *gamíns* as a burden and nuisance to the city.[23] These blame-laden reports of street children lead to their dehumanization, which is at the foundation of hate crime. The *gamíns* are no longer seen as children who live on the streets due to economic circumstances, parental abuse, or other forces beyond their control. To the public, they become violent and unconscionable delinquents who must be harshly punished. Like other hate crimes, the murders of street children in Colombia have a direct relationship to the "notions of social normalcy and moral acceptability" found in Colombian society.[24]

Due to the widespread perception of street children as criminals and delinquents, the children are constantly subjected to mistreatment and abuse, including police brutality. Police officers frequently detain the children, forcing them to relinquish their money or stolen goods in exchange for being released without a beating. Periodic police campaigns to eliminate street children from the downtown area have been cruel and abusive. Bogotá policemen will sometimes beat *gamíns* and shave their heads to humiliate them in front of their friends. The police also zealously patrol park fountains where the children bathe and where police have a legal right to remove the children by force. In one well-publicized case of police abuse, an officer caught a young boy stealing a gold chain from a male pedestrian. The officer dragged the boy to the pedestrian, who proceeded to savagely beat the child as the police officer and other bystanders watched.[25]

By far the ugliest forms of punishment waged against street children are the periodic "clean-up operations," which occur while the *gamíns* sleep in the city's isolated areas. There are seldom any witnesses, and the raids are rarely reported. Consequently, the only evidence of violence comes from a variety of ethnographic data, studies undertaken by human rights agencies, and occasional newspaper accounts.

In February 1994, a fact-finding delegation of politicians and community organizers from Chicago traveled to Bogotá to meet with Colombian human rights advocacy groups and activists. During a visit to a children's program in Ciudad Bolívar, one of Bogotá's poorest barrios and the site of frequent social cleansings, a child expressed his fear that he would one day be a victim of social cleansing. When asked why he thought he and his friends were being targeted, he responded, "I don't know. Maybe they don't like our haircuts or clothes, or the kind of music we listen to."[26] Since 1990, more than five hundred children have been assassinated in Ciudad Bolívar, many of them street children.[27]

Sometimes the assassins leave signs on the children's corpses that state "I was a thief" or "I was a drug addict." In some cases, the hands of a corpse are mutilated to show other thieves what punishment is in store for them should they be caught.[28] In downtown Bogotá on August 12, 1993, professionally lettered placards invited delinquents and other indigents to their own funerals. The placards were signed by "your generous hosts," including anonymous businesspeople, civic groups, and the "good people" of the community. Although one placard was placed within two blocks of a police station, no one was ever detained for the incident.[29]

Available evidence suggests that although many businesspeople, civic groups, and "good people" of the community support and sometimes finance social cleansings, the actual murders are committed by death squads or paramilitary organizations and individuals within the police force. Statistics cited by the Andean Commission of Jurists concluded that 56 percent of social cleansings between January and September of 1993 involved police or other state agents, 18 percent involved paramilitary groups, and the rest of the crimes were committed by unidentified perpetrators.[30]

Fieldwork informants indicate that police were involved in most of the killings of street children during 1987 and 1988, and recent investigations have produced similar evidence. These observations concur with those of Gilberto Dimenstein in Brazil, who explains, "The police are convinced that they are doing what the community wants them to do: getting the 'delinquents' off the streets."[31] Some Colombian police officers may also feel frustrated by the nation's lack of social and public order and are distrustful of the judicial system. Consequently, they take justice into their own hands and punish accordingly. Furthermore, the officers' typically low salaries create discontent and cause individual officers to accept off-duty security jobs. Local businesspeople and shopkeepers frequently hire off-duty policemen to eliminate street children and other social undesirables who threaten the security and profitability of their businesses.

Recently, paramilitary groups have become active in social cleansing crimes in Bogotá, and one group calls itself, "Death to *Gamíns*."[32] According to Colombian scholar Carlos Rojas, more than forty social cleansing groups have been identified in Colombia.[33] These groups see themselves as providing an alternative solution to social problems such as delinquency, poverty, homosexuality, and lack of security. Not only do the groups kill "undesirables," but they effectively force marginalized groups to remain within specific city zones. They threaten the "undesirables" with further killings if they expand beyond established boundaries.

LAW ENFORCEMENT AND JUDICIAL RESPONSES

The law enforcement and judicial responses to social cleansings in Colombia have been minimal. In Colombia, few crimes are reported to the police. In 1992, only twenty out of every hundred crimes in the country were reported to the authorities; of those reported crimes, only 4 percent were fully investigated and resulted in trial and sentencing procedures.[34] Esmerelda Ruiz of the Colombian Public Defender's Office on Children and Families described the lenient sentencing for crimes against children: "If someone kills a twenty year old, they get a minimum of fifteen years in jail. If they kill a child, they get between one and three years."[35]

Although the bodies of street children are regularly found in the streets of Bogotá, few of the murders are reported to the authorities. Between January and October of 1993, only twelve murders and twenty cases of mistreatment against street children were denounced in Bogotá.[36] The children themselves are unlikely to report the crimes for fear of becoming the next victims. Neighborhood residents may also be reluctant to report social cleansing crimes because of suspected police participation and fears of retribution.

The Colombian judicial system is under constant international pressure to oppose drug trafficking and under intense national pressure to maintain public security. As a result, the problem of social cleansing of street children is given a lower priority and receives fewer legal resources than crimes related to the drug war and political violence. Furthermore, the judicial system is not under any pressure to confront social cleansing crimes; widespread attitudes of apathy and tolerance implicitly condone the killings as well as diminish public pressure to stop the murder.

If the social cleansing crimes against street children were actively investigated, police participation in many of the killings would make the crimes difficult to prosecute. Members of the Colombian police force, because of their military status, are likely to be tried within the jurisdiction of a separate military court system and outside the domain of civil courts. The separate military system not only has its own military judges but does not allow civilians, including witnesses, inside the courtroom.

"WE'RE NOT DISPOSABLES, WE'RE CITIZENS"

Like hate crimes and social cleansings in other Latin American countries, Colombian hate crimes are difficult to document, and the perpetrators are difficult to prosecute. The social cleansing of street children in Colombia is expected to continue and will probably increase due to further urbanization, deteriorating economic conditions for large segments of the population, cutbacks in already meager social programs, and a continued lack of legal and judicial resources.[37] As Kelly, Maghan, and Tennant conclude about hate crimes in general, any effective solutions to alleviate social cleansing must involve larger social, economic, and political forces that go beyond the resources and capabilities of the law enforcement community.[38]

Attitudes of apathy and prejudice toward street children need to be addressed by the larger community. As long as society continues to stigmatize, dehumanize, and label street children as "disposable," social cleansing crimes are not likely to generate any public outcry. Recently, marginalized groups in Bogotá have organized themselves to bring attention to social cleansings. On September 27, 1993, a group of courageous street children, prostitutes, and indigents stopped traffic in Bogotá during an organized city march. Their rallying cry was, "We're not disposable; we're citizens."[39] Colombian human rights organizations and community groups continue to pressure the state to end social cleansings but lack widespread societal support for their efforts.

Both the law enforcement and judicial systems need more resources and reform.[40] The judicial system must publicly prosecute and sentence the perpetrators of hate crimes to eliminate an environment of private justice that erodes public confidence in the system. Further reforms and strategies might include the appointment of special task forces and prosecutors to investigate social cleansings and paramilitary groups, sensitivity training for police officers, legal sanctions against officers accused of violence toward street children, and restrictions on police participation in off-duty security employment.[41] Increasing police salaries would also be an important strategy for building morale and keeping individual officers from taking off-duty assignments.

Recently, international human rights groups like Amnesty International and America's Watch have devoted increasing attention to the plight of street children in Latin America. Their attention is important but must be accompanied by law enforcement and judicial reforms, as well as significant changes in social attitudes and public perceptions. As long as hatred is fueled and widespread violence continues to escalate, Colombia's street children will have little protection against future social cleansings.

NOTES

1. Roman Villarreal (1993), "Ciudad Bolívar: el precio de ser joven," *Cien Días* (Bogotá) 4(14): 30–33.

2. Although racism and racist crimes are not unknown in Colombia, social cleansings of street children do not appear to be racially motivated. Colombia has a populations of 30.8 million—70 percent *mestizo*, of mixed descent; 22 percent of European descent; 6 percent of African descent; and 2 percent indigenous (Jenny Pearce [1990], *Colombia: Inside the Labyrinth* [London: Latin America Bureau], 48–61). Although descendants of African slaves and indigenous groups can be found in all parts of Colombia and have fought for their rights via political movements, their populations are regionally concentrated in Colombia's coastal and rural areas.

3. Gilberto Dimenstein (1991), *Brazil: War on Children* (London: Latin America Bureau), 20; U.S. House Select Committee on Hunger (1991), *Street Children: A Global Disgrace*, 102d Cong., 1st sess., 313–15. Estimates of the number of street children killed in Brazil are often much higher, but documentation is difficult to obtain. Scheper-Hughes and Hoffman cite Brazilian federal police figures of five thousand children who were murdered in Brazil between 1988 and 1990 (Nance Scheper-Hughes and Daniel Hoffman [1994], "Kids Out of Place," *Report on the Americas*, 47, no. 6 [NACLA], 21–24). However, this figure reflects all children who were murdered, not just street children.

4. Comisión Andina de Juristas Seccional Colombiana (1993), "Overview of Human Rights and International Humanitarianism in Colombia During 1993"

(Bogotá: Comisión), 97–103; Alvaro Guzmán Barney (1988), "Escenarios de la violencia en Cali," in *Colombia: Democracia y Sociedad,* ed. by Nora Segura de Camacho (Bogotá: CIDSE and FESCOL, 1988), 313–38; Alvaro Camacho Guizado (1988), "Dimensiones de lo público y lo privado en la violencia urbana en Cali," in *Colombia: Democracia y Sociedad,* 291–312.

5. The statistics we present on deaths due to social cleansings and political violence in Colombia were obtained from a variety of journals and reports; however, all of the statistics originate from the internationally respected Colombian research institute, CINEP (Centro de Investigación y Educación Popular), which collects data on political violence and social cleansings from Colombian newspapers. Because very few killings of street children are reported to the police, much less published in newspapers, our statistics come from the most reliable source available. They clearly underestimate the number of street children who have been killed in social cleansings.

6. Comisión Intercongregacional de Justicia y Paz (1992), *Justicia y Paz* (Bogotá) 5(4): 67.

7. Comisión Andina de Juristas Seccional Colombiana (1993), 1.

8. Lewis Aptekar (1988), *The Street Children of Cali* (Durham, N.C.: Duke Univ. Press).

9. Jonathan Hartlyn (1988), *The Politics of Coalition Rule in Colombia* (New York: Cambridge Univ. Press), 2.

10. Comisión Andina de Juristas Seccional Colombiana (1993), 1.

11. Comisión Andina (1993), 1.

12. Comisión de Estudios sobre la Violencia (1988), *Colombia: Violencia y Democracia, Informe presentado al Ministerio del Gobierno* (Bogotá: Universidad Nacional de Colombia and COLCIENCIAS, 1988), 68.

13. Washington Office on Latin America (1989), *Colombia Besieged: Political Violence and State Responsibility* (Washington, D.C., 1989), 38–49, 51–61.

14. Estimating the number of street children in Colombia and other countries is extremely difficult for several reasons. The street children are a mobile population who actively avoid detection by the authorities, and confusion often occurs about the definition of *gamín.* A *gamín* may be defined as a child who has no contact with his family, a child who has sporadic contact with his family, or a child who remains in contact with his family and sometimes stays at home. If the first definition is employed (as is normally the case), lower estimates are produced. Finally, public authorities attempt to downplay the problem of street children by consistently presenting low estimates and criticizing higher figures. For further information on the problems associated with street child population estimates, see Aptekar (1988) and Dimenstein (1991).

15. The data on Bogotá's street children come from Julia Greider-Durango's fieldwork, from 1987 to 1988, which includes personal accounts of street children, social workers, researchers, and journalists. Additional data were collected

in 1990, 1991, and 1993. The book *Musarañas* (1978, Bogotá: Andigraf), written by Father Javier de Nicoló and his colleagues at the Bosconia La Florida program for street children, was also an invaluable source of information.

16. Javier Baena (1988), "Los niños callejeros: entre el crimen y el abandono," *El Espectador* (Bogotá), July 14, p. 1B.

17. During an interview in 1988, a Colombian social worker gave the following account. In 1984, Hector Babenco's film, *Pixote,* was shown for the first time in Bogotá. *Pixote,* a documentary about street life of the *gamíns* of São Paulo, Brazil, opened the eyes of many Colombians who had previously ignored the problems of street children in their own country. The film produced a widespread reaction of horror and disbelief that children were living in such life-threatening conditions in the urban underworld. *Pixote* was shortly banned by the Colombian government because of its strong content. Before the film was banned, the Comité de Trabajadores Voluntarios (CTV), a volunteer work force of Colombians and North Americans was invited by the Colombian press to a private screening of *Pixote.* The CTV brought along twelve Bogotáno street children. While the adults flinched at the movie's graphic violence, the *gamíns* did not blink an eye. When asked their opinion of the film, the boys responded "boring."

18. U.S. House Select Committee on Hunger (1991), 17.

19. Over 96 percent of Colombia's population identifies itself as Roman Catholic (Pearce [1990], x). Historically, the Catholic Church was allied closely with the Conservative Party. Following La Violencia, church leaders worried that links between the Church and political violence would lead to the sullied reputation of the Church. As a result, the leaders decided to remove the Church from politics altogether. Currently, the Colombian Catholic Church is among the more conservative in the region; and as Levine notes, Colombian prelates "are regarded throughout Latin America as leading spokesmen for current Vatican policy in the region" (Daniel H. Levine [1992], *Popular Voices in Latin American Catholicism* [Princeton, N.J.: Princeton Univ. Press], 69). Not surprisingly, the Colombian Catholic Church has neither encouraged nor experienced the development of liberation theology in Colombia. Although individual church leaders and priests—most notably from the Jesuit order—have denounced social cleansings in Colombia, the Church itself has taken no position.

20. The following observations come from a variety of settings and sources, including interviews with Colombian social workers and community organizers, and conversations heard in Bogotá's markets, buses, and shops.

21. Suzanne Wilson (1989), "Political Power and the Colombian Middle Class" (paper presented at the annual meeting of the Midwest Sociological Society, St. Louis, Mo., Mar. 12–15).

22. Father Javier Giraldo Moreno (1994), interview by Julia Greider-Durango, Chicago, Mar. 15.

23. Aptekar (1988), 82–84.

24. Robert J. Kelly, Jess Maghan, and Woodrow Tennant (1991), "Hate Crimes: Victimizing the Stigmatized," in *Bias Crime: American Law Enforcement and Legal Responses*, ed. Robert J. Kelly (Chicago: Office of International Criminal Justice, Univ. of Illinois at Chicago), 41.

25. "Enérgico rechazo a golpiza a un gamín" (1987), *El Tiempo* (Bogotá), Sept. 16, p. 3A.

26. Alynne Romo, member, Steering Committee of the National Colombia Human Rights Network (1994), interview by Julia Greider-Durango and Suzanne Wilson, Chicago, Mar. 12.

27. " 'Limpieza Social' en Colombia y Brasil: Exterminio de los pobres" (1993), *Reporte de Derechos Humanos* (Bogotá) 1(7): 4.

28. Carlos R. Rojas (1993), "Ojo por ojo, diente por diente," *Cien Días* (Bogotá) 6(24): 12–13.

29. " 'Limpieza Social' " (1993), 4.

30. Comisión Andina de Juristas Seccional Colombiana (1993), 1.

31. Dimenstein (1991), 38.

32. Lori Heise (1991), "Killing the Children of the Third World," *Washington Post Outlook*, Apr. 26, p. A9.

33. Rojas (1993), 12.

34. "The Injustices of Colombia's Justice System" (1993), *Bulletin of Justice and Peace* (Bogotá) 1(9): 16.

35. Isabel Cristina Mendoza (1994), "Colombia no nos quiere," *El Tiempo* (Bogotá), Jan. 9, p. 31.

36. "Más de 3,700 ñeros sobreviven en 45 parches" (1993), *El Espectador* (Bogotá), Dec. 2, p. C2.

37. Pearce (1990), xi.

38. Kelly, Maghan, and Tennant (1991), 42.

39. " 'Limpieza Social' " (1993), 1.

40. Although the Colombian judicial system has undergone several reforms under the impetus of the drug war, the results of the reforms have been questionable. The reforms, intended to target drug traffickers, have in practice targeted political opposition groups. In 1991, the Colombian Congress enacted a new *Code of Criminal Procedures*, which introduced special courts and a system of "faceless justice." Any Colombian accused of a drug or "terrorist" crime may be jailed without formal charges, without time limits, and without bail. Defendants and their lawyers testify to a "faceless judge" who sits behind a one-way mirror and whose voice is distorted. The Centro de Investigación y Educación Popular, in a study of cases tried under the new law, found that the "vast majority" of defendants tried by this system have "nothing whatsoever to do with drugs or terrorist activities" ("Injustices of Colombia's Justice System" [1993], 110).

Furthermore, although the 1991 constitution eliminated the "state of siege" in Colombia, the federal government may declare a "state of emergency," which effectively bypasses judicial and legislative channels. During these periods, the president can legislate by decree and suspend individual and collective rights in order to restore order.

41. Dimenstein (1991), 73.

7. The Emergence and Implications of American Hate Crime Jurisprudence

James B. Jacobs

Politics and constitutional concerns probably pose an insuperable barrier to passing laws punishing group libel and hate speech in the United States.[1] However since 1980, there has been a steady movement among American states to criminalize, recriminalize, and increase punishments for intentionally injurious *behaviors* that are motivated by certain types of prejudice and hate.[2] Most of these targeted behaviors are already covered by "generic" crime categories, but the new hate crime genre splinters, or perhaps "deconstructs," generic crime categories, creating a new family of specialized hate crimes. In effect, American criminal jurisprudence is experiencing the kind of legal transformation that has already taken place during the past several decades in other areas of law, especially civil rights and employment.

The new hate crime legislation needs to be distinguished from an older genre of federal and state criminal laws dating back to the period of the Reconstruction following the Civil War.[3] Those laws were aimed explicitly against the Ku Klux Klan and, among other things, outlawed private paramilitary organizations, the wearing of hoods in public places, and conspiracies to violate the rights of black people. The federal criminal laws punishing civil rights violations remain on the book but are used infrequently and almost always as a backup when state and local criminal prosecutions for generic criminal offenses have gone seriously awry.[4]

By contrast, the current wave of hate crime legislation has not been motivated primarily by organized paramilitary hate groups like the KKK but by unorganized individual acts of hate. Moreover, while the most serious acts of violence are already heavily sanctioned under the law of homicide, rape, and arson, the most significant contribution of the new genre of hate crimes to criminal jurisprudence is probably its focus on low-level offending, in some cases, at the borderline between expressions of opinion and prejudice and the perpetration of assault, intimidation, menacing, and vandalism.[5]

Much of the formulating, writing, and lobbying for hate crime legislation has been carried out by the Anti-Defamation League (ADL) of B'nai B'rith, which has been tracking anti-Semitism for many years. Its model hate crime statutes have served as a basis for many states' legislation.[6] That legislation and more far-reaching variations have been strongly supported by many civil rights and minority advocacy groups, including the Washington Lawyers' Committee for Civil Rights under Law, the National Institute Against Prejudice and Violence, and California's Racial, Religious and Ethnic Crimes Project, the National Organization of Black Law Enforcement Executives, the Southern Poverty Law Center, and the National Gay and Lesbian Task Force. As far as I know, there have been no interest groups opposing such legislation, although some Congressmen and New York state legislators balked at including gays and lesbians with the other victimized groups, apparently fearing that it would be a step toward including homosexual men and women under the umbrella of civil rights legislation.

While many states have passed the ADL's model laws, other states have crafted their own statutes, adding more groups, types of wrongdoing, and remedies, including in some cases, civil analogues to the criminal statutes.[7] Beyond legislation, many police departments and a few prosecutors' offices have created antibias units to investigate, report, and prevent hate crimes.

In 1990, Congress passed the *Hate Crime Reporting Act*, which requires the U.S. Department of Justice to collect national data on "crimes that manifest evidence of prejudice based on race, religion, sexual orientation, or ethnicity, including where appropriate, the crimes of murder, nonnegligent manslaughter, forcible rape, aggravated assault, simple assault, intimidation, arson, and destruction, damage, or vandalism of property."[8] Consequently, a new category of criminal offense, the hate crime, has officially arrived, both reflecting and encouraging a new way to think about social pathology in American society.[9]

In New York City, public attention has been quickly drawn to the idea of hate crime. The public now expects an announcement of "bias" or "nonbias" in highly visible interracial and other intergroup offenses. Journalists, advocacy group spokespersons, and other public commentators demand that various crimes be labeled bias-related and protest when they are not.[10]

What accounts for the proliferation of hate crime law? What types of hate crime laws are there? To what extent are those hate crime laws consistent with traditional criminal law principles and to what extent a departure or innovation? What problems, if any, of criminal justice administration do such laws raise? What problems should we expect this new genre of legislation to solve? Ultimately, what if anything, can these laws tell us about the feasibility of using criminal law to suppress group libel and hate speech?

THE NEW WAVE OF HATE CRIME LEGISLATION

The long-term impetus for the 1980s hate crime legislation undoubtedly is the American Civil Rights movement that, since World War II, has pressed forward the interests and aspirations of one "minority group" after another—blacks, women, prisoners, physically and mentally handicapped, and most recently gays and lesbians. As the Civil Rights movement has gained strength and legitimacy in American society, minority groups have become more empowered and increasingly committed to, and skilled in, asserting group rights and demands. Not surprisingly, more individuals have come to see themselves, or at least present themselves, as members of disadvantaged or victimized minority groups.[11] As a result, American society has experienced a profound proliferation of group consciousness, and American politics has come increasingly to be dominated by competition and conflict among groups. The emphasis upon the interracial and intergroup aspect of traditional crime is a logical consequence of this societal and political transformation.

The perception that hate crime is an increasing phenomenon has no doubt also been a factor propelling the new legislation. The advocates of new hate crime legislation at the federal, state, and local levels have asserted throughout the 1980s that the United States is experiencing a rising tide of religious, racial, and homophobic violence.[12] The Anti-Defamation League, which has been tracking anti-Semitism, reports a steady increase in anti-Semitic incidents. Similar reports are offered by groups that advocate the rights of blacks and gays and lesbians.[13] Because United States law enforcement agencies have not collected historical data on hate crimes, the statistics that provide the justification for hate crime legislation have been collected and reported to the public by the groups that most strenuously advocate such legislation.

Nevertheless, the belief that a broad spectrum of hate crimes is on the rise in the United States has widespread support and is frequently cited as fact in academic articles and books, newspaper stories, government reports, and political debate. For example, a recent bill offered into the New York state legislature states:

> The legislature finds and determines that there has been an alarming increase in the incidence of gang assaults and bias-related violence committed because the victim is a member of a class or group identifiable by factors including, but not limited to race, creed, color, national origin, sex, disability, age, or sexual orientation. There is growing public concern that such crimes of violence are committed because of prejudice or hatred aimed at an entire class or group of people. Gang assaults and bias-related crimes undermine the freedom that forms the foundation of what should be an open and tolerant society. These crimes vitiate the goodwill and understanding that is essential to the working of a pluralistic society. They are the antithesis of what this nation and state stand for. Accordingly, the legislature finds that gang- and bias-related crimes should be prosecuted and punished with appropriate severity.[14]

I do not mean to imply that the data offered by the civil rights and advocacy groups are consciously inflated or even inaccurate, but American crime statistics are notoriously unreliable, and the hate crime accounting that has been done by private groups suffers from even more potential reliability problems than traditional crime statistics. What appears to be a "crime wave" may in fact be explained by a greater conceptualization of, and willingness to report, certain crimes as bias-related and by a more widespread and aggressive system for collecting and recording information about these offenses.[15]

For the most part, politicians have been receptive to claims that hate crime is a steadily escalating problem. American politicians long ago learned that crime legislation is cheap and symbolically potent. It does not require allocation of new resources, and it often assuages important constituencies. Interest groups often feel strongly about the importance of having a particular social problem recognized through criminal legislation, and politicians are usually happy to comply. Not surprisingly, in recent decades, we have often seen claims about crime waves deflated after systematic study.

TYPES OF HATE CRIMES LAWS

Hate crime legislation is really a family of legislation, including reporting statutes, civil rights laws, new substantive crimes, and sentencing laws. Each of these juridical forms raises interesting issues for criminal law theory and criminal justice administration.

In my opinion, the current wave of hate crime legislation is more reflective of greater intolerance to discrimination, negative stereotyping, and hate mongering than it is to higher and more severe levels of racial, religious, and homophobic violence. We have a movement to hate crime legislation because our sensitivity to, and distaste for, group prejudice and hatred have sharply increased, rather than because we are being drowned in a tidal wave of hate crime.[16]

HATE CRIME REPORTING STATUTES

The federal government, as well as several states and cities, have passed laws or administrative regulations requiring the police to investigate and report hate crimes. The 1990 *Federal Hate Crimes Statistics Act* states:

> The Attorney General shall acquire data for the calendar year 1990 and each of the four succeeding calendar years about crimes that manifest evidence of prejudice based on race, religion, sexual orientation, or ethnicity, including where appropriate the crimes of murder, nonnegligent manslaughter, forcible rape, aggravated assault, simple assault, intimidation, arson, and destruction, damage or vandalism of property.[17]

All hate crime legislation, including reporting statutes like the federal act, face a difficult challenge in defining hate crime. What kinds of behavior, driven by what kinds of motivation, against what kinds of victims, constitute the offense? The federal law does not cover crimes against women, the elderly, members of political groups, labor unions, or right-to-work groups.[18] Furthermore, the federal law covers some, but not all, generic crimes when motivated by bias.

Putting aside the question of defining what kinds of prejudices and bad motives ought to qualify as bias crimes, there is bound to be a great deal of subjectivity in identifying any particular event as a hate crime. How can the police tell whether a particular crime "manifests prejudice," or was committed "on account of" or "because of" the victim's membership in a particular group?

The complexity and subjectivity of the labeling decision is illustrated by the following guidelines of the New York City Police Department's bias unit, established "to monitor and investigate acts committed against a person, or place because of race, religion, ethnicity, and sexual orientation."[19]

CRITERIA
1. The motivation of the perpetrator;
2. The absence of any motive;
3. The perception of the victim;
4. The display of offensive symbols, words, or acts;
5. The date and time of occurrence (corresponding to a holiday of significance, i.e., Hanukkah, Martin Luther King Day, Chinese New Year, etc.);
6. A commonsense review of the circumstances surrounding the incident (consider the totality of the circumstance);
   a. The group involved in the attack;
   b. The manner and means of the attack;
   c. Any similar incidents in the same area or against the same victim;
7. The statements, if any, made by the perpetrator.

QUESTIONS TO BE ASKED
1. Is the victim the only member or one of a few members of the targeted group in the neighborhood?
2. Are the victim and perpetrator from different racial, religious, ethnic, or sexual orientation groups?
3. Has the victim recently moved to the area?
4. If multiple incidents have occurred in a short time period, are all the victims of the same group?
5. Has the victim been involved in a recent public activity that would make him or her a target?

6. What was the modus operandi? Is it similar to other documented incidents?

7. Has the victim been the subject of past incidents of a similar nature?

8. Has there been recent news coverage of events of a similar nature?

9. Is there an ongoing neighborhood problem that may have spurred the
   event?

10. Could the act be related to some neighborhood conflict involving area
    juveniles?

11. Was any hate literature distributed by or found in the possession of the
    perpetrator?

12. Did the incident occur, in whole or in part, because of a racial, reli-
    gious, ethnic, or sexual orientation difference between the victim and
    the perpetrator, or did it occur for other reasons?

13. Are the perpetrators juveniles or adults, and if juveniles, do they under-
    stand the meaning (to the community at large and to the victim) of
    the symbols used?

14. Were the real intentions of the responsible person motivated in whole
    or in part by bias against the victim's race, religion, ethnicity, or sexual
    orientation, or was the motivation based on other than bias, e.g.: a
    childish prank, unrelated vandalism, etc.?

   Note: If after applying the criteria listed and asking the appropriate questions, substantial doubt exists as to whether or not the incident is bias-motivated or not, the incident should be classified as bias-motivated for investigative and statistical purposes.

   Remember: The mere mention of a bias remark does not necessarily make
   an incident bias-motivated just as the absence of a bias remark does not make
   an incident nonbias. A commonsense approach should be applied and the
   totality of the circumstances should be reviewed before any decision is made.
   Any questions should be referred to the Bias Incident Investigating Unit.

These guidelines demonstrate that there is much greater subjectivity in
identifying bias crimes than in identifying traditional generic crimes. It
is also telling that the guidelines require that doubt be resolved in favor
of the bias crime determination.

It is hard to predict what will be learned from these hate crime statistics. Will they provide useful information about American society that
will become the basis for sound law enforcement and social policy? Will
they provide "more heat than light" because of the subjective and politicized nature of the labeling process? What will we be able to infer from a
statement like, There were five thousand hate crimes in the United States
in 1992; or, from the statement, There were five hate crimes per 100,000

population? What will count as a lot or a little? Will this kind of accounting paint an unduly pessimistic picture of American race, ethnic, gender, and sexual orientation relations and set off controversies about double standards as to whether some people's victimizations are more serious than other people's?

No matter what numbers come up, they will likely be cited as proof of a massive problem. If so, the consequence may be to set off competition and conflict between representatives of different groups and spark a controversy about which groups are being most mistreated by which other groups. The unanswered question is whether this focus on the racial, ethnic, religious, and sexual orientation aspects of crime will lead to less hate and more harmonious intergroup relations or to a more balkanized, divided, and conflict-ridden polity? Hate crime labeling may be as socially divisive, or more so, than hate crime itself.

SUBSTANTIVE HATE CRIMES

There are two general types of substantive hate crimes.[20] One type criminalizes highly expressive and symbolic speech that aims or is likely to offend certain minority groups. Another type recriminalizes behavior that is already criminal if it is motivated by certain kinds of bias, prejudice, negative stereotypes, and hatreds.[21]

Criminalizing Hate Speech and Symbolism

The St. Paul, Minnesota ordinance, which was declared unconstitutional by the United States Supreme Court, states:

> Whoever places on public or private property a symbol, object, appellation, characterization or graffiti, including but not limited to a burning cross or Nazi swastika, which one knows or has reasonable grounds to know arouses anger, alarm, or resentment in others on the basis of race, color, religion, or gender, commits disorderly conduct and shall be guilty of a misdemeanor.[22]

This law bristles with First Amendment problems. On its face, it makes all sorts of expressions potentially criminal—from paintings to signboards to photographs and movies. Under the St. Paul ordinance, a person's display of a symbol could be criminal even if the intent was to force an audience, no matter how painfully, to confront objectionable symbols with the perhaps misguided hope that the result would be salutary, cathartic, politicizing, or whatever. Furthermore, St. Paul's ordinance could be interpreted to criminalize all sexually explicit magazines, movies, and rap music since it is arguably "likely to cause resentment based upon gender."

The St. Paul ordinance, like many new hate crime laws, also suffers from vagueness in that it leaves a person having to guess at what actions mixed with expression are permissible.[23] For example, could one legally protest the view of the Catholic Church or of a church prelate on abortion or birth control? These questions illustrate how sensitive a matter it is to make content-based prohibitions on symbolic expression, no matter how distasteful.

From the standpoint of a criminal code, hate crime laws like St. Paul's lie at the boundary between criminal and noncriminal. It defines an offense or misdemeanor at the low end. The punishment is likely to be light. In high-volume urban criminal courts, like New York City's, crimes of this level rarely result in jail time. Indeed, a very high percentage of such cases are simply dropped by the prosecutor.[24] Consequently, if hate crime statutes are meant to have more than purely symbolic significance, that is, to have a significant effect on repressing hate or at least crimes based on hate, it would be necessary to promote this category of offense to a higher level of seriousness.[25] In the criminal courts of America's big cities, this would require additional resources or significant reordering of priorities. Prosecuting significantly more individuals for hate crimes would mean prosecuting significantly fewer individuals for some other crimes.

Hate crime statutes that prohibit expression invite political trials. Some offenders will no doubt "volunteer" for prosecution in an effort to gain even more publicity for their "cause." While many persons who engage in offensive speech and graffiti of the kind apparently envisioned in the St. Paul ordinance are juveniles or antisocial young people acting on impulse (and this appears to be the situation in the St. Paul case itself), a small number of offenders are engaged in systematic hate mongering. Some of them, far from desiring to hide their offending, may be interested in advertising it in order to gain adherents, publicity, and sympathy. Prosecuting such individuals could result in political trials that give publicity to the offenders' racist, sexist, or anti-Semitic views, while allowing the defendants to posture themselves as martyrs for the First Amendment. In addition to publicity, some hate crime defendants may attract sympathy and followers or even stimulate copycat crimes. In other words, potential "costs" are associated with hate crime jurisprudence.

For these reasons, it would seem preferable to deal with intimidations at the borderline between expression and assault with generic criminal law statutes on harassment and menacing. Burning a cross on another person's property could certainly be prosecuted as arson, vandalism, or disorderly conduct. In addition, town or state legislatures could make it a crime to burn any object on another person's property—and an aggravated form of the offense to burn any object on another person's property with the intent to inflict emotional distress or with the intent to intimidate or threaten that person from engaging in future behavior. This would avoid content-based judgments about what kinds of expression are unacceptable and what kinds of group sensitivities are entitled to special legislative recognition.

Recriminalizing Behavior That Is Already Criminal

A second kind of substantive hate crime law prohibits behavior that is already criminal, if it is motivated by racist, homophobic, or certain other undesirable impulses and motivation. For example, in 1982, New York State, following the ADL model, passed the following amendment to its aggravated harassment statute:

> A person is guilty of aggravated harassment in the second degree when, with intent to harass, annoy, threaten or alarm another person, he . . . strikes, shoves, kicks, or otherwise subjects another person to physical contact, or threatens or attempts to do the same because of the race, color, religion, or national origin of such a person. Aggravated harassment in the second degree is a class A misdemeanor.[26]

In effect, this statute elevates ordinary harassment to aggravated harassment if it is committed because of race, color, religion, or national origin. This statute raises three key issues.

Which Bigotries Are Covered? All hate crimes cover offenses motivated by racial, religious, and ethnic prejudice. Several state hate crime statutes, and bills pending before the New York State legislature, include prejudice based upon sexual orientation. Some states also include crimes motivated by bias based upon gender, age, and mental and physical handicap. Herein lies a key problem for criminal jurisprudence. Should the law count some peoples' victimization (and, if so, whose) as more serious than others? This might strike some people as dubious and even insulting. Is it "worse" morally or sociologically to be victimized on account of being gay than to be victimized on account of being old, female, or handicapped, or for being a union organizer, a right-to-work advocate, or an abortion rights proponent or opponent? Does it make sense jurisprudentially, sociologically, or politically for criminal law to begin moving down this road? If so, which group memberships are entitled to this heightened attention and penalty structure? To add further complexity, should special victim status for criminal law purposes vary from city to city, or even from neighborhood to neighborhood, depending upon the demographic composition?

As the number of prohibited prejudices and victims' sensibilities increases, a bias crime statute would embrace more and more aggressor/victim combinations. One major issue is whether hate crimes should include offensive behavior motivated by gender prejudice. This would sweep under the hate crime umbrella a large percentage of crimes committed by men against women, including rape and sexual child abuse.[27]

Another important issue is whether only crimes by members of the racial, ethnic, gender, and religious majority against minority group members will count as hate crimes—in effect, a kind of affirmative action law. Will crimes by members of minority groups against the majority and against other minorities also count as hate crimes?[28] Affirmative action in the crime context makes much less sense, than it does in the employment or educational admissions contexts where the goal is to increase educational diversity, remedy past employment discrimination, and open up more opportunities for underrepresented groups.

While intraracial crime far exceeds interracial crime, statistics at least for the United States as a whole show that with respect to interracial crimes, whites are more likely to be the victims of blacks and other minorities than they are to be the perpetrators of crimes against these groups.[29] While some law review writers have advocated that hate crimes should only encompass harms perpetrated by whites against members of minorities, all state hate crime statutes include offenses perpetrated by minority group members against members of majority as well as against other minority groups.[30]

What constitutes an offense based upon ethnicity or national origin may present some difficult and awkward problems in a complex multiethnic society. For example, are "Hispanics" a single group, or should an assault by a native-born Nicaraguan against a native-born Puerto Rican be cognizable as a hate crime?[31] What about crimes between blacks born or descended from Haitians and those born or descended from Jamaicans? Such questions could be endlessly multiplied.

What Crimes Are Included? The ADL model hate crime law is labeled "intimidation" and criminalizes at an aggravated level the offenses of trespass, criminal mischief, harassment, menacing, and assault when they are motivated by reason of actual or perceived race, color, religion, national origin, or sexual orientation. New York's hate crime offense is limited to aggravated harassment.[32] It is difficult to see why, if hate crime is an appropriate category of criminality, it ought not apply to all types of offending behavior so that any crime motivated by wrongful prejudice will be defined as an aggravated form of the core offense and be punished more severely than it would be if it were motivated by run-of-the-mill motivations and impulses such as mean-spiritedness, selfishness, or lust.

How Much Wrongful Motivation Must Be Proven? Hate crime laws apply special punishment to crimes committed "because of," "motivated by," or "on account of" certain kinds of discreditable prejudices. They require proof of a causal relation between a certain motivation and a certain criminal behavior. However, there is some ambiguity and imprecision in how strong that causation must be. Could a defendant successfully defend himself by claiming that while he was prejudiced against the victim on account of national origin, he would have committed the crime anyway because, for example, he needed the money? Alternatively, should a prosecutor interpret the hate crime laws to cover situations in which prejudiced motivation played any role in the defendant's choice of victim? If the former interpretation prevails, prosecutors will face enormous difficulty in proving that the defendant was solely or even primarily motivated by prejudice. If the latter interpretation prevails, prosecutors will have a much easier job; all or most intergroup crime, to some extent, consciously or unconsciously, is arguably motivated by prejudice, bigotry, and negative stereotypes.[33] However, it is likely that other factors will also be operative—pecuniary motive, jealously, personal dislike, sexual obsession, or just plain antisocial character. Every crime, like all human behavior, flows from a mixture of complex motivations that are hard to disentangle. It is probably for this reason that Anglo-American criminal law does not usually deal with motivation.

How will the defendant's wrongful motivation be proved? In some cases, racism, anti-Semitism, or homophobia will be blatant, because, for example, the defendant shouted epithets.[34] If, however, the defendant carried out his assault silently, would it be permissible for the prosecution to prove his hateful motivation by introducing evidence of the hate books and pamphlets the offender subscribes to and reads, the hate groups of which he is a member, and the hate conversations and humor he engages in with family, friends, and coworkers? If the law allowed this kind of proof, it would raise serious First Amendment problems.

MAKING HATE CRIMES A SENTENCING ENHANCER

Some statutes deal with the subject of hate crime as a sentencing issue. Pennsylvania law classifies a variety of offenses one degree higher if they are motivated by hatred of the victim's race, color, religion, ancestry, or national origin.[35] In effect, this increases the maximum sentence if the judge finds that the offense was motivated by one of the enumerated prejudices. While this scheme avoids some problems discussed previously, from a jurisprudential standpoint it raises the same core problems— whether a crime deserves more punishment because it is motivated by values, beliefs, and impulses that the majority has defined as abhorrent.

HATE CRIMES AS CIVIL RIGHTS OFFENSES

Some hate crimes are modeled after the federal criminal civil rights acts, which make it a crime to conspire to violate a person's federal or constitutional rights or, if acting under color of law, to subject any inhabitant to the deprivation of any rights, privileges, and immunities secured or protected by the Constitution or laws of the United States.[36] A satisfactory interpretation of this federal crime has been no easy matter for the U.S. Supreme Court and lower federal courts. In particular, confusion has surrounded the mental element of these offenses, the state action requirement, and the determination of which rights are secured by the Constitution and laws of the United States.[37] Moreover, these statutes are used very sparingly.

A Massachusetts statute states:

> No person, whether or not acting under color of law, shall by force or threat of force, willfully injure, intimidate, or interfere with, or attempt to injure, intimidate or interfere with, or oppress or threaten any other person in the free exercise or enjoyment of any right or privilege secured to him by the

constitution or laws of the commonwealth or by the Constitution or laws of the U.S.[38]

A civil rights–type criminal statute like this one has a number of advantages over the hate crime statutes discussed previously. On its face, it is "neutral" and not content-based. It does not select some wrongful motivations for aggravating the offense and for sentence enhancement. Indeed, it applies to individuals not groups. The reach of this kind of statute, however, might be difficult to contain depending upon how broadly "rights and privileges" are defined. For example, the following proposed New York statute, a combination of hate crime and civil rights crime law, defines rights so broadly and vacuously that practically every criminal act could also be prosecuted as a civil rights hate crime.[39]

> A person is guilty of bias-related violence or intimidation in the second degree when, with the intent to deprive an individual or group of individuals of the exercise of civil rights because of the individual's or group of individuals' race, creed, color, national origin, sex, disability, age, or sexual orientation, such person intentionally, knowingly, or recklessly causes damage to the property of another or causes injury to another individual.
> "Civil rights" are defined very broadly to include:
> a. applying for and enjoying employment; b. applying for or enrolling in any school or college: c. applying for or using housing accommodations and commercial space; d. using public streets, roads, highways, bridges, alleys, avenues, driveways, sideways, thoroughfares, boardwalks, parks, and public spaces. . . . g. enjoying the security of one's own person.

In effect, this bill would transform into a hate crime practically any injury generated by one of the enumerated hate motives. Presumably, every violent crime or street crime, including murder, rape, robbery, and assault, is committed with an intent to deprive a person of the enjoyment of the "security of his or her own person." If, in addition, it was committed by a member of one group against a member of another group, it could plausibly be charged and prosecuted under this proposed law, although the prosecution would still have to prove that the perpetrator launched his attack because of the victim's membership in a particular group.

IS NEW HATE CRIME LEGISLATION NECESSARY?

Having reviewed a number of significant constitutional, jurisprudential, and administrative problems raised by the new genre of hate crime legislation, we need to ask how persuasive the rationale for this legislation is, and whether the problems it means to address are not or could not adequately be addressed under "generic" criminal laws. Several rationales are essentially based upon the view that perpetrators of hate crimes deserve more severe punishments than perpetrators of generic crimes.

THE IMPACT OF HATE CRIMES ON THE VICTIMIZED GROUP

One rationale for the new hate crime laws is that they provide a more severe sanction for a type of crime that has repercussions beyond the immediate victim. Hate crimes, it is argued, put many members of the victim's group in fear of being victimized by the group to which the aggressor belongs, and they therefore undermine social stability.[40]

Although this rationale is plausible, it is not entirely persuasive. First, practically all crimes, especially street crimes, have repercussions beyond their immediate victims. In American cities, the fear of random street violence is intense. Nightly media accounts of crimes in the subways, parks, and streets feed enormous apprehensions about personal safety and are a prime cause of flight from cities to suburbs. The repercussions of crime are intense in more specific contexts as well. For example, all the residents of an apartment building or school are deeply affected and sometimes traumatized by a murder, rape, or other serious crime.

If the rationale for the new hate crimes depends upon the wider social and social-psychological repercussions of such crimes, there is no escaping the need for empirical verification. There is a need to investigate the repercussions of the whole range of aggressor/victim combinations and how much damage they do to the social fabric. This kind of inquiry itself could have negative political and social ramifications. Advocates of this rationale should be aware that the vast majority of American street crimes involves perpetrators and victims who belong to the same racial and ethnic groups. In interracial cases, the aggressor is more likely to be a member of a racial minority and the victim to be white.[41] It is not obvious, especially in urban areas where racial minorities are the demographic majority or near majority, that white-on-black crimes are more socially destablizing than black-on-white crimes, or that either is more destablizing than the intraracial warfare that threatens the survival of some inner-city neighborhoods.

The situation is different when it comes to gender and age. Women are overwhelmingly victimized by men, the elderly by youth, and gays and lesbians by heterosexual males. Consequently, if a case is to be made for enhanced penalties based upon the wider group impacts of street crimes, it is probably strongest for males attacking females, the young attacking the old, and heterosexuals attacking gays and lesbians.[42]

THE CONFLICT-GENERATING POTENTIAL OF HATE CRIMES

A slight variation on the above argument is that what makes hate crimes more serious than other offenses in the same generic crime category is that they increase the possibility of retaliation and wider societal conflict. One can certainly think of situations in which this is plausible. In America, interethnic and interracial assaults have the greatest potential for retaliation and intergroup conflict. Indeed, the kind of interyouth gang warfare dramatized by the movie and play, *West Side Story*, is very much a part of the urban history of the United States. In New York City, one often hears through the media of one interracial attack being a random "retaliation" for a previous interracial attack. However, nonracial intergroup aggressions seem to have a much lower conflict-generating potential. For example, street assaults and rapes have not led to random retaliation by women against men; neither gay bashing nor anti-Semitic violence and vandalism have led to wide-scale retaliations.

To accept as a rationale for hate crime legislation the potential of crimes involving certain offender/victim configurations to trigger retaliation would lead to a perverse result. Only crimes against groups whose members are likely to retaliate would be defined as hate crimes. Crimes against groups whose members are too intimidated or too peaceful to retaliate would not count as hate crimes.

DISPROPORTIONATELY SEVERE IMPACTS ON THE INDIVIDUAL

Another rationale for punishing hate crimes more seriously than other crimes is that they have a more severe emotional and psychological impact on victims than other crimes in the same generic offense category. This argument is based upon an empirical claim which, although plausible, has not yet been demonstrated. Indeed, an empirical research study of hate crime in New York City appears to have found no significant differences in the injuries sustained by hate crime victims and a matched sample of "ordinary" crime victims.[43] In fact, the researchers found that many hate crime victims whom they interviewed were surprised and annoyed by all the attention they were getting from the police department.

Even if we were to accept the claim that hate crimes inflict greater suffering, distress, and injury than nonhate crimes, some distinctions would be necessary. For the most serious crimes, obviously including murder, it does not seem likely that the aggressor's bias motive would add much, if any, additional harm to the victim. When the enormity of the crime is great, the marginal additional harm caused by the offender's prejudice against the victim's group would seem quite small. For less-serious crimes, the significance of the prejudice might be greater. A person might interpret being knocked down in the street by a gang of rowdy youth as less serious than being knocked to the ground by a gang of youth chanting epithets about the group of which the victim is a member.

The most difficult issues are at the margin of criminal law. Burning a cross on the lawn of a minority family's home is more hurtful and threatening than burning a piece of trash. Likewise, defacing someone's home with a swastika is much more threatening than defacing it with unrecognizable graffiti. The symbolic import of the burning cross as a Klan symbol and the swastika as a Nazi symbol carries a venomous message and perhaps an implied threat of future attack.

The question is whether criminal law should be in the business of outlawing certain symbolic expressions and not others. After all, there are many words and symbols that are hurtful and threatening. For example, painting a picture of an embryo on the house of a doctor who performs abortions or on the house of a woman who has had an abortion would be more hurtful than run-of-the-mill graffiti. The point is that expression, and especially highly symbolic expression, can frequently be painful and hurtful.

Therefore, perhaps the best way to handle these problems at the border between criminality and expressive speech is by vigorous enforcement of generic, not content-based, criminal laws. Burning a cross on someone's lawn constitutes trespass, criminal mischief, vandalism, and possibly assault and arson. The advantage of using generic criminal laws is not having to draft a law that picks and chooses among acceptable and unacceptable epithets, insults, and expressions. The disadvantages of using generic criminal laws is that they may have less symbolic impact and inadequate penalty structures. The symbolism issue will be dealt with later. As for adequacy of penalties, it would be an understatement to say that American sentencing law is well known for its severity. However, always sentencing hate crime offenders to the maximum prescribed punishment would raise the same issues that have just been considered—whether certain expressions and offender/victim configurations warrant more severe treatment by the criminal justice system. However, prosecutorial discretion can be much more finely tuned to take diverse circumstances into account. It does not lead invariably to treating all assaults based upon certain enumerated hate motives as more serious than all assaults that are not.

DETERRING HATE CRIMES

The justifications for hate crime legislation considered in the previous section mostly center on "just deserts"—do criminals with certain kinds of hate motives deserve more severe punishment? A different justification is that hate crime legislation is necessary to deter hate crimes from occurring in the first place.

In the area of hate crimes, we are dealing with marginal deterrence. Since the behaviors that hate crime laws are aimed at suppressing are already criminal, the question is how many additional crimes will be deterred by threatening potential offenders with an aggravated version of the offense or with higher maximum or minimum penalties? This is an empirical issue. However, even if some marginal effect could be produced at some level of draconian punishment, it is not necessarily clear that those penalties should be imposed. If the minimum punishment for every crime were raised to life imprisonment, there would undoubtedly be fewer crimes in all categories, but other considerations have led to the scaled system of punishments we now have.

In any event, perpetrators of hate crimes might not be particularly sensitive to small increases in maximum possible sentences. Hate crimes are not crimes of negligence or inadvertence where a perpetrator's behavior might be changed by calling his attention to the risk to which he is exposing others. People do not deface synagogues and cemeteries or burn crosses inadvertently. Many hate crimes involve intentionality. Consequently, it may be difficult to produce much marginal deterrence by enhancing penalties.

According to data from New York and Los Angeles, the majority of hate crimes appear to be committed by teenagers; this is also relevant to the question of deterrence. In New York City in 1990, more than 50 percent of arrests for hate crimes were of individuals under the age of nineteen (in 1989 more than 60 percent of arrestees were under the age of nineteen), and more than 20 percent were of individuals under the age of sixteen.[44] Young people who commit such crimes often have confused and antisocial personalities. And they often commit the crimes with peer support. They are unlikely to be concerned about whether their crimes violate one offense category or two.

Ironically, when juveniles commit hate crimes or any other crimes, they are not charged with specific criminal law offenses but with being delinquent. Consequently, hate crime laws would not apply to juveniles, unless the juvenile justice law was amended to make juvenile hate crime offenders prosecutable under those specific laws.

Marginal deterrence may also be achieved by increasing the risk of apprehension. It could be argued that the new hate crime laws are justified because they will change police and prosecutorial priorities so that certain intergroup crimes receive more investigative and prosecutorial attention than intragroup crimes. This is certainly one of the explicit purposes of the New York City Police Department's bias unit, which nevertheless is successful in making arrests in only about one-third of the cases it handles.

In evaluating the plausibility of enhancing the risk of catching and prosecuting bias crime offenders, a distinction should be made between serious and nonserious crimes. On the one hand, with or without bias crime legislation, high-visibility interracial homicide cases already receive top priority and maximum police and prosecutorial attention, at least in New York City. On the other hand, serious crimes against gay and lesbian victims have not traditionally received as much police and prosecutorial attention, and much less media attention, as interracial crimes. Bias crime legislation might enhance the attention and resources they receive.

It is easy to imagine an explicit policy of giving higher priority to less-serious crimes when they can be labeled hate crimes. This could involve devoting more investigative resources or pressing prosecutions more vigorously. Such selective policing and prosecuting could be carried out administratively without new substantive or sentencing law. (Of course, it could also be argued that new substantive and sentencing law is a way of directing the police and prosecutors to engage in just such selective law enforcing.)

These observations about selective investigation of hate crimes also raises the same question we confronted earlier—should some crimes be treated more seriously because of certain bad motives of the perpetrators and, if so, why? One final point needs to be made. Our assessment of the wisdom and desirability of deploying more police and prosecutorial resources to hate crimes might turn on whether we are talking about adding disproportionately more resources to hate crime cases or simply allocating the same resources to these cases that are allocated to nonbias crimes in the same generic offense category. For example, to the extent that gay bashing was traditionally ignored by the police, bias crime legislation might equalize resources devoted to such cases. Of course, this result could be achieved by administrative directive as well as by criminal legislation.

The "bottom line" is whether we wish to direct police and prosecutorial officials to enforce the criminal laws in the most color-blind way possible, ignoring insofar as possible the race, sex, or sexual orientation of offenders and victims, or whether we want to direct law enforcement officials to enforce the criminal laws in the most color-conscious way possible, prioritizing cases on the basis of racial, ethnic, religious, gender, or sexual orientation combinations of aggressors and victims. It is hard to predict whether such "color-maximizing" enforcement of the criminal laws would have more negative than positive social and political ramifications. Perhaps there is some optimal level of color-conscious enforcement, but one wonders whether the American police and prosecutorial agencies can formulate and implement policies that are subtle enough to find their way to that optimal level.

The Importance of Symbolic Denunciation

Much of the momentum toward passage of new hate crime legislation, like much criminal law, is driven not so much by the belief that more criminal law will lead to less crime, but by the belief that criminal law is the appropriate vehicle for "making a statement" about the abhorrence of certain conduct.

In New York State, Governor Mario Cuomo, Attorney General Robert Abrams, other politicians, and minority group advocates have again and again demanded more hate crime legislation for just this reason. In an open letter dated August 16, 1991, to members of the New York state legislature, Governor Cuomo stated that "as government, our single most effective weapon is the law. I implore you to support the *Bias Related*

Violence and Intimidation Act I have proposed, and make it clear to the people of this state that behavior based on bias will not be ignored or tolerated."[45]

After the killing of Yusef Hawkins, a black youth, in Bensonhurst and the beating of three Jewish students at Brooklyn College by ten black assailants, Attorney General Abrams said that the proposed *Bias Related Violence and Intimidation Act* "would send a message that hate crimes will be severely punished."[46] David Wertheimer, executive director of the New York City Gay and Lesbian Anti-Violence Task Force, advocates hate crime legislation, because "violence-motivated bigotry and bias should be identified as a unique category of a crime. Prejudices based on race, ethnicity, religion, disability, sex, or sexual orientation are related and often lead to physical attacks, and this violence cannot be tolerated in our society."[47] The U.S. Senate *Report to the Federal Hate Crimes Reporting Statute* also declares that "the very effort by the legislative branch to require the Justice Department to collect this information would send an additional important signal to victimized groups everywhere that the U.S. Government is concerned about this kind of crime."[48]

The message and signal sending that hate crime proponents advocate is different from deterrence that is aimed at potential perpetrators of hate crimes. Governor Cuomo, Attorney General Abrams, and others seem to be concerned with directing a statement of moral support to the minority communities and their advocacy groups. In effect, their goal is to put their abhorrence of racism, homophobia, sexism, and anti-Semitism on the record in the strong and unambiguous terms that criminal law signals. This political and educative use of criminal law is no stranger to American society and has a legitimate, perhaps important, role to play in our system of law and jurisprudence. However, it should be used carefully, lest it raise expectations that cannot be met and set in motion a continuous escalation of criminal laws and penalties that generates counterproductive results.

We ought to be mindful of the mess created by the continuous proliferation and escalation of criminal laws and punishments in the area of illicit drugs. Despite mountains of laws, hundreds of thousands of arrests, and overflowing criminal courts, jails, and prisons, we have failed to suppress the use and abuse of illegal psychoactive drugs. Will criminal law be any more successful in suppressing the kind of abhorrent racism, sexism, homophobia, and other prejudices that blight a free society? One might conclude that such prejudices cannot be repressed out of existence. The extent to which they can be ameliorated and reduced will depend upon "institution building" and bold, creative leadership.

The counterproductive dangers of hate crime legislation have already been suggested. Probably the most important is the First Amendment rights and values that may be trampled upon in the rush to denounce and punish attitudes and conduct that the majority deplores. History teaches that the same arguments used today to denounce cross burnings and swastikas can be used tomorrow to denounce unpopular social and political ideologies and policies. Indeed, the logic of hate crime legislation could lead to censoring all kinds of sexually explicit expression and perhaps to censoring the views of one side or the other in the abortion controversy.

Another possibly important counterproductive consequence of hate crime legislation could be the further deterioration of America's complex race and ethnic relations. In New York City, some portion of the citizenry believes that the media and the police are more sensitive to hate crimes involving black and Hispanic victims than to hate crimes involving black and Hispanic perpetrators.

Progress in combating group hatred and prejudice by means other than criminal law should not be ignored. Norms about speech and behavior that offend others have changed dramatically during the last several decades, even to the point where some observers charge that students and professors dare not voice opinions that are not deemed "politically correct" according to prevailing liberal or conservative orthodoxy. Whether or not this is an exaggeration is not the point. What is significant is that attitudes, sensitivities, norms, and behavior have all changed in many sectors of America society.

During the last decade, the United States has experienced the largest immigration in its history, much of it from Latin America, Asia, and to a lesser extent, Africa, but also including significant numbers of Russians, Eastern European, and Middle Eastern peoples. To a remarkable extent, these populations have settled into American society without provoking organized or even disorganized resistance and hostility. The current reactions to new immigrants are far more civilized and hospitable than the treatment of immigrants early in the century. This has occurred without using the criminal justice system in an all-out effort to repress xenophobes.

CONCLUDING REFLECTIONS

Ultimately, the issue under consideration is the appropriate role of criminal law in a free society. Ought criminal law to be mobilized to a much fuller extent than it has been historically in aid of suppressing prejudice, bias, and hate? Can criminal law play a positive role in ameliorating group hatred and prejudice, or will its deployment in this area produce more negative than positive effects?

One way to think about the issue is whether it is wise policy to emphasize the racial, gender, sexual, and religious components of as many crimes as possible. Ought we to move away from generic criminal laws and toward specialized criminal laws that meet the concerns of particular victimized groups? If so, it is possible that eventually calls will be heard for even more deconstruction of criminal law. Perhaps, it will be said that the victimization of blacks and gays are too different to be dealt with in a single hate crime statute and that different substantive and sentencing laws are necessary.

On reflection, it is a constant source of amazement that people who share the same goal of moving toward a more tolerant society, which respects diversity and treats individuals with respect and dignity, differ so sharply about the best means to attain that goal. Perhaps the key difference is between those who believe that the best path is one that emphasizes group rights and entitlements and those who believe that the best path is one that emphasizes individual entitlements and rights.

NOTES

1. See L. Bollinger, *The Tolerant Society: Freedom of Speech and Extremist Speech in America* (New York: Franklin Watts, 1986), 48–54.

2. According to the Anti-Defamation League, *Hate Crime Statutes: A 1991 Status Report*, thirty-two states have passed hate crime laws based on or similar to the ADL model law, twelve states have other forms of hate crime laws, and five states have not passed any hate crime legislation ([Washington, D.C.: ADL, 1991], 34–41).

3. The major civil rights statutes of the Reconstruction Era include the *Civil Rights Act of 1866*, 1 ch. 31, 14 Stat. 27 (1866); the *Enforcement Act of 1870*, 2 ch. 114, 16 Stat. 140 (1870); and the *Civil Rights Act of 1871*, 1 ch. 22, 17 Stat. 13 (1871), popularly known as the "Ku Klux Klan Act."

4. For example, in 1990, sixty-four prosecutions were commenced by the U.S. Department of Justice; see *Annual Report of the Director of the Administra-*

tive Office of the U.S. Courts 1990 at 185 (Washington, D.C.: Government Printing Office, 1990).

5. For example, see the St. Paul Minnesota cross-burning statute that the U.S. Supreme Court declared unconstitutional in *R.A.V. v St. Paul*, 112 S.Ct. 2538 (1992).

6. See Anti-Defamation League, *Hate Crime Statutes*.

7. The Anti-Defamation League has proposed two model laws covering institutional vandalism and intimidation.

8. Pub. L. No. 101–275, 104 Stat. 140 (1990). The U.S. Department of Justice delegated responsibility for hate crime statistics collection to the FBI. See 28 C.F.R., Pt. O. sec. 85(m). The FBI assigned the role of developing procedures to its Uniform Crime Reporting section. See also James B. Jacobs and Barry Eisler, *The Hate Crime Statistics Act of 1990* 29 Criminal Law Bulletin 99 (1993).

9. In 1988, Congress passed the *Religious Vandalism Act*, criminalizing intentional damage of religious property and obstruction of a person's employment of free exercise of religious beliefs. 18 U.S.C. sec. 247(b) (1). State analogues to this statute have existed for many years. See, for example, *Tex. Penal Code* ann. sec. 42.09 (Vernon 1974).

10. Failure to label some interracial crimes against white victims as bias crimes has led journalists to denounce double standards and hypocrisy. See, for example, J. O'Sullivan, *Do the Right Thing, Suppress Crime: Racial Aspects of New York City Crime*, 4119 National Review 13 (Oct. 13, 1989); L. Anderson, *Crime, Race, and the Fourth Estate*, 4220 National Review 52 (Oct. 15, 1990). See also James Sleeper, *The Closest of Strangers: Liberalism and the Politics of Race in New York* (New York: Random House, 1990).

11. See J. Epstein, *The Joys of Victimhood*, New York Times Magazine, July 2, 1989, 20.

12. See J. M. Fernandez, *Bringing Hate Crimes into Focus*, 26 Harvard Civil Rights and Civil Liberties Law Review 261–93 (1991); see note, *Combatting Racial Violence: A Legislative Proposal*, 101 Harvard Law Review 1270–86 (1988); G. Padgett, *Racially Motivated Violence and Intimidation: Inadequate State Enforcement and Federal Civil Rights Remedies*, 75 Journal of Criminal Law and Criminology 103–38 (1984).

13. Klanwatch Project of the Southern Poverty Law Center, *Hate Violence and White Supremacy: A Decade Review 1980–1990* (Montgomery, Ala.: SPLC, 1990); Anti-Violence Project, National Gay and Lesbian Task Force, *Anti-Gay Violence, Victimization, and Defamation 1989* (Washington, D.C.: NGLTF, 1990).

14. *Comprehensive Bias and Gang Assault Act*, N.Y.S. 6220, 214 Laws of the Res. Sess. sec. 1 (1991).

15. An excellent example would be the near-hysteria a decade ago about missing and kidnapped children. Similarly, the whole subject of drugs and drug

abuse is awash with inflated rhetoric and dubious data. The passage of crime legislation also may be viewed as a mechanism by which politicians legitimate a conception of their own "essential goodness in relation to others." See S. Steele, *The Content of our Character* (New York: Knopf, 1980).

16. For example, despite intense media attention on the subject of bias crime in New York City in the last year, the police department's bias crime unit reports very steady figures during the last three years.

17. See: Or. Rev. Stat. sec. 181.550 (1)(1989); Va. Code ann. sec. 528.5A (1991); Ariz. Rev. Stat. ann. sec. 131–504, 1604 (1989).

18. Eight members of the House Judiciary Committee expressed their disappointment that the federal act "does not go far enough and include violence by and against union members." H.R. Rep. no. 101–109, 101st Cong., 1st sess., at 7 (1989).

19. New York City Police Department, *Bias Incident Investigation Unit* (N.Y.P.D. document, Sept. 1991).

20. Many states have a whole family of so-called "anti-Klan" statutes that are not dealt with in this section. See, for example, N.C. Gen. Stat. secs. 1412.214.12.15 (1981, and supp. 1985), which forbid secret societies that have the circumvention of laws as a purpose and wearing masks on public ways and burning crosses on other persons' properties. Tennessee has a statute called the *Night Riding Statute*, which prohibits persons from disturbing the peace or intimidating citizens through threats or other improper means. Tenn. Code. ann. sec. 392–706 (1982).

21. Other statutes make it an offense to desecrate or damage religious property or a cemetery. They also prohibit the formation of paramilitary organizations and the wearing of masks.

22. *R.A.V. v St. Paul*, 112 S.Ct. 2538 (1992). See also: *State v Mitchell*, 113 S.Ct. 2194 (1993) in which the Supreme Court upheld a statute enhancing the punishment for offenses motivated by bias.

23. See note, *The Void for Vagueness Doctrine in the Supreme Court*, 109 Univ. of Pennsylvania Law Review 67 (1960).

24. In 1990, 44 percent of misdemeanor charges that were filed in the New York City criminal court were simply dismissed. Of those defendants convicted, 75 percent received no more than fifteen days in jail. K. Subin, *The New York City Criminal Court: The Case for Abolition*, Occasional Paper Series (New York: Center for Research in Crime and Justice, New York Univ. School of Law, 1992), 91–104.

25. For further development of this point, see James B. Jacobs, *Implementing Hate Crime Legislation: Symbolism and Crime Control*, symposium issue, 3 Annual Survey of American Law 18–34 (1992–93).

26. N.Y. Crim. Proc. Law sec. 240.3 (McKinney 1982).

27. See R. Pellegrini, *Rape Is a Bias Crime, New York Times*, May 27, 1990, p. 13.

28. For an argument that only crimes by whites against blacks should be punished as hate crimes, see *Combatting Racial Violence: A Legislative Proposal* 1270, supra note 12; M. Fleischauer, *Teeth for a Paper Tiger: A Proposal to Add Enforceability to Florida's Hate Crimes Act*, 17 Florida State Univ. Law Review 697–711 (1990); and *R.A.V. v St. Paul*, 112 S.Ct. 2538 (1992). See also *State v Mitchell*, 113 S.Ct. 2194 (1993) in which the Supreme Court upheld a statute enhancing the punishment for offenses motivated by bias.

29. U.S. Department of Justice, Bureau of Justice Statistics, *Sourcebook of Criminal Justice Statistics 1990*, NCJ 13–0580 (Washington, D.C.: Government Printing Office, 1991), table 3.40 at 278 and table 3.55 at 261.

30. See note, supra note 12.

31. See *Labels Mask 'Latino' Diversity*, 22(3) Ford Foundation Letter 10–11 (1991): "The term 'Hispanic voters' rolls easily off the tongues of pollsters and politicians, suggesting a monolithic ethnic group whose members share the same values. However, in the first broad analysis of the political attitudes and practices of Mexicans, Puerto Ricans, and Cubans, who comprise a large majority of all Hispanics, the Latino National Political Survey reveals differences that defy conventional wisdom about the nation's fastest growing population group" (10).

32. There are currently a large number of bills pending before the New York legislature that would greatly expand the reach of the hate crime category.

33. Interestingly, the Illinois attorney general has interpreted that state's hate crime statute, based on the ADL model, as requiring wrongful prejudice to be "the sole motivating factor." By contrast, some statutes explicitly state that it is sufficient to prove guilt that the defendant's act was in part motivated by a wrongful prejudice.

34. Racial, ethnic, and other epithets, of course, can have different meanings to different speakers. Some people use them with the conscious intent of imposing hurt, distress, and humiliation. Other people use them in a more unthinking way, or even as a kind of banter. Some people who tell ethnic jokes that depict a particular group in a negative light claim not to intend any hurt.

35. 18 Pa. Cons. Stat. sec. 2710 (1991).

36. *Civil Rights Act*, 18 U.S.C. secs. 24–142 (1988).

37. Padgett, supra note 12. See *U.S. v Ehrlichman*, 546 F.2d 910 (D.C. Cir. 1976).

38. Gen. L. ch. 265, sec. 37 (1988).

39. Memorandum from Mario M. Cuomo, governor of the State of New York to the New York legislature (Apr. 23, 1991), on file with the Albany Governor's Press Office.

40. See *Hate Crime Statistics Act of 1988: Hearing Before the Subcommittee on*

the Constitution of the Senate Committee on the Judiciary, 100th Cong., 2d sess. 24–041 (1988) (testimony of the American Psychological Association), 1003–7.

41. Supra note 29.

42. See *Hate Crimes: Confronting Violence Against Lesbians and Gay Men,* ed. P. Herek and M. Berrill, (Washington, D.C.: National Gay and Lesbian Task Force, 1992).

43. Chris Maxwell (a researcher on the project), interview by author, New York City, Oct. 1991.

44. New York City Police Department (Sept. 1991), 9.

45. Mario M. Cuomo, governor of the State of New York, letter to the New York legislature, Aug. 16, 1991.

46. A. Abramovsky, *Bias-Motivated Crime, Part 3,* 74 New York Law Journal 3 (Nov. 9, 1989), citing Robert Abrams's letter to Senate Majority Leader Ralph Marino, dated Oct. 12, 1989.

47. D. M. Wertheimer, *Victims of Violence: A Rising Tide of Anti-Gay Sentiment,* USA Today, Jan. 1988, 54.

48. S. Rep. no. 21. 101st Cong., 2d sess. 1588C–1594C (1990).

8. Spectacular Punishment and the Orchestration of Hate: The Pillory and Popular Morality in Eighteenth-Century England

Antony E. Simpson

istorically, many examples of bias and malice appear in the substance of the law, in its applications, and in the numerous theories of legal philosophy. The law is not some detailed coda of immutable rules but is an expression of traditional, moral, and generalized beliefs set in the crucible of immediate circumstance. Most importantly, the law is an expression of prevalent power relations; of all successful social institutions, the law is the means for translating the reality of power into a more or less acceptable system of state authority. As social circumstances change, notions of power and authority change. Consequently, conceptions of the law are both vibrant and dynamic. They must continually change but in ways that recognize both new realities and the continuance of legal and social traditions.

Different characterizations of modern common law systems emphasize equity and consistency, both of which require some bureaucratic legal machinery. Traditional functional analysis assumes that these requirements emerge from the will of a "collective consciousness" and interprets legal ritual as serving to define the ever-changing boundaries of permissible behavior.[1]

Consistency is a brief phenomenon that embodies equal treatment of similar cases heard during the same period of time, while *equity* is recognized by conflict theorists as an innate feature of common law systems. One view suggests that the law is the principle "ideological formation" of the dominant class it governs, but it exists as a social, rather than individual, phenomenon. As a social phenomenon, it is beyond the control of individual interests and is, as a whole, unamenable to direct manipulation through conscious conspiracy. Although it may be manipulated in particular situations, the law must always in some sense represent the interests of all social groups. If it does not, then it is not law as we know it but is simply a bald expression of state power. As an instrument of repression and coercion, it can have little authority.[2] E. P. Thompson stated: "If the law is evidently partial and unjust, then it will mask nothing, contribute nothing to any class's hegemony. The essential precondition for the effectiveness of law, in its function as ideology, is that it shall display an independence from gross manipulation and shall seem to be just."[3]

The law, even in the most politicized societies, comes to some extent to recognize the diverse cultural and economic interests of all constituents. The direction and nature of legal change can, therefore, be used as a framework for examining the changing balance of political and economic powers. It can also be used to examine the ways in which the state comes to terms with traditional and subcultural beliefs, which may command strong allegiance but which are not strongly represented in the political power structure. The state, as Antonio Gramsci explained, does not have a monopoly over all ideology.[4] Nor do competing ideologies represent the complete belief systems within a society. To be successful the state, especially through its legal system, must in some way recognize the culture and beliefs of those whose political awareness is distinguished only by its potential. Assured of this recognition by the state, all of society can be persuaded to accept the legitimacy of the authority of the existing power structure.

Because of its dramatic social and legal changes, England in the eighteenth century has been greatly analyzed, because its sophisticated, although premodern, legal system enabled a small, dominant class to rule by using ritual to inspire fear and deference and by threatening awful public punishment for the most severe infractions against it.[5] The subsequent transformation of that system in the early decades of the nineteenth century has been interpreted as a challenge to meet the needs of burgeoning commercial and financial interests of a more effective system of law enforcement and the related emergence of new concepts of discipline and subservience to authority.[6]

One further approach emphasizes the importance of the late eighteenth century as a transition between premodern, or "repressive," and modern, or "autonomous," systems of law.[7] These two systems are quite distinct. The modern system emphasizes the certainly and consistency of punishment, independence from political processes, procedural fairness, and other attributes only achievable within the kind of bureaucratic framework that did not exist previously.[8] The patrimonial premodern system emphasized principles over legal rules, the flexibility of precedent, and the primacy of law determined by judges.

Following an argument developed by Douglas Hay, systematic reliance on ritual and occasional public and awe-inspiring punishment was a natural consequence of both the function and the structure of criminal justice in the eighteenth century. As Hay and Foucault suggest, punishment as a public spectacle served two distinct but related functions. As ritual, it emphasized the connections between the apparatus of criminal justice and the ruling class, whose members monopolized the principal offices of government. Events on the public scaffold served to buttress ceremonies such as "the traditional, and calculated, panoply" of the assizes. These and other powerful judicial rituals celebrated the power of the state and of those individuals who controlled it, in the personal and nonbureaucratic fashion of the day.[9]

Ritual also constituted the only powerful way by which the almost unlimited power of the sovereign and his functionaries could be demonstrated. Ritual was not intended to convey the state's ability or intention to punish all transgressions against it. Certainty of punishment was the ambitious objective of later times. As Foucault and Ignatieff state, efforts to instigate punishment required the kind of powerful bureaucratic organization that the eighteenth-century elite was unwilling to tolerate or finance. Public order was not an issue for rural landowners, as it later became for the urban bourgeois.[10] In the eighteenth century, intimidation of the masses and the exaction of the deference was important. Ritual punishment illustrated the knowledge and the power of the sovereign and the heinousness of affronts to him or his agents:

The atrocity of a crime was also the violence of the challenge flung at the sovereign; it was that which would move him to make a reply whose function was to go further than this atrocity, to master it, to overcome it by an excess that annulled it. The atrocity that haunted the public execution played, therefore, a double role: it was the principle of the communication between the crime and punishment. . . . It provided the spectacle with both truth and power; it was the culmination of the ritual of investigation and the ceremony in which the sovereign triumphed.[11]

These functional characteristics explain many of the elaborations of capital punishment and the mode of its imposition in the eighteenth century. Discretion ensured that a capital conviction did not necessarily result in an execution. Most, indeed, did not.[12]

The extraordinary capacity of the sovereign to grant mercy undoubtedly served to reinforce his judicial power and the rewards of deference: "The wretched thief begging on his knees for forgiveness is not a literary conceit, but a reality described in many legal depositions."[13] The capacity to forgive existed when the reprieve process was arbitrary or was conducted according to rational and consistent criteria.[14]

Further elaboration of ritual occurred at the discretion of the authorities to increase the severity of pre- or postmortem punishment. Traitors, including counterfeiters, could be hanged, drawn, and quartered. Although death by torture never occurred after the mid-eighteenth century, it was ordered as late as 1867 and almost occurred in 1803.[15] Sir Samuel Romilly and other penal reformers of the nineteenth century repeatedly cited the awful punishment for treason as epitomizing the barbarity of the past and the unwillingness of supposedly enlightened nineteenth-century thinkers to accept change.[16] Hanging in chains was usually reserved for pirates and perpetrators of exceptionally vicious murders but was also used as punishment in the nineteenth century. Although this ritual did not affect subsequent physical executions. It certainly aggravated a prisoner's ordeal.[17]

Postmortem punishments occurred frequently until the 1830s. Gibbeting and other kinds of corpse mutilation were used extensively and with apparent success, if the object was to have been the aggravation of punishment by humiliating a body after execution. The bodies of executed felons were sometimes insulted in extraordinary ceremonies.[18] In the most widely vilified instances of postmortem mutilation, the bodies of executed felons were given to surgeons for dissection. People's hatred of "burking"—the conveyance of bodies from whatever source to the surgeons for dissection—was widespread and was often expressed by crowds at a scaffold. Serious rioting often resulted when bodies of the executed were to be subjected to a final indignity.[19]

SPECTACULAR PUNISHMENT AND POPULAR CULTURE

Various barbarisms associated with the scaffold occurred long after the emergence of a bureaucratic, autonomous, and modern system of law by the 1830s. Although spectacular punishment was clearly functional in the eighteenth-century premodern system, it became a positive embarrassment to a modern system. A legal system that emphasizes certainty of punishment, rationality, equity of process, and bureaucratic functioning does not seem to be one likely to celebrate the public scaffold. The rioting and brutality associated with public executions were unacceptable to a modern age that supposedly sought modification of the spirit instead of abuse of the body. However, public executions continued in England until 1868.[20] But the debauchery and violence associated with them probably escalated due to the proliferation of urban centers and consequent increases in the attendant crowds.[21]

The triumph of bureaucracy over patrimonialism in the legal system was complete and has been well documented. The rituals surrounding public punishment, especially on the scaffold, seem to reflect needs and beliefs that were traditional, usually apolitical, and strong enough to require formal expression. Postmortem mutilations of the executed were not horrifying to crowds because of values instilled in them by the ruling class. The physical quartering of a body after execution was quite inimical to the many myths and customs associated with the gallows. These reflected popular beliefs concerning the sanctity of the body and the magical properties of the corpse of the condemned.[22] Disfigurement of the corpses of felons may also have disturbed crowds, because it reminded them that revival of the dead—always a faint possibility in an age of botched executions—was no longer possible.[23]

The attraction of the public to the place of execution was a dramatic illustration of the almost unbridled power of the state. However, public executions also gave the condemned an opportunity to display personal courage, which could be rewarded by crowd reactions of support. Displays of courage were traditional and quite stylized; some dying men attempted to kick off their boots before they expired.[24] Those guilty of dishonorable crimes could seek some kind of worldly redemption by taking heroic stances during the last minutes of their lives, or perhaps for the first time in their lives. An individual's carriage on the gallows was more important to him than to the state. Penitent or not, condemned criminals frequently felt a compelling need to explain themselves to the crowd. Heroic behavior on the gallows followed long-standing tradition. Henry Fielding observed in 1751 that "the thief who is hanged today hath learned his intrepidity from the example of his hanged predecessors."[25]

As a public event, capital punishment was surrounded by legal and populist ceremonies. During its use, the most elaborate procession to the gallows—from Newgate to Tyburn—was abandoned in 1783 primarily because of attacks on public officers and even rescue attempts. However, processions to public executions continued because of policies of directing perpetrators of especially heinous offenses to the places where their crimes had been committed.

Opportunity for public confession undoubtedly served to demonstrate the justice, if not the mercy, of the state when criminals were appropriately penitent. It also served to reinforce the public's image of the state as a gatherer of knowledge and an investigator of fact; to Foucault, public confession highlighted the intimate connection between "truth and power." The result of public confession was also not entirely under the control of the authorities. Speeches by dying convicts usually expressed contrition and acceptance, perhaps because the last-minute reprieves were no means unknown.[26] However, impenitents who raved against the nature of the state's actions and the legal process that had brought them to the gallows reinforced the righteousness of the state and the crowd.[27] Ritual was a way for the working class to express their beliefs as well as a demonstration of the power of the law and the power of the elite. Most importantly, a public execution was popular entertainment. It was enjoyed by all spectators as a dramatic carnival where everyone had an opportunity to strongly express themselves about the crimes being punished and the character or circumstances of the condemned criminal.

The aristocratic elite accepted unruly expressions of the populace because the power of the elite rested in their ownership of land. Aristocrats were not concerned with the creation of an orderly urban working class or smooth commercial traffic. The eighteenth-century ruling class was not greatly bothered by public disorder. For a long time, it had been unwilling to create the kind of bureaucratic structures necessary to restrain disorder. Furthermore, the values of the aristocracy were not so very different from those of the working class. Aristocrats and workers generally share a lack of interest in restraint, sobriety, thrift, and deferred gratification, which distinguish the middle class. They also, for their own reasons, both approve in theory of values like honor, bravery, and fidelity. Some argue that working-class and aristocratic value systems diverged only when the elite assumed that privacy was a worthwhile value.[28]

The elite's tolerance of crowd activity should not, however, be interpreted as a meeting of antibourgeois hearts and minds. The system of law in the eighteenth century was intended primarily to allow a small group to rule with the consent of the ruled and without the creation of a state apparatus. The system was political, although members of the elite may have been apolitical. Analyses of the "moral economy" of crowds in this period suggest that their values were certainly traditional but based upon political reality. George Rudé, reviewing the literature of popular protest at this time, suggests that the notion of crowd values existing in isolation from current political reality was outmoded by the early part of the eighteenth century.[29] Traditional values certainly flourished for a long time but were constantly modified by both supporters and enemies of the state. What E. P. Thompson called "the sharp jostle of experience" modified traditional values.[30] Particular events could affect and perhaps transform the outlooks of people on particular issues.

Disturbances outside of metropolitan London also reflected the celebration of traditional politicized views.[31] Thompson's analysis of the nationwide riots, which frequently occurred over the price and quality of bread, indicates how mobs did not have to be politically astute to become a threat to the state. Thompson is not analyzing planned conspiracies executed for explicitly political ends. The riots were organized locally and appear to have been spontaneous.[32] However, both ideology and the exercise of political power were at issue. The riots seem to have been motivated by deeply felt convictions about the right of working people to purchase food at a "just price," and by belief that, in manipulating prices, vendors were exceeding the rules of permissible behavior. That the "riots" commonly centered on the crowds' insistence on buying bread at what they considered to be fair prices, and not on the outright confiscation of food, underscores the issue of permissible behavior. Many of the gentry, including justices of the peace, supported the crowds.

If the motivations of the crowds are characteristic, then a separate and volatile "moral economy" of the urban crowd would have posed a constant and troublesome challenge to a state ill-equipped to contain its often violent expressions.[33] The mob's propensity to use electoral and other political issues as excuses for riot was legendary and is well docu-mented.[34] Attempts to control the ideology or mentalities of the populace was therefore an essential feature of the state.[35] This was because of the demands of a unique social transformation and because of the need to inhibit the development of a politicized, unrestrained urban population. When the crowd could be placated, the state had every reason to do what was needed to placate it.

Patterns of disorder in London were rather different from those in the provinces. Metropolitan riots could have a variety of causes but were rarely about food. They also represented a traditional morality, but one moderated by xenophobia, anti-Catholicism, nascent class awareness, and, in the first half of the century, Jacobitism. Disorders in London, as in the provinces, were probably the major important form of communi-cation between people and their rulers.[36] Urban riots were, however, likely to be manipulated politically and to serve a central function in the political process.[37] From the 1780s, rioting in London and elsewhere ap-pears to have developed a class-based political sense. The politicization of English society after the 1780s and the class antagonism associated with later popular protest began to develop.[38] In London, the political conno-tations of disorder were affected by the memories of the Gordon Riot of 1780, in which three hundred people died and twenty-five were executed for related crimes. The power of unrestrained mob behavior acted as a strong discouragement to politicians attempting to manipulate crowds during previous innocent times.[39]

THE SPECTACLE AND SECONDARY PUNISHMENT

The scaffold ritual was not the only dramatic and spectacular punish-ment dealing with life and death. Supposedly nonlethal punishments ex-isted, which were intended to expose culprits to humiliation, discomfort, and pain, but not death. At these punishments, spectators did more than express their opinions from the sidelines. At some of them, the audience took an active role in the administration of the sentences and helped de-termine the severity with which they were executed.

These spectacular secondary punishments may be considered in two groups: those in which the authorities had complete control over the se-verity of the punishments and those in which responsibilities could po-tentially be delegated to the crowd. In the first group, torture was only considered in English law as a pretrial way of extracting information and was never, in legal theory at least, considered as a punishment. Torture had vanished from the judicial scene by the end of the sixteenth century, although its revival was considered by the Privy Council in 1628. Its disappearance is generally ascribed to the development of the jury system and relaxed standards of proof, which made the existence of confessions less important in securing convictions in criminal trials.[40] Mutilation was extensively used before and during the seventeenth century and was usually added to other punishments.[41] Mutilation associated with the punishment for high treason was not used after the 1745 rebellion. Branding usually on the hand and in open court was retained as the traditional punishment for manslaughter. It was effectively ended in the late 1770s by the practice of striking a cold iron on the hand—the literal "slap on the wrist." The principal use of branding to mark a vagrant for permanent identification was abandoned in 1744.[42] Mutilation was, therefore, rarely used as a punishment during the eighteenth century.

Whipping and other punishments to shame lawbreakers were generally prescribed for misdemeanors, but the courts had tremendous discretion over them. Punishments for most felonies were mandated by statute law, but those for misdemeanors were generally subject to common law. At the discretion of the court, fines could be combined with whippings or imprisonment. The discretion, like the number of offenses to which it applied, was very broad.[43] Ignominious punishment was an option for the courts in a great range of circumstances.

Whipping has enjoyed a long history in English penal sanctions. Public whipping of women was abolished in 1817; and the whipping of men, except in the armed forces, in 1862.[44] Private whippings continued to occur in England until 1948. In certain bizarre situations, they occurred in England until 1993.[45] Until the early nineteenth century, public whippings were awarded liberally. Whipping at the back of a cart was primarily reserved for vagrants and applied as a persuasive means of escorting them out of town. As with other ignominious punishments, the severity of a sentence very much depended on the way the punishment was applied. In the absence of detailed historical analysis of whippings, this punishment was probably not usually severe.[46] Public whippings were punishments under the complete control of the authorities. Most reports suggest that its applications were unpopular and correspondingly mild. They were never fatal and do not seem to have caused considerable pain. Edward "My Hearty" Wright was publicly whipped more than fifty times during his long career and survived to be capitally convicted at least once.[47] His punishments can hardly have been consequential and certainly were no deterrent. Wright's experience was not unusual; most press accounts of public whippings emphasize their unpopularity as humiliating but not necessarily painful ordeals.[48] Communities found public whippings unacceptable due to the courts use of this punishment for vagrancy, while excluding its use in the punishment of moral infractions.[49]

However it was applied, public whippings were under the direct control of the courts that imposed them. Other punishments, the severity of which depended on their reception by participating audiences, included the pillory and the stocks.[50] Imposition of an hour or two in the stocks was generally a rural punishment, although it was sometimes used in London. An offender's hands were free but his legs were confined. Women seem to have escaped punishment in the stocks. Restricted offenders could, with their hands, protect themselves against abuse, especially from missiles thrown by crowds. However, the stocks in rural and urban areas were reserved largely for drunkards.[51] Given the licentious society of eighteenth-century England, it is not surprising that no records exist of people in the stocks being subjected to physical abuse. Apart from indicating an unsurprising tolerance for the alcohol addicted, the experience of people in the stocks reveals little about the moral or political concerns of English crowds.

THE PILLORY: SPECTACULAR PUNISHMENT AND COMMUNITY JUSTICE

The pillory represented the only punishment where spectators could often determine its severity. Someone subjected to it would be stood, usually for an hour and perhaps on several occasions, facing a crowd and with neck and hands pinioned. In the absence of state control, crowd reactions at the pillory became expressions of popular morality, and the pillory had stronger associations with popular and traditional notions of community justice than to the judicial system. Theoretically, the pillory was a punishment only for the public humiliation of a culprit. As an almost exclusively urban phenomenon, it probably exposed to the public the faces of criminals whose activities were characterized by guile and misrepresentation. Its early use for frauds and tricksters and later use for perjurers strongly suggests exposing criminals publicly.[52] No legal justification existed for the state to use this punishment to inflict physical harm. The obligation of the state to protect a person in the pillory was accepted in Elizabethan times and appears to have been accepted until the end of the seventeenth century.[53] Titus Oates, a perjurer who had forsworn the lives of five innocent men, was pilloried several times each year between 1685 and 1689. He was pelted and abused, but the authorities took care to protect him from harm. The lord chief justice was at the pillory to ensure fair play, as were many of Oates's supporters. Eyewitness accounts described in detail the severity of the regular whippings, which were a related part of Oates's punishment.[54] Seventeenth-century penal philosophy accepted abuse, even mutilation, of a pilloried culprit, but only if the aggravated penalty was inflicted by the state.

By the early eighteenth century, state-inflicted abuse had ended, but the severity of the pillory had become characterized by the uncertainty of the experience. One authority, writing in 1730, commented on the transformation of the pillory from an instrument of state justice to a vehicle for mob rule and complained of the apparent unwillingness of the authorities to intervene on behalf of the ritual's victim.[55]

The abdication of state responsibility became generally acceptable, partly because of the importance of the pillory as the standard punishment for perjury. Until the nineteenth century, the courts were somewhat ambiguous about the nature of perjury. It was established early as an indictable offense, but seventeenth-century legal opinion was reluctant to transform it from a misdemeanor into a felony because such action would serve to discourage submission of testimony to the Court of Star Chamber. During the eighteenth century, certain kinds of perjury were subsumed within other offenses and transformed into capital offenses. These offenses generally included activities associated with forgery and designed to acquire property fraudulently. However, falsely swearing away people's lives—the offense of which Oates was convicted—remained a misdemeanor, although such behavior was widely perceived as tantamount to murder.[56]

English society in the eighteenth century undoubtedly regarded corruption as widespread in urban courts.[57] An established practice was the payment of substantial rewards or "blood money" to those responsible for the conviction of people accused of robbery, theft, and other capital felonies. The practice continued until the nineteenth century. A consequence of a system of law enforcement that relied on private efforts, the practice created a class of professional "thief-takers" who used false testimony to achieve profitable convictions. Their strong links to the criminal subculture enabled them to profit from the recovery of stolen property.

Scandals involving thief-takers and their perjuring away of human lives erupted during the century. The infamous Jonathan Wild operated openly and successfully from 1712 until his conviction on related capital charges and execution in 1725.[58] Four thief-takers, also known to have brought about the deaths of possibly innocent people, were convicted of perjury in 1756.[59] In 1816, eight men, including a police officer in London and a patrol officer in Bow Street, were convicted for perjury. Their conspiracies appear to have been discovered through the misuse of the judicial process and before loss of life.[60] However, after the conviction, the lord mayor of the city stated that he knew personally of thirty cases in the previous ten years in which innocent lives had been sworn away by informers seeking statutory rewards.[61]

Informing for "blood money" was not the only way in which the law could be manipulated by professional criminals. Extortion under threat of prosecution for real or imagined crimes was common and frequently involved allegations of sexual misconduct. This kind of blackmail was difficult to substantiate in law, and few were convicted of it.[62] Those who were convicted were frequently exposed at the pillory. Of the ten blackmailers convicted of crimes relating to false accusation of rape in the city courts, five were punished at the pillory.[63] The experience of two of them, convicted in the same case, were described in accounts. Robertson and Hunt, pilloried in 1755, were "so severely treated by the Mob, that it is much doubted whether they will live to undergo the other Part of their Punishment, which is seven Years Transportation."[64] These two criminals were not professional extortionists and appear to have been motivated by a desire for personal revenge rather than financial gain. Nonetheless, the mob hated them with a revenge that was as thorough as that of the criminals.

Eleven of the eighteen people convicted of misdemeanors relating to blackmail under allegations of homosexual misconduct were also placed in the pillory. John Newarks and George Butts, punished in 1756, devised a novel but unsuccessful way of lobbying the crowd for support: "These villains had the unparalleled impudence before they mounted the pillory, to distribute several written papers reflecting on the honor of the gentlemen who prosecuted them, in order to obtain favor from the populace, but it had a contrary effect."[65] They do not appear to have been injured, but Samuel Scrimshaw and James Ross, convicted of a similar offense three years later, were. They were "severely pelted." However, a police officer endeavoring to protect them inadvertently killed a member of the crowd with his sword. The fury of the mob was diverted from the two blackmailers, and the constable had some difficulty making his escape.[66] The bizarre killing at the pillory was a fortunate event for Scrimshaw and Ross, but its ultimate cause was mob antipathy toward the two men and their crimes.

Strong difference in the attitudes of the courts and the populace existed toward blackmail. Extortion under allegation of heterosexual misconduct was only regarded seriously when false testimony put an innocent man's life in jeopardy. In most circumstances, the courts regarded the offense lightly.[67] The benign attitude of the courts was in all probability due to many instances of blackmail actually reflecting the traditional and extralegal practice of having a perceived injury "made up" through an apology and sometimes a payment of money, offered in some public forum.[68]

Blackmail under allegation of homosexual practice was regarded very differently because of the professional and organized nature thought to characterize this form of extortion but also because such allegations were felt to be much more damaging to those charged with them.[69] Very few misdemeanor prosecutions for this kind of blackmail occurred after the 1770s. The courts in a dramatic and persistent sleight of hand transformed this kind of blackmail into the capital crime of robbery. Blackmailers making accusations of homosexuality were regularly convicted on capital charges. In the early nineteenth century, they became a sizable proportion of those convicted of robbery.[70] This shift in legal substance and practice is a telling indicator of the growing public antipathy toward male homosexuality.

The hatred of informers and others produced by a primitive system of law enforcement was widespread. The use of the pillory to punish perjurers probably diverted public attention toward the behavior of the offenders and away from the inadequacy of the system that had produced them. Exposure of miscreants to the ritual and uncontrolled punishment by the crowd enabled the state to express its own condemnation of offenses by allowing the crowd to demonstrate its own strong feelings. Preserving a barbaric and uncertain mode of punishment probably served to legitimize a very questionable state institution.

At the pillorying of four thief-takers in 1756, the state assigned only two officers to protect them. Egan was quickly killed by stoning, and Salmon was badly, perhaps fatally, injured. Berry died in prison some years later, and M'Daniel, the ringleader, survived the pillory and a prison sentence to embark upon a career as a soldier in India.[71] The lengthy judicial debate, which had led the court to decide that the four could not be tried for murder, resulted in a compliment to the impartiality of the proceedings: "The obligation on the judges in England to adhere strictly to the letter of the law, when favorable to criminals, never appeared more conspicuous than in the case of these miscreants."[72]

The uncertainty of the pillory could be mobilized in other political circumstances. Severe attacks against the state could be countered with capital prosecutions for treason. Only in times of open rebellion against the Crown in 1715 and 1745 were cases of treason tried with any degree of success. Lesser offenses, frequently involving scurrilous attacks in print against the Crown or its agents, could be subject to misdemeanor prosecutions for criminal, seditious, or blasphemous libel. In these prosecutions, the image of the pillory could be invoked as a deterrent to the disrespectful, and the uncertainly of its use could be manipulated effectively. Authorities could, in deciding whether or not to protect an individual, change a humiliating punishment into one at the pillory where the punishment was decided by a demonstrative crowd. In 1703, Daniel Defoe was sentenced to the pillory for libel. His terror of the pillory was occasioned by his fear of a possibly homicidal mob. However, his exhibition "was an occasion of triumph and not of ignominy to him. A ring of admirers was formed round the place of punishment, and bunches of flowers instead of handfuls of garbage were thrown at the criminal."[73] The government did protect him, and the famous painting of the occasion by Eyre Crowe shows the military occupied primarily with the control of those anxious to bestow bouquets upon the victim.[74] The government also enjoyed another triumph. Recognizing Defoe's fears, his Whig friends negotiated with the authorities; Defoe would be given official protection at the pillory in return for information about the publishers of his offending pamphlet.[75] In negotiation, the authorities could use the pillory as an instrument for political intrigue and repression. Reliance upon the application of the law rather than its content gave the government a potentially powerful way to assail sedition and dissent.

The ritual at the pillory could not always be manipulated by the authorities. Rich or popular culprits could mobilize forces to protect themselves, whether their offenses were political or not.[76] The authorities could intervene at the pillory in other ways. Dr. Shebbeare, pilloried for libel in London, had a considerate undersheriff to hold a parasol over his head to shield him from the sun.[77] The appearance of the protective undersheriff undoubtedly gave the crowd a message about the level of misbehavior that would be tolerated. If protective policies failed, authorities could, if they wished, curtail the punishment.[78] They could also increase it; at the 1732 pillorying of Eleanor Beare, an abortionist, the court officers removed the protective headgear worn by Beare.[79] As a consequence, she appears to have been severely injured.[80]

Imaginative means could be employed to protect culprits when generally appropriate. For one rich perjurer, officials kept the crowd much further from the pillory than was the norm before the event; they also cleared the area of any debris that could be thrown at the perjurer. The convict's possession of wealth was probably the main determinant of protective official policies.[81]

Use of the pillory to deter political enemies of the state was not effective in the last half of the eighteenth century, because of the chance that those punished would attract the sympathy of the crowd. Its use for overtly political purposes was revived at the end of the century and probably reflects the failure of the authorities to secure more than a few capital convictions for treason.[82] Misdemeanor prosecutions for libel and related offenses were made successfully in large numbers.[83] Prosecutions to combat dissent with threats of the pillory were ultimately unsuccessful. In 1812, Daniel Eaton, a longtime Freethinker, had been publishing the works of Tom Paine in spite of seven state prosecutions against him during a twenty-year period.[84] Eaton's pillorying was an unmitigated disaster for the government. He was cheered and applauded by a crowded of fifteen thousand people who seem to have been complimenting his courage as much as his principles.[85] The occasion was more than just a personal triumph for Eaton, his supporters, or the movement they represented; it demonstrated to the government that the pillory was no longer a threat to its political opponents.[86] The pillory, which the state had been able to manipulate, could now be turned against the authorities. The government decided three years later to abolish the pillory as punishment for offenses other than perjury.[87] By 1830, the pillory was virtually never used, and by 1837, it was defunct in law.[88] The timing of its effective demise is perhaps significant. The London Metropolitan Police, England's first bureaucratized police force, was founded in 1829.[89] With it came an effective system of prosecution and the abandonment of the old entrepreneurial and frequently corrupt system of law enforcement. The need for a severe curb on perjury became diminished.

Legislative discussion of the rationale for abolition of the pillory emphasized the uncertainty of its outcome—the characteristic that had historically given it its distinctive power.[90] That discussion indicates how much the failure of the pillory to terrorize Daniel Eaton constituted a failure for government policy. The court ordered Eaton pilloried outside Newgate Prison. According to Lord Ellenborough, the lord chief justice, the court believed him to be the probable object of violence and wanted to take him to a place of safety if he was injured.[91] Lord Ellenborough's expert opinion underscores the intent that Eaton's punishment was to be more than mere public humiliation. That Eaton was not injured reveals the state's intentions toward him and the embarrassment of its defeat. Furthermore, Eaton's punishment had been most unusually advertised in the newspapers the day before he was pilloried.[92]

It is tempting to relegate the pillory to history as an archaic and supposedly primitive mechanism of punishment against the human body, as Foucault considers it.[93] Too much power can also be assigned to authorities to regulate events at the pillory. A jurisdiction could decide in some cases to award or withhold protection, but it is very doubtful if any unit of government always felt confident to control the setting. A state, which could not generally suppress riots and which abolished the Tyburn procession because of difficulties in containing violent reactions, would not have felt certain of its ability to control the crowd at the pillory.[94] Elizabeth Canning, convicted of perjury in 1754, was spared traditional punishment, because the lord chief justice feared that violence might erupt if she were pilloried.[95] In normal circumstances, however, the authorities may have felt no pressing obligation to protect people at the pillory.[96] There, expressions of rage were expressions of popular morality and traditional notions of community justice; they were not directed at the state.

Urban riots represented traditional group values and to some extent were politicized. The lower classes were very familiar with other formal ways of expressing their values. The "skimmington," the "stang ride," and other forms of "rough music" were traditional, ritualistic ways by which rural communities would publicly shame and sometimes assault wife-beaters, cheats, and others who transgressed moral boundaries.[97] "Rough music" survived the transition from the country to the city, and from the premodern to the modern world, it was extensively used in all settings against informers, crimps, strikebreakers, enclosures, witches, and unpopular officials.[98] These rituals were more than just statements of popular values. They were intended to cause the permanent humiliation and perhaps physical chastisement of offenders.[99] A common urban variation of "rough music" was the ritual submerging in water of pickpockets and homosexuals as an alternative to invoking the process of law.[100] Ducking was not just a token punishment because culprits were sometimes subjected to lengthy ordeals that they did not survive. The sometimes deadly nature of this form of rough justice was fully recognized.[101] The courts also informally recognized it as standard popular practice, and rarely was anyone punished for deaths related to ducking.[102]

In these forms of "rough music" and at the pillory, violence was considerable. Punishment was administered formally, ceremoniously, usually at a distance, and was the result of applying a community standard, not an individual or collective whim.[103] Neither kind of punishment can be equated with generalized street violence. A pattern drawer named Clark was stoned to death in Bethal Green in 1771. Clark had provided the principal evidence against two men who had been convicted and executed, but he was ritually pelted with bricks by a crowd of two thousand. It took three hours for him to die.[104] Although these illegal executions were not always tolerated openly—several people were arrested for Clark's murder and two were subsequently executed.[105] Such executions commonly occurred in eighteenth-century London.[106] Even at the end of the century, serious public disturbances were as frequent in London as hanging days, and a significant number of them were occasioned by extralegal demonstrations of community justice that resulted in loss of life.[107]

THE PILLORY AND POPULAR VALUES

The demise of the pillory has been generally linked by scholars to the inability of the state to contain violence at the pillory.[108] However, its treacherous nature as a state weapon against radicals was the immediate cause of its downfall.[109] During its long existence, the pillory, because it represented a mobilization of popular feeling through the judicial process, was a unique and direct link between an elite-dominated criminal justice system and traditional lower-class values. Little attention has, however, been paid to the use of the pillory as a setting for examining the nature and strength of popular values.

It is difficult to analyze patterns of imposing the pillory in a particular jurisdiction because it was a penalty not often used. Individual courts applied local policies in imposing it and invoked different policies regarding its administration and control.[110] Many criminal penalties were ordered by eighteenth-century courts but were never applied. It is impossible to know how many individuals ordered to the pillory actually suffered punishment there. Press coverage of the spectacle of the pillory is unreliable about its incidence; most pilloryings were not reported. Incidents involving excessive violence might usually have attracted the attention of the press, but in a world where public riots were commonplace, individual incidents might go unreported. William Cobbett, in justifying his view that the state intended to harm Daniel Eaton in the pillory for his blasphemous libel in publishing the works of Tom Paine, noted the punishment given to a convicted perjurer, pilloried at the same pillory the previous day. According to Cobbett, the perjurer was almost killed.[111] Yet the event was not reported in the press of 1812—a time when riots in London were becoming rare, and the pillory itself had become obsolescent.

The many detailed accounts that are given in the press are unreliable indicators of the violence that may have occurred. Some are very descriptive of crowd animosity.[112] As indicators of the injuries suffered by a culprit, they are likely instances of eighteenth-century journalistic hyperbole.[113] Victims were typically and consistently described as "severely pelted."[114] It is impossible to know precisely what "severely pelted" meant or to adduce from it the level of violence applied or injury incurred. When injured offenders were reported to have died after being pilloried, the causes of their death are unclear. Many sentences to the pillory were accompanied by prison terms. Deaths from typhus and other diseases in Georgian prisons were many. When Salmon, one of the notorious thief-takers of 1756 was badly injured in the pillory and later died in prison, his injuries may not have been the fatal elements of his punishment.

Nonetheless, reports of crowd behavior at the pillory do reflect the popular morality of the time. Perjury can occur in a variety of situations and legal contexts.[115] Perjury involving falsely informing for reward money on individuals who were later executed invariably attracted the extreme animosity of crowds. Organized displays of such animosity were by no means injurious to the state. In fact, they drew attention to the low-level snitches within an incompetent law enforcement system and away from the system that encouraged them. Those who perjured in other contexts could, at the pleasure of the crowds, be treated with consideration.

Other offenders sent to the pillory included individuals convicted of attempted rape, particularly in cases involving children. The City of Westminster used the pillory for rapists.[116] So did the courts in the county of Surrey and in London.[117] Those punished for child molestation usually suffered; however, not every court used the pillory for this offense. The petty and quarter sessions of the criminal courts in the City of London convicted twenty-eight men for attempted rape between 1740 and 1816 but pilloried none of them, although almost half of all cases involved attempted rape against children.[118] However, the courts in the city regularly sent to the pillory individuals convicted of the misdemeanor of "assault with intent to commit sodomy"—a phrase used to address propositioning and a variety of consensual acts.

Eighteenth-century society was much more concerned with homosexuality than with heterosexual misconduct. Its concern strengthened in the early nineteenth century when homosexuals were frequently executed. In the early 1760s, however, homosexuals were increasingly being arrested on noncapital charges. Many of these prosecutions in London resulted from activities directed at homosexuals frequenting public places known to be favored by them. The activities were well organized by small groups of prosecutors motivated by concerns for public order, antigay sentiment, or even monetary consideration. Elsewhere in London, prosecutors raided "molly houses" or homosexual clubs, and prosecutions resulting from these raids almost invariably resulted in noncapital prosecutions.[119] Homosexuals were undoubtedly treated harshly by the courts. Sodomy, rape, and associated misdemeanors or "assaults with intent" were parallel offenses in law. Prosecutions were theoretically subject to identical standards of proof, although sodomy cases in courts involved consensual acts and were therefore victimless. Despite the legal difficulties of prosecuting sodomy as a capital felony or as a misdemeanor, sodomy was dealt with very severely in law. Court statistics indicate that the Old Bailey, where all capital cases originating in London and most other parts of the metropolitan area were tried, heard fewer cases of sodomy than of rape. However, accused sodomites stood a much greater chance of being convicted than accused rapists. If convicted, sodomists were likely to be executed. Cases of sodomy as a misdemeanor were generally tried in the city quarter sessions in London; a few were heard in the Old Bailey. During the century, twice as many accused sodomites as accused rapists were prosecuted, and they were more likely to be convicted than rapists.[120]

Use of the pillory for homosexual offenders is another reflection of a greater preoccupation with them than with heterosexual predators. The preoccupation was more than a reflection of an elite judicial perspective. The system of prosecution was a private one, and it was generally individuals, not the courts, who initiated cases. Once a charge was made, it was heard by a magistrate in London who was very much a member of the national elite.[121] If the magistrate chose, the case was heard by a grand jury and subsequently if a true bill were found, by a trial jury. Members of these juries were not members of the upper classes. Juries were dominated by shopkeepers, tradesmen, and others of the "middling" orders.[122] Juries did not determine punishment, but they did deliver verdicts with a knowledge of what the punishment was likely to be. Pillorying of convicted sodomites had at least the tacit approval of the middle classes.

London was not consistent in its use of the pillory during the eighteenth century. Between 1741 and 1763, homosexuals were routinely pilloried, but after 1763, the pillory was rarely used. During the next half century it was used only twice: in 1773 and 1779.[123] In 1810, London revived the pillory for homosexual offenses, and five of the ten men convicted in that year were sentenced to it. It was used again in 1813 for a convicted sodomite. The pillory was then abandoned for all purposes by the city, and most homosexuals convicted on capital charges were not put in the pillory.[124] Nonetheless, in practice and in the popular mind, the pillory was closely associated with homosexual offenders, and violent crowd reactions occurred when "unnatural crimes" were the focus of punishment.[125] In nineteenth-century London, six members of the infamous "Vere Street coterie," habitués of a "molly house," were pilloried in the city of Westminster of 1810. Even at this late date for the use of the pillory, the spectacle had been orchestrated in a classic way. A well-motivated crowd prepared for the punishment days in advance, and easy access of the miscreants was provided in the procession to the pillory and at the punishment itself.[126] More than a hundred officers helped prevent several of the culprits from being killed. However, it was believed that had the weather not been dry, deaths would have occurred due to the crowd smothering the offenders with wet debris.

Extremely hostile and persistent judicial attitudes developed toward homosexuals in early nineteenth-century Britain, because of the greatly increased propensity of the state of execute individuals convicted capitally on charges of sodomy. However, reliance of this propensity assumes previous tolerance.[127] Eighteenth-century society often did not want to execute sodomites or to prosecute them on capital charges.[128] However, intolerance of homosexuals was strongly evident. Changing British law to permit capital prosecutions of only blackmailers threatening accusations of homosexual misconduct is a dramatic consequence of fears that only blackmail was a threat to harshly antipathetic social attitudes.

The elite created and changed the law and controlled most of its administration, although other social classes populated juries and the ranks of prosecutors. The general populace had opportunities to express its feelings in various spectacular and formal settings. Harsh punishments administered by the state were only problematic when the audience was unsympathetic to the messages being conveyed. Harsh punishments administered by the crowd within a state structure were only problematic when the uncontrolled nature of the crowd's violence cast doubt on the ability of the authorities to maintain public order. Spectacular punishments of both kinds have potential as indicators of the values of both the government and the populace.

The pillory was used as a state weapon against dissenters, although its success was due to the independence of popular feelings. Events at the pillory suggest strong popular animadversion of two particular groups: informers and homosexuals. Qualitative evidence about these events do not reveal the strength of such animadversion. Systematic analysis of events at the pillory offers the possibility of providing additional evidence.

In the year 1763, press reports described ten pilloryings involving sixteen people.[129] One individual was punished for attempted rape, five for fraud, six for perjury, and four for homosexual offenses. Andrew Brady, a sixty-year-old shoeblack was punished in Westminster for "ravishing Sarah Gregory, a girl of ten years old and giving her the foul disease."[130] Reports of Brady's treatment suggest crowd animosity but do not describe the extent of crowd violence. Brady was "severely pelted by the mob whilst standing, and all the way to the Gatehouse." No injury was reported, however, and the press did not report incidents at two additional times he was sentenced to the pillory. However, another man was sentenced to the pillory for "ravishing" in the same year that he committed suicide in prison before sentence could be imposed.[131]

Accounts of the six perjurers indicate much more favorable treatment than Brady received. A group of three perjurers were treated well, even generously, by the crowd, and "their tears and grey hairs drew such compassion from the people, that instead of pelting they collected money for them."[132] More than advanced age probably assured favorable treatment for these perjurers. Their crime had no connection to "blood money" but involved a civil suit relating to the ownership of an estate in Leicestershire. Another perjurer named Benjamin Franklin, who had committed his crime with the intention of defrauding the bankruptcy commissioners, was not apparently molested.[133] The only case involving perjury in the criminal courts was that of a man and wife who had sworn a false alibi for a man later convicted of robbery. On the pillory at Croyden in Surrey, the couple described the circumstances to the crowd and as a result was "not the least insulted."[134] The mob at the pillory had generally little interest in the punishment of nonviolent criminals or others whose perjury was not related to informing for profit.[135]

The five frauds who were pilloried in 1763 included three sailors and a woman who were guilty of obtaining money under false pretenses. They were treated well, and "no one attempted to pelt them."[136] A man named Parsons, the main mover in the affair of the "Cock Lane ghost," had concocted an elaborate and profitable fraud linking necromancy and blackmail. His sophisticated fraud deceived some of the press for a time. Parsons had compounded his fraud with the gulling of the London public, a clear affront to the smart Cockneys of the city. When the venue of his punishment was announced, "a great mob was assembled, and, to the scandal of humanity, had prepared every offensive ingredient, in order to make a sacrifice of that unhappy and ruined man." The authorities did not make him stand at the pillory. When he finally did undergo his punishment, the public had changed its attitude. "He was not in the least pelted, but rather pitied, and about ten guineas were collected for him by the spectators." He stood at the pillory two more times and did well on both occasions, being treated kindly and receiving more money.[137]

The other three reported pilloryings of 1763 involved four homosexuals. Treatment given was markedly different in each case. Thomas Powell was treated well by a crowd that behaved "with the greatest decency and order," attributable in part to his punishment being in the better-governed jurisdiction of London.[138] The second pillorying occurred in Kent and resulted from the consensual sexual activity between two men, one of whom was a clergyman and a baronet. "The populace pelted the Divine suitable to his crime" but no other evidence indicates a level of violence.[139] The third homosexual, "who stood on the pillory at Bow, for sodomy, was killed by the mob." The coroner's jury brought in their verdict of willful murder, and some individuals were taken into custody.[140] Prosecution in this murder was, however, halfhearted. No indictments were brought by the corner's jury, and positive action was only achieved when a private prosecution was brought by a gentleman who had witnessed the death. Two men, Richard Bacon and Samuel Rogers, were tried at the assizes in Essex and acquitted. Two others, Thomas Drybury and John Drybury, were indicted by the grand jury but were never apprehended.[141] The only positive result of court action in this last case was to ascertain that the victim, Daniel Lobley, had been stoned to death and had not died from strangulation, smothering, or other causes.

The events of 1763 suggest that crowds were capable of generosity as well as violence; they also appeared to display a collective morality that was not always predictable. Too much should not, however, be made of the decent treatment given to Thomas Powell who was punished in London. Other cases of homosexuals pilloried in London at the same time were likely to involve the restraint of crowds by effective law enforcement.[142] In other jurisdictions, the experience was different. Outside of London, only one instance was reported of a homosexual being treated well in the pillory. In 1764 in rural Cambridgeshire, a fifteen-year-old miscreant, Jonathan Glynn, was not molested by the populace, who were pretty numerous on this occasion. The lad was fully sensible of his crime and the indulgence he received, for which he kneeled down and thanked the public."[143] Pilloried homosexuals were not treated as well as Jonathan Glynn in London.

Many people were described in newspapers as being ordered to the pillory, but no accounts of their experiences were later provided. A lack of reportage did not necessarily indicate benign treatment; newspapers did not generally report Lobley's death. Moreover, reports in newspapers of the same event are often so similar as to suggest identical provenance. Nonetheless, similar reports of one event indicate that popular values were being expressed at the pillory. Rough treatment of homosexuals appears to be more than a general inclination on the part of a "fierce and volatile" crowd ready and willing to mete out violence to pilloried individuals, without regard for the nature of their offenses.[144]

POPULAR VALUES AND DEATHS IN THE PILLORY

Approaches to assessment of public morality suffer from the disadvantage of relying too heavily on the wording of newspaper accounts, which are characterized by rote language, exaggeration, and great selectivity. However, the spectacle at pillories resulted in fatalities, and violent death is a finite indicator of extreme crowd reactions and of the strength of the moral outrage that causes death. If patterns of such deaths are found to be arbitrary, crowd violence at pillories can be seen as generalized and aimless. A search of primary sources from 1730 to 1830 yielded at least six instances of people who probably died in the pillory between 1729 and 1786.[145] The number is conservative, because it excludes cases in which pelted individuals were reported to have been badly injured during their ordeals. The number is expansive in that it includes individuals who reportedly died within a day or two of their ordeals—the assumption being that the gaol fever endemic in Newgate Prison can be discounted as a cause of death in such cases. All deaths in the pillory or associated with it occurred in London, which reflects the contemporary practice of defining this punishment as an urban phenomenon.

Deaths of pilloried criminals occurred in 1729, 1732, 1756, 1763, 1777, and 1780. Two other deaths occurred in 1759 and 1786 when members of a crowd were killed by constables endeavoring to protect their charges. The additional two deaths seem to reflect the general level of violence at pillories. The circumstances of these eight deaths closely resemble the pattern of violence identified for 1763. One involved forgery; one, extortion; three, perjury; three, homosexuality.

The forger, a man named Hale, died in 1729, three days after being in the pillory. He falsified a promissory note, and the crime was purely a commercial transaction involving a threat to property. It is not known why he attracted the ire of the crowd, if indeed he did. His injury could have resulted from over-enthusiasm rather than malice.[146] Another death occurred at the pillorying of Aylett (variously Ayelette or Aylette) for perjury in 1786. He was a wealthy attorney who had abused his office as a member of Parliament to avoid a writ of debt. As was predicted in the press, his experience in the pillory was eased by the extraordinary measures—attributed to Aylett's wealth and privilege—taken by the city to protect him. The death that occurred was of a member of the crowd killed by the police. Tremendous ill feeling had been expressed toward the culprit by the press, and one account later regretted that Aylett had not been the fatality. The crowd's dislike was attributable to Aylett's profession, or his place in it, as well as to his blatant abuse of his position. Regret was expressed that he had not been made "a striking example of the herd of base pettifogging law practitioners [that] are the leaches of society, ever feeding upon the blood and vitals of their fellow creatures."[147] Aylett's co-conspirator, Christopher Atkinson, a former member of Parliament had stood in the pillory the previous year and had been similarly well protected and came to no harm.[148]

The two perjurers actually killed in the pillory were professional thief-takers who specialized in testifying against the innocent for reward money.[149] The case of the four convicted in 1756 has already been described. The violence at the pillory was considerable, and one or perhaps two of the pilloried convicts were killed. In 1732, John Waller, alias Trevor, was a professional perjurer who operated in the circuit courts, swearing on behalf of the prosecution at trials for robbery. When he was finally convicted of perjury and sentenced to the pillory, a group of men, including one who had lost a brother to Waller's practices, planned to— and did—kill him in the pillory. A coroner's jury, which had plenty of evidence as to their identities, chose not to indict the group. Two men were, however, eventually convicted and executed for Waller's murder.[150] Only these capital convictions resulted in deaths at the pillory and occurred because of the obviously premeditated nature of Waller's murder.

The deaths in 1763, 1777, and 1780 were all of homosexuals. Daniel Lobley died from stoning. Little effort was made to bring his tormentors to trial, and his death attracted relatively little attention. In 1777, Ann Marrow was pilloried for fraud. She had been convicted of adopting male disguises and had participation in marriage ceremonies with unsuspecting women, ostensibly to appropriate their savings. Reports of her activities emphasized her deviant sexuality, and some omitted mention of the criminal aspects of her behavior. Her punishment was publicized in advance, an unusual circumstance. In the pillory, she was stoned, at least blinded, and, in some accounts, killed.[151] At the time, people who were convicted of fraud were rarely punished in the pillory, and if they were, they were not badly treated.

Lesbianism was neither legally proscribed nor informally sanctioned, except to the extent that society in the eighteenth century went to extraordinary lengths to deny its existence.[152] Women dressing and passing as men were frequently mentioned, but unlike their male counterparts, their sexual preference was almost never described.[153] The savagery of the crowd against Ann Marrow can only be understood as a reaction of people forced to confront an aspect of female sexuality with which they did not care to become familiar. Marrow's crime was rare but not unique. In 1746, Mary (alias Charles, alias George, alias William) Hamilton was convicted at Taunton quarter sessions in Somerset as "an uncommon, notorious cheat" for posing as a man to "marry" approximately fourteen women. Hamilton's motivations were not addressed directly, but reports of the case clearly suggest a sexual purpose.[154] She was sentenced to six months in prison and public whippings at four locations.

The last death of a homosexual in the pillory occurred in 1780.

William Smith, a plasterer, and Theodosius Reid, or Read, a coachman, were tried at St. Margaret's Hill after being caught together in a coffee house. Although accounts vary, one of them, probably Reid, certainly died; the other man may have died. Evidence exists that Reid was forced into a device that was too high for him and too small to fit his head properly. A coroner's jury decided on a verdict of "Strangled in the Pillory." Contemporary opinion, including that of the jury and Edmund Burke, a member of Parliament, agreed that the "severity of the mob" was at least a strongly aggravating factor in Reid's death.[155] Reid died because of bad luck, bad management, and the animosity of the crowd.

The only death that occurred at the pillorying of an extortionist was in 1759 when a member of the crowd was killed by a constable protecting Scrimshaw and Ross.[156] The two culprits had extorted or had attempted to extort money from a man who they threatened to expose or prosecute because of his homosexuality. At the pillory, they aroused the crowd's traditional hatred of informers and homosexuality. The crime practiced by Scrimshaw and Ross aroused such public antipathy that it later came to be a capital offense. If they had been convicted of extortion by blackmail fifteen or twenty years later, they would have faced the gallows.

Clearly, the populace was not altogether arbitrary in its behavior at the pillory, and the crowd generally expressed its own standards of moral conduct. Of the eight documented deaths, two cases involved false swearing to ensure a criminal conviction; three involved homosexuality; and a sixth reflected a combination of homosexuality and perjury—two prime objects of crowd resentment.

CONCLUSION

Public executions allowed crowds to express their feeling or actively engage in the death of the condemned.[157] Relatively little effort was made by authorities to control the nature of the ritual, and involvement of the crowd was an effective public means of demonstrating the neutrality of the law.[158]

The pillory allowed crowds to participate in punishments more directly and formally. With its strong connections to traditional forms of community justice, and with rioting and rowdiness as expressions of political communication, the pillory provided a familiar and structured setting for the expression of popular beliefs. A state that relied on ritual and participatory expressions of morality controlled popular feelings when it could. That the pillory did not seem to work well when manipulated in highly politicized contexts does not detract from its value. Violence at the pillory cost the state very little. It was, in fact, valuable in providing a legitimate place to celebrate the universal moral values the state was supposed to represent. Informers and homosexuals were hated by the mob, but their existence or punishment had no political implications at the pillory. The state's acceptance of crowd values at the pillory reflected its purpose of incorporating traditional values within a legal structure dominated by an elite.

The hatred of "blood money" informers and perjurers came easily to the populace. The state had little objection to seeing individual perjurers become the objects of popular resentment that might otherwise have been directed at the system that produced them. Working-class animosity toward homosexuals existed generally and is well documented in contemporary sources.[159] Recent explanations of that animosity address its more virulent nineteenth-century forms and focus on state concerns for using moral pressures to limit diversity of thought and behavior. The sources of these pressures are the need for a regimented, family-oriented workforce and a desire by the state to defuse ideas contrary and subversive to conventional beliefs.[160]

However, in England in the eighteenth century, people were relatively immune to moral direction or control. They were immune to the downward mobility experienced by many males who moved to urban areas. Reduced social status is often accompanied by a search for other sources of esteem and means of assertion. Attitudes of urban males toward gender issues, including female and male sexuality, undoubtedly changed during these times. These changes may have been caused by compensatory notions of "masculinity," which, as in modern society, constrain and inhibit while providing a way to express superiority.[161] Whatever caused these changes, the virulent popular feelings of hatred were concentrated and expressed through legal structures of the eighteenth century.

The legal system of the time was not characterized by cruelty and incompetence. Modern assessments frequently focus on its sophistication and suitability for its apparent purposes.[162] Acceptance of the extralegal violence at the pillory should be seen as a function of the system eager to adapt itself to the beliefs of the governed, especially in relatively unimportant matters. Moreover, a society ruled by aristocrats was not always antithetical to mass violence and the values it represented. Violence was only perceived as a liability to the state when it subverted the needs of a growing middle class and when it became associated with political concerns for public order.[163] The failure of the use of the pillory against radicals like Daniel Eaton may have been the immediate cause of the pillory's demise. That failure, however, represented a new and general change, because the state could no longer rely on crowd reactions to reflect purely traditional values.

The use of the pillory against political dissent implied a strong threat of exposing miscreants to unrestrained mob violence, as evidenced by the reaction of Daniel Defoe to the prospect of his punishment in 1703.[164] The pillory had been, in the early eighteenth century, an effective weapon of deterrence, but attempts to use it against political dissidents failed in the 1790s and later, not because the mob had been subdued but because the state had come to misjudge the temper of the mobs.

Use of the pillory against homosexuals had no overtly political connotations. Nor does it appear to have been used to deter. The frequent violence against homosexuals undoubtedly served as cathartic demonstrations of collective and intense feelings about sexual behavior. The demonstrations also served as reminders of how dangerous a place the pillory could be when the punishment was arbitrated by a crowd that could at whim be rowdy, energetic, fickle, but always moralistic.

Intelligently mobilizing hateful feelings for purposes that are ultimately political is scarcely unknown in recent history. Reasons for the persistence of hate frequently lie more in the circumstances of its mobilization than in the nature of the feelings mobilized. In practice, violence at the pillory was directed against informers and homosexuals. The state supported a system that encouraged the first and was not particularly threatened by the second. Attacks against these people did not bolster state interests directly. However, a state structure allowed popular feelings about informers and homosexuals to be expressed freely and physically. It certainly helped legitimize the system by providing public reinforcement of the values of the system to the people it ruled. The use of the pillory may have manipulated the antipathies of the very lowest elements of society, but analyses of rioting London mobs agree that they represented a broad cross section of the population.[165] The few indications of the composition of crowds at the pillory also agree with the analyses.[166] Strong expressions of feelings, whether gestures of support or of hate, were not limited to the lowest social strata.

The notion of the pillory as a vehicle for conveying infamy alone contains its own contradiction. As Edmund Burke appreciated in 1780, the creation of formal and well-attended spectacles for the imposition of humiliation inevitably implies a strong potential for violent punishment. A ritual of physical confrontation between an offender and society stimulates expressions of feeling. The formal structure of the pillory channels passionate feelings while subjecting those feelings to some social constraint: "For there is so little distance between the object of public shame and public detestation, that one produces the other: detestation then naturally begets outrage, and the law which meant a lesser punishment produces in the end the greatest of all punishments."[167] The legal system of eighteenth-century England demonstrated an advanced appreciation of the manipulation of hateful public feelings as a weapon of political power.

NOTES

1. This approach is very Durkheimian in nature. A major expression of it is represented by Kai T. Erikson (1966), in *Wayward Puritans: A Study in the Sociology of Deviance* (New York: John Wiley).

2. Colin Sumner (1979), *Reading Ideologies: An Investigation into the Marxist Theory of Ideology and Law* (London: Academic Press).

3. E. P. Thompson (1978), "Eighteenth Century English Society: Class Struggle Without Class?" *Social History* 3: 139.

4. Antonio Gramsci (1971), *Selections from the Prison Notebooks*, trans. Quintin Hoare and Geoffrey Nowell Smith (New York: International Publishers).

5. Douglas Hay et al., eds. (1975), *Albion's Fatal Tree: Crime and Society in Eighteenth-Century England* (New York: Pantheon).

6. Michael Ignatieff (1979), *A Just Measure of Pain: The Penitentiary in the Industrial Revolution, 1750–1850* (London: Macmillan); Michel Foucault (1979), *Discipline and Punishment: The Birth of the Prison,* trans. Alan Sheridan (New York: Vintage Books).

7. The characterizations are those of Philippe Nonet and Philip Selznick (1978), *Law and Society in Transition: Toward Responsive Law* (New York: Harper Colophon).

8. Succinct accounts showing the technical differences between the two systems as they existed in England are included in J. H. Baker (1977), "Criminal Courts and Procedures at Common Law," in *Crime in England 1550–1800*, ed. J. S. Cockburn (Princeton, N.J.: Princeton Univ. Press), 43–57; and A. H. Manchester (1978), "Legal Administration," in *Crime and Law in Nineteenth Century Britain,* ed. W. R. Cornish et al. (Dublin: Irish Univ. Press), 111–52.

9. Hay et al. (1975).

10. David Philips addresses the changing concerns of a society increasingly influenced by the urban bourgeois in his discussion of the issues surrounding the protracted efforts to establish a modern police force (David Philips [1980], " 'A New Engine of Power and Authority': The Institutionalization of Law Enforcement in England 1780–1830," in *Crime and the Law: The Social History of Crime in Western Europe since 1500,* ed. V. A. C. Gatrell, Bruce Lenman, and Geoffrey Parker [London: Europa], 1550–89). Those efforts began in 1770 but were not successful until 1829. See also Allan Silver (1967), "The Demand for Order in Civil Society: A Review of Some Themes in the History of Urban Crime, Police and Riot," in *The Police: Six Sociological Essays,* ed. David J. Bordua (New York: John Wiley), 124.

11. Foucault (1979), 56.

12. By the late eighteenth century, only about a third of those capitally convicted in England and Wales were actually executed (Baker [1977], 43).

13. Hay et al. (1975), 41.

14. Two recent studies suggest that the reprieve process was indeed one based on identifiable criteria (Peter King [1984], "Decision-Makers and Decision-Making in the English Criminal Law, 1750–1800," *Historical Journal* 27: 25–58; and Richard Mackesy [1993], "Lethal Lottery or Coherent Scheme? Executions and Rationality in Eighteenth Century England" [Ph.D. diss., City Univ. of New York]). However, given the large number of cases involved and the primitive state of the organizational ways of reviewing them, it is clear that the process was frequently unpredictable in individual cases.

15. When Colonel Despard and his associates were executed for treason in 1803, they came close to receiving the full penalty for their offense. Only the direct intervention of the king caused the most barbaric elements of the punishment to be remitted (*Notes and Queries* [1908], 10th series, 10 [Oct. 31]: 354–55; and *Notes* [1880] 6th series, 1 [June 12]: 476–77).

16. See Romilly's famous speech on the subject in the House of Commons in 1813 (Sir Samuel Romilly [1820], *The Speeches of Sir Samuel Romilly in the House of Commons,* ed. William Peter [London: James Ridgway], 462).

17. When a group of smugglers was sentenced to death in 1749, five were ordered to be hanged in chains and the other two to be "hung only as common malefactors." The latter were said to have been greatly relieved by their good fortune. When the other five were fitted with chains on the day of their execution, the process of fitting seems to have caused them more distress than any other part of the proceedings (Cal Winslow [1975], "Sussex Smugglers," in Hay et al., 119–66).

18. The body of William Jobling, hanged in Durham in 1832 for the murder of a magistrate, was carried fifteen miles to Jarrow by an escort that included a troop of hussars and two companies of infantry. There the corpse was stripped, smeared with tar, reclothed, and gibbetted. The surreptitious removal of the

body some days later was an example of many attempts by the populace to thwart punishment of a postmortem nature (*Notes and Queries* [1930] 158 [May 17]: 357–58).

19. Peter Linebaugh (1977), "The Ordinary of Newgate and His Account," in *Crime in England 1550–1800*, 246–69.

20. The abolition of public executions was greatly delayed by efforts of total abolitionists who reasoned that removing executions from public view would serve to undercut potential support for repealing the death penalty in its entirety (David D. Cooper [1974], *The Lesson of the Scaffold* [London: Allen Lane]).

21. The crowd at the execution of Henry Fauntleroy, the gentleman forger, in 1824 was estimated to comprise 100,000 people (*Annual Register* [1824], 66, part 2: 163). In the previous century, crowds were never of a compatible size at executions.

22. James Boswell observed at one execution that "no less than four diseased persons had themselves rubbed with the sweaty hands of malefactors in the agonies of death, and believed that this would cure them" (quoted in Thomas W. Laqueur [1989], "Crowds, Carnival and the State in English Executions, 1604–1868," in *The First Modern Society: Essays in English History in Honor of Lawrence Stone,* ed. A. L. Beier, David Cannadine, and James M. Rosenheim [Cambridge: Cambridge Univ. Press], 341).

23. Peter Linebaugh (1975), "The Tyburn Riot Against the Surgeons," in Hay et al., 65–117.

24. See *Gentleman's Magazine* (Mar. 1733), 154; *Annual Register* (1805), 47: 369–70.

25. Quoted in Cooper (1974), 98.

26. William Fox, twice capitally convicted, was granted a reprieve "just as the cap was pulling over his eyes" (*Gentleman's Magazine* [Apr. 1777], 198).

27. Linebaugh (1977); J. A. Sharpe (1985), " 'Last Dying Speeches': Religion, Ideology and Public Execution in Seventeenth-Century England," *Past and Present*, no. 107 (May): 144–67. Contemporary published sources may lead us to underestimate the numbers of condemned who flouted their crimes on the gallows. An obituary of Paul Lorrain, longtime ordinary of Newgate, commented on his practice of falsifying confessions for those who were unrepentant: "It is certain the good man thought it a Matter of Consequence to the State, as well as his own private Emolument, that a Person publicly convicted of Crimes should not go out of the world with Lye in his Mouth" (*The Country Journal: or, The Craftsman* [Apr. 26, 1735], 78). A very rewarding perquisite of the ordinary was the publication of the last speeches of the condemned (Linebaugh [1977]).

28. E. P. Thompson (1974), "Patrician Society, Plebeian Culture," *Journal of Social History* 7: 382–405.

29. George Rudé (1980), *Ideology and Popular Protest* (New York: Pantheon).

30. Thompson (1978), 164.

31. Metropolitan London comprised the small and centrally located City of London, the larger city of Westminster, and urbanized parts of the home counties: Essex, Hertfordshire, Middlesex, and Surrey. Each of these jurisdictions had its own government, including petty and quarter sessions. Felonies committed in London and Westminster and in the county of Middlesex were heard in the Old Bailey. The other counties heard felonies in assizes courts.

32. E. P. Thompson (1971), "The Moral Economy of the English Crowd in the Eighteenth Century," *Past and Present*, no. 50 (Feb.): 76–136.

33. Thompson (1971), 91.

34. For riots originating in electoral disputes, see Max Beloff (1938), *Public Order and Popular Disturbances: 1660–1714* (London: Oxford Univ. Press); John A. Cannon (1973), *Parliamentary Reform: 1640–1832* (Cambridge: Cambridge Univ. Press); and Nicholas Rogers (1978), "Popular Protest in Early Hanoverian London," *Past and Present*, no. 79 (May): 70–100. For the riots of 1710, see Geoffrey Holmes (1976), "The Sacheverell Riots: The Crowds and the Church in Early Eighteenth-Century London," *Past and Present*, no. 72 (Aug.): 55–85. For the Wilkesite and Gordon riots of 1768 and 1780, see George Rudé (1964), *The Crowd in History: A Study of Popular Disturbances in France and England, 1730–1848* (London: John Wiley), 50–65. For discussion of riot as a traditional and apolitical form of working-class expression, see John Stevenson (1979), *Popular Disturbances in England 1700–1870* (New York: Longman), 47–50. A discussion of riot and other forms of disorder as "community politics" is given in John Bohstedt (1983), *Riots and Community Politics in England and Wales 1790–1810* (Cambridge: Harvard Univ. Press).

35. *Mentalités* connotes group views that are more traditional than political. For a discussion of them as a concept, see Michel Vovelle (1977), "Le Tourant des Mentalités en France 1750–1789: La 'Sensibilité' Pre-Révolutionnaire," *Social History* 5 (May): 65–29; and Rudé (1980).

36. Bohstedt (1983), 5.

37. Bohstedt (1983), 209.

38. E. P. Thompson (1963), *The Making of the English Working Class,* (New York: Vintage Books); Mick Reed and Roger Wells, eds. (1990), *Class, Conflict and Protest in the English Countryside: 1700–1880* (London: Frank Cass), 136.

39. J. P. de Castro (1926), *The Gordon Riots* (Oxford: Oxford Univ. Press).

40. John H. Langbein (1977), *Torture and the Law of Proof: Europe and England in the Ancien Regime* (Chicago: Univ. of Chicago Press), 135–40.

41. Three Puritans convicted of blasphemy in 1637 were cruelly mutilated after being placed in the pillory. All their injuries were inflicted by the state and not by the crowd (T. B. Howell [1816–28], *A Complete Collection of State Trials and Proceedings for High Treason and Other Misdemeanors from the Earliest Period to the Year 1783* [London: Longman and others], 3: 749–55).

42. William Andrews (1899), *Bygone Punishments* (London), 138–42.

43. Sir James Stephen described the existence by 1839 of ninety-six classes of misdemeanor, many of which were common-law offenses that could also be prosecuted as statutory crimes. Consequently, a tremendous range of criminal behaviors could be subject to corporal punishment (Sir James F. Stephen [1883], *A History of the Criminal Law of England* [London: Macmillan], 1: 489–90).

44. Anthony Babington (1968), *The Power of Silence: A History of Punishment in Britain* (London: Robert Maxwell), 16–24; Sir Leon Radzinowicz (1948–68), *A History of English Criminal Law and Its Administration from 1750*, 4 vols. (London: Stevens and Sons), 1: 57–183.

45. The Isle of Man, which has its own judicial system, recently bowed to international pressure and initiated plans to abolish the practice of birching juvenile offenders. It also repealed the statute under which adults engaging in consensual homosexual activity could be given life imprisonment (Tony Farragher [1993], "Isle of Man to Scrap Birch at a Stroke," *The Guardian*, Mar. 6, sec. 1, p. 5).

46. A bibliography of the lash is as odd as it is extensive. Reverend William M. Cooper's work includes forty-nine chapters, but legal scholars will be dismayed to learn that only one addresses whipping as a penal sanction. Chapters such as "The Birch in the Boudoir" take pride of place (William M. Cooper [n.d.], *A History of the Rod in All Countries from the Earliest Period to the Present Time* [London: William Reeves]).

47. *Annual Register* (1806), 48: 457.

48. When a court in a town in Kent ordered a public flogging in 1815, the mayor sought volunteers to carry out the sentence. When none were forthcoming, he offered to pay any soldier in the nearby barracks who would undertake the task. When none was forthcoming, he was obliged to do the job himself (*Annual Register* [1815], 57: 72–73).

49. Andrews cites a number of examples of popular reactions against public whippings (Andrews [1899], 209–26).

50. Other punishments included the ducking stool, the bridle, the scold, and the branks. These usually represented punishments awarded informally and occasionally by local communities and without benefit of legal process. By the eighteenth century, these punishments can only be regarded as part of a traditional, perhaps obsolescent system of rural community justice. They had no place in the law (John W. Spargo [1944], *Juridical Folklore in England: Illustrated by the Ducking Stool* [Durham, N.C.: Duke Univ. Press], 284–329).

51. John Chamberlayne specifically identified the stocks as punishment for "Drunkards, Vagabonds, prophane Swearers, loose, idle, disorderly Persons, Nightwalkers, and the like" (John Chamberlayne [1718], *Magnae Britanniae Notitia, or, The Present State of Great Britain* [London: Timothy Godwin], 192). Andrews discusses the use of the stocks almost exclusively for drunkenness and

suggests that their use was ordered by magistrates until at least the late nineteenth century (Andrews [1899], 186–200). In the eighteenth century, stocks were regarded as the punishment only for egregious drunkenness. In the course of a trial for seditious libel in 1811, the spending of an hour in the stocks was described as the common punishment for drunkenness, but only when the offender was "very riotous indeed" (Howell [1816–28], 31: 539).

52. Chamberlayne noted pillorying as the common punishment for "Forgery, Cheating, Libelling, False Weights and Measures, Forestalling the Market, Offenses in Baking and Brewing" (Chamberlayne [1718], 191–92). A lengthy list of crimes for which the pillory was used before the early eighteenth century is included in Llewellyn Jewitt (1861), "The Pillory, and Who They Put in It," *The Reliquary* 1 (Apr.): 209–24.

53. A man being pilloried in the sixteenth century almost lost his life through strangulation when the rotted boards beneath his feet gave way, leaving him hanging by his neck and hands. A court awarded him damages from the town for its negligence (Andrews [1899], 157).

54. Thomas B. Macaulay (1913), *The History of England from the Association of James the Second* (London: Macmillan), 1: 476–84; Jane Lane (1949), *Titus Oates* (London: Andrew Dakers), 318–22.

55. "As to the Pillory, that is intended only to expose the offender to shame and infamy, and to mark him out to the public, as a person not fit to be trusted, but to be shunned and avoided by all creditable and honest men: never did the law design that he should be exposed to the peltings of a mob, or the assaults and injuries of a furious rabble, where the prisoner is so disguised as to defeat one main design of setting him there, which was, that he might be publicly known and observed. It is indeed a surprising neglect, that no effectual care has hitherto been taken to suppress these practices, especially considering the fatal consequences which have sometimes ensued from them, even to the loss of the poor man's life. . . . He is at that time in the hands of justice, and justice ought to protect him: when a man is at liberty, he is in many cases able to defend himself; but when he is in the custody of the law, and is thereby disabled from being his own defender, the law ought to be his security and defense against any injurious treatment" (Sollom Emlyn, ed. [1730], *Complete Collection of State Trials, and Proceedings for High Treason, and Other Crimes and Misdemeanors,* 2d ed. [London], 1: xxxvi–xxxvii).

56. Michael D. Gordon (1980), "The Invention of a Common Law Crime: Perjury and the Elizabethan Courts," *American Journal of Legal History,* Apr. 24, 145–70; Sir William Holdworth (1945), *A History of English Law,* 3d ed. (London: Methuen), 4: 407–80.

57. Professional perjurers openly offered their services to the criminal courts in the 1720s (Gerald Howson [1970], *Thief-Taker General: The Rise and Fall of*

Jonathan Wild [London: Hutchinson], 141). A century later the Old Bailey was still having difficulties with perjurers who made careers of swearing to assets they did not possess so that their employers could qualify for bail (London Central Criminal Court *Proceedings* [Mar. 3, 1835] 1: 708–24).

58. Howson (1970), 141.

59. Howell (1816–28), 19: 809.

60. *Annual Register* (1816), 58, part 2: 314–18; *The Whole Four Trials ...* (1816). The men were convicted of conspiracy at Middlesex quarter sessions and sentenced to lengthy prison terms. Because of a change in the law in 1816, the court could not, fortunately for them, send them to the pillory.

61. John D. Potter (1965), *The Fatal Gallows Tree* (London: Elek Books), 164–65.

62. The word *blackmail* was not used in this context until the nineteenth century. Previously, *extortion* was always used, despite the fact that its origins as a legal term involved misuses of authority for personal gain by government officials.

63. *R. v D'Arcy and Walker* (Dec. 1754), Corporation of London *Sessions Minute-Book* (hereafter *LSMB*); *R. v Robertson and Hunt* (1755), *Old Bailey Proceedings* (hereafter *OBP*), sessions ending Oct. 25; *R. v Kite* (1762), *OBP*, sessions ending Apr. 23. This finding is based on a comprehensive search of the records of the Corporation of London quarter sessions and the Old Bailey.

64. *Whitehall Evening-Post: or, London Intelligencer* (Nov. 25–27, 1755), p. 107.

65. *Gentleman's Magazine* (Mar. 1756), 147.

66. *Annual Register* (1759), 2: 99–100.

67. A barmaid, after her second attempt to extort money with accusations of rape, was told by the judge: "You should not play these tricks, young woman" (*R. v Foy* [1782], *OBP*, sessions beginning Dec. 4).

68. The ways in which the courts accepted this traditional means of redress and sometimes facilitated it are explored in Antony E. Simpson (1986), "The 'Blackmail Myth' and the Prosecution of Rape and Its Attempt in Eighteenth Century London: The Creation of a Legal Tradition," *Journal of Criminal Law and Criminology* 77: 101–50.

69. Gangs of professional criminals specializing in homosexual blackmail operated throughout the century. Horace Walpole's brother was a victim of a gang's allegation in 1751. Lord Castlereagh, the foreign minister, committed suicide in 1822 after being harassed by blackmailers. For a discussion of the widespread nature of homosexual blackmail, see Antony E. Simpson (1984), "Masculinity and Control: The Prosecution of Sex Offenses in Eighteenth Century London" (Ph.D. diss., New York Univ.), 509–84.

70. For discussion of how this transformation of the law was achieved outside of the legislature, together with consideration of its social context, see Antony E.

Simpson (1986), "The Development of the Law of Blackmail in Georgian England: Common Law Creation of a Capital Felony" (paper presented at the annual meeting of the American Society of Criminology, Atlanta, Oct.).

71. *Annual Register* (1762), 5, part 1: 75; Howell (1816–28), 19: 814.

72. *Annual Register* (1762), 5, part 1: 75.

73. William Minto (1869), *Daniel Defoe* (New York: Harper), 40.

74. A reproduction of this painting appears in William Lee (1869), *Daniel Defoe, His Life, and Recently Discovered Writing, Extending from 1716–1729* (London: J. C. Hotten).

75. Paul Dottin (1928), *The Life and Strange and Surprising Adventures of Daniel Defoe,* trans. Louise Ragan (London: Stanley Paul), 103–5.

76. Richard Baggs was pilloried for homosexual practices in Bristol in 1732, and the crowd "had resolved to use him severely." A large and armed group of miners hired by Baggs prevented an attack (*Gentleman's Magazine* [Sept. 2, 1732], 97–106).

77. House of Commons, *Parliamentary Debates* (Apr. 6, 1815) 30: 354–56.

78. A perjurer named Kelly, although well protected by "a very powerful posse of constables," had to be removed early "lest he should be entirely smothered." The report concludes: "So much for informers" (*The Times* [London] [Dec. 3, 1789], p. 3).

79. Another account, quoted in Jewitt ([1861], 209–24) states that she had previously been acquitted of murder in which a man was poisoned, and she was suspected of killing two other people with poison.

80. Andrew Knapp and William Baldwin, eds. (1819), *The New Newgate Calendar* (London: Cundee, 1819), 1: 428–30.

81. "It was formerly said, that the punishment of the *pillory* rendered a man infamous; but it will be found, that *gold leaf* will *guild* over every species of *guilt*" (*University Daily Register* [Nov. 28, 1785], p. 3). See also *The Times* (London) (Nov. 28, 1786), p. 2.

82. In 1798, between seventy and eighty people were arrested for treason, but no indictments were obtained against them. In the same year, five other people were tried for high treason, and all were acquitted (*Annual Register* [1799], 41, part 1: 195–201).

83. Clive Emsley (1981), "An Aspect of Pitt's 'Terror': Prosecutions for Sedition During the 1790s," *Social History*, May 6, 155–84.

84. Thompson (1963), 97, 604–5.

85. See the detailed account of Eaton's Pillorying in *Cobbett's Weekly Political Register* (June 13, 1812), 21: 748–49.

86. The government seems to have been extraordinarily slow to take a point that had been made decades ago. Subjecting radicals to the pillory was done at mid-century and again in the 1790s, but results generally were unfavorable to the

state (J. M. Beattie [1986], *Crime and the Courts in England: 1660–1800* [Princeton, N.J.: Princeton Univ. Press], 466; Stevenson [1979], 50, 165).

87. The pillory was outlawed for offenses other than perjury in 1816 and abolished altogether in 1837 (House of Lords, *Parliamentary Debates,* 56 Geo. III, c. 138 and 7 Will. IV & 1 Vic., c. 23).

88. Peter James Bossy was sentenced to the pillory for perjury in 1830. It was reported to be the first time in twelve years that this penalty had been given by a London court (*The Times* [London] [Apr. 23, 1830; June 5–6, 1830]).

89. Philips (1980).

90. House of Commons, *Parliamentary Debates* (July 5, 1815), 31: 112–27; (July 10, 1815), 31: 114–243; and (Feb. 22, 1816), 32: 803–5.

91. House of Commons, *Parliamentary Debates* (July 5, 1815), 31: 11–24.

92. *The Times* (London) (May 26, 1812), 3.

93. Foucault (1979), 8.

94. In the City of London, now London's financial district, scenes of rowdiness or violence were not tolerated. The pillorying there of Thomas Powell for "sodomitical practices" was attended by a crowd that behaved "with the greatest decency and order." Its behavior was not, however, attributable to tolerance of homosexuality but to "the good government of the city of London, and the respect which will always be paid by the people to the preference of the Magistrate, in the execution of his duty" (*Lloyd's Evening Post, and British Chronicle* [Dec. 21–23, 1763], pp. v, 1, 7–9). For discussion of the superior administrative structure and arrangements of the city, see C. J. Harman (1963), "The City Justices and Justice Rooms," *Guildhall Historical Association Transactions* 3: 33–38; and George Rudé (1971), *Hanoverian London: 1714–1808* (Berkeley: Univ. of California Press), 118–42.

95. The judge may in fact have been worried about violence on the part of Canning's many supporters. Her conviction resulted from her well-publicized allegations of abduction, which were eventually disproven but which were nonetheless widely believed (Lillian de la Torre [1945], *'Elizabeth is Missing,' or, Truth Triumphant: An Eighteenth Century Mystery* [New York: Knopf]).

96. J. M. Beattie suggests that, in the first half of the century, severe treatment of pilloried offenders often occurred with the tacit approval of the authorities. Sporadic efforts to protect the punished were generally more usual after 1750. Francis Place, who lived in London, believed that the authorities would generally tolerate a certain amount of violence when the crowd was hostile. Containment seems to have been the most practical policy (Beattie [1986], 614–16).

97. E. P. Thompson (1972), " 'Rough Music': Le Charivari Anglais," *Annales: Sociétiés, Économics, Civilizations* 27e année (Mar.–Apr.): 285–312.

98. Bohstedt (1983), 89; Stevenson (1979), 48–49.

99. Thompson (1972), 291–94.

100. One account referred to ducking as "the usual discipline" meted out to such offenders (*Whitehall Evening-Post, or London Intelligencer* [Oct. 24, 1755], pp. 107–9). One suspected homosexual was apprehended by a crowd that "carried him to a pump, stripp'd him almost naked, and pump'd him till he was almost dead" (*Whitehall Evening Post, or London Intelligencer* [Feb. 4–6, 1755], p. 2).

101. A citizen apprehended a man who had picked his pocket but refused to give the culprit to the mob because: "If I leave him to your Mercy you will whip him to Death, or drown him." The pickpocket was convicted and sentenced to transportation for seven years (*R. v Wenscot* [1743], *OBP,* sessions beginning Sept. 7).

102. John Fray, the instigator of a ducking resulting in the death of a pickpocket, was convicted of manslaughter for his part in the death (*OBP,* sessions beginning Sept. 24, 1785). At his trial, the judge observed to the jury that "this common error of punishing pickpockets by ducking is a thing that happens, we all know, very frequently . . . it is never accompanied with an intention by the parties acting in it of taking away the life of the offender." The judge added that such action was not strictly justifiable, "but yet, gentlemen, we are to consider, that we are men, and that the law gives some indulgence to the infirmities of human nature." Fray was imprisoned for six months and fined one shilling. Fray was probably only prosecuted because the pickpocket, a boy, had pleaded to be prosecuted rather than ducked and averred his inability to swim. The boy had been thrown in the river several times, and Fray was the last man to throw the boy into the river to his death.

103. Thompson (1972), 284. Thompson suggests that these structural characteristics distinguish these forms of punishment from lynching. His view perhaps fails to appreciate the consistency of the ritual use of lynching and its reliance as an institution on community support. See James M. Inverarity (1976), "Populism and Lynching in Louisiana, 1889–1896: A Test of Erikson's Theory of the Relationship Between Boundary Crises and Repressive Justice," *American Sociological Review* 41: 262–80.

104. *Gentleman's Magazine* (Apr. 1771), 189–90.

105. Six or seven were arrested. Robert Campbell and Henry Stroud were convicted of murder and hanged at the scene of their crime. Popular support for them was demonstrated by the large crowd attending the execution. A feared rescue attempt was thought to have been deterred by the presence of an unusually large number of officers (*Annual Register* [1777], 14, part 1: 96, 122).

106. Two months after the Clark stoning, a soldier who had given evidence for the Crown in a murder case was attacked by a mob. He was extricated with great difficulty by a group headed by two courageous aldermen (*Gentleman's Magazine* [June 1771], 231). For other examples of impromptu mob violence against informers, see Beattie (1986), 134–35.

107. Stevenson defines a "riot" as an event involving three or more persons, "mutual intent," and loss of life. He identifies 223 riots as occurring in London between 1780 and 1821. Of these, 10 were instances of "community justice" (Stevenson [1979], 306–7).

108. Ignatieff notes that the nature of events at the pillory was primarily a function of "the crowd's tacit support of the authorities' sentence" (Ignatieff [1989], 21). Stevenson characterizes the pillory as " 'licensed' community justice, which could backfire if the authorities misjudged the temper of the spectators" (Stevenson [1979], 50).

109. William Cobbett, an eyewitness to the pillorying of Daniel Eaton, described how Eaton was lauded and the court officers present were jeered: "This it was that was the real cause of putting an end to the punishment of the pillory!" (quoted in Thompson [1963], 605).

110. The courts of eighteenth-century Surrey used the pillory as a sentence approximately once every eighteen months, usually for homosexual offenses or child molestation (Beattie [1986], 465, 615). The Old Bailey imposed it most often for perjury, the indictable misdemeanor most likely to come before this court. It was occasionally given to homosexuals by the courts of the City of London but never to those convicted of attempted rape.

111. Thompson (1963), 605.

112. A convicted homosexual pilloried in London in 1762 was stripped naked by the crowd, which then "pelted and whipped him till he scarcely had any signs of life left; he was once pulled off the pillory, but hung by his arms till he was set up again and stood in that naked condition, covered with mud, till the hour was out, and then was carried back to Newgate" (*Gentleman's Magazine* [Aug. 1762], 549). Such accounts are common.

113. Newspapers were notorious for their exaggeration. The dramatist Richard Sheridan was reported severely wounded by Captain Mathews in his famous duel in 1772—one of the last duels with swords in England. The bloody nature of the encounter was thought to have diverted the subsequent interest of potential duelists from swords to pistols. Sheridan, apparently in relatively good health, was said to have enjoyed his short convalescence by reading newspaper accounts of his imminent demise (R. Crompton Rhodes [1933], *Harlequin Sheridan: The Man and the Legends, with a Bibliography and Appendices* [Oxford: Basil Blackwell], 49).

114. "Severely pelted" was the only description given of the treatment given to William Spence, convicted at Westminster quarter sessions of "attempted sodomy" (*London Evening-Post* [Feb. 26–29, 1778]). Such abbreviated descriptions were frequent.

115. Informing for reward money characterized the system for enforcing the law in its entirely until 1829. All retailers and others subject to excise taxes, licensing, and other regulations were subject to the attentions of informers anx-

ious for bribes or a share of the fines imposed by the courts. Informing was a well-organized and professional activity and was fully recognized. For examples of the routine expressions in the press of public distaste for informers, see *Gentleman's Magazine* (Sept. 3, 1733), 11–12; *Monthly Review* (Apr. 24, 1761), 218–21; *London Evening-Post* (Jan. 31, 1764); and (Feb. 2, 1764), p. 14; *Morning Chronicle, and London Advertiser* (Dec. 26, 1776), p. 28; *General Evening Post* (Mar. 24–26, 1785); *Universal Daily Register* (Jan. 18, 1786), p. 6; *The Times* (London) (Aug. 15, 1816), pp. 8–10; *Annual Register* (1822), 64, part 1; part 2: 176–80. A contemporary account of the intimate association between paid informing and the law enforcement system is given in Robert Holloway (1817), *A Letter to Sir Richard Ford, and the Other Police Magistrates upon the Prevalence of Gaming, and the Infamous Practices of Common Informers* (London: Vaughan Griffiths). See note 135 below.

116. Two cases of rape were reported in the press in 1766 (*Annual Register* [1766], 9, part 2: 84; *St. James's Chronicle, or British Evening-Post* [Jan. 28–30, 1766]).

117. Beattie (1986), 467, 615.

118. The total of twenty-eight men excludes people convicted of the lesser charge of simple assault. For discussion of the substance and application of the law of rape, patterns of its persecution, and victim characteristics, see Antony E. Simpson (1987), "Vulnerability and the Age of Female Consent: Legal Innovation and Its Effect on Prosecutions for Rape in Eighteenth Century London," in *Sexual Underworlds of the Enlightenment,* ed. G. S. Rousseau and Roy Porter (Manchester: Manchester Univ. Press), 181–205.

119. Simpson (1984), 437–45, 482–500.

120. Between 1730 and 1830, 294 men were tried for rape in the Old Bailey. Fifty-one were convicted, and of these, 28 were actually executed. Comparable figures for accused sodomites are 71 tried, 26 convicted, and 16 executed. In all courts handling indictable misdemeanors in the City of London, 81 men were prosecuted for attempted rape, and 37 were convicted. Of the 169 prosecuted for "attempted sodomy," 97 were convicted. Allegations of "attempted sodomy" heard by city magistrates were likely to be sent to a grand jury. Allegations of attempted rape were taken less seriously and were likely to be adjudicated summarily. For statistics documenting these findings, see Simpson (1984), 81–114, 821–22, 823, and 828–31. Related text discusses the development of the law in sexual offenses, the patterns and techniques of their prosecution, and their relationship to social structure and popular thought.

121. Nicholas Rogers (1979), "Money, Land, and Lineage: The Big Bourgeoisie of Hanoverian London," *Social History* 4: 437–54; Lucy Sutherland (1956), "The City of London in Eighteenth Century Politics," in *Essays Presented to Sir Lewis Namier,* ed. Richard Pares and A. J. P. Taylor (London: Macmillan), 49–74.

122. Beattie (1986), 378–99; Thomas R. Forbes (1978), *Crowner's Quest* (Philadelphia: American Philosophical Society); Thompson (1963), 468.

123. *R. v Smith alias Snooke* (1773), *LSMB*, Nov.; *R. v Coleman* (1779), *LSMB*, May. Thirty-six men were convicted of attempted sodomy between 1764 and 1809 (Simpson [1984], 820–21). Courts in the urbanized parts of Surrey tended to abandon use of the pillory after the 1760s (Beattie [1986], 615).

124. B. R. Burg (1983), *Sodomy and the Perception of Evil: English Sea Rovers in the Seventeenth Century Caribbean* (New York: New York Univ. Press), 29.

125. Francis Place, a contemporary observer, retained this view (Stevenson [1979], 50).

126. A lengthy contemporary newspaper account of pillorying of the "vere street coterie" is quoted in Henry S. Ashbee (1969), *Index of Forbidden Books* (1877; reprint, London: Sphere), 330–34. The unreliability of press reporting is indicated by a different account of the event that states that "no accident of any note occurred" (*Annual Register*, [1810], 52, part 1: 280–81).

127. For a discussion and documentation of eighteenth-century judicial and popular attitudes concerning homosexuality, see Simpson (1984). These sources also provide support for the related observations in the paragraphs that follow.

128. From approximately 1796, men capitally convicted in the Old Bailey of homosexuality would be executed almost every other year. Previously, executions for homosexuality in this jurisdiction occurred only in 1730 and 1776 (Simpson [1984], 828–31).

129. The year is chosen, because it represents the beginning of a period when homosexuals, who engaged in unacceptable, noncapital, public acts, were starting to be prosecuted regularly. A pillory death was also known to have occurred in 1763.

130. *Lloyd's Evening Post, and British Chronicle* (July 27–29, 1763). Brady must have been convicted of *attempted* rape as this crime when completed was a capital one. However, newspapers of the time commonly refer to such misdemeanors as "rapes." The description reflects the difficulties of prosecuting sexual assault as a capital crime and the consequent tendency to pursue the lesser charge.

131. James Reyley was convicted at the Salisbury (Wiltshire) assizes (*London Chronicle* [July 23–26, 1763]).

132. *Annual Register* (1763), 6, part 1: 79–80.

133. The report does not actually say how Franklin was treated, but public tolerance is assumed because of the lack of any mention of violence (*London Chronicle* [Aug. 20–23, 1763]).

134. *London Chronicle* [Aug. 6–9, 1763]. The crowd might not have been so tolerant if they had known that the robber was a professional who, on the scaffold some days later, publicly confessed to two unrelated murders (*London Chronicle*, [Aug. 11–13, 1763]).

135. Nonetheless, resentment against informers was by no means limited to those who swore falsely against the innocent in criminal trials. Throughout the century, there was tremendous antipathy toward those who informed on vendors for disobeying local regulations on trade. In the early part of the century, there was great ill feeling for those informing for rewards on unlicensed sellers of liquor. During two months in 1738, attacks on and prosecutions of these informers occurred regularly, sometimes daily. Informers were injured and sometimes killed. (*London Evening-Post* [Jan. and Feb. 1738]). By 1750 the government, anxious to maximize excise revenue from the sale of liquor, had greatly tightened its licensing system (Peter Clark [1983], *The English Alehouse: Social History. 1200–1830* [London: Longman], 166–94). Informers' activities and attacks on them had decreased in the 1750s, but informing against tradesmen for profit continued until the early nineteenth century. See note 78.

136. *London Chronicle* (Sept. 22–24, 1763).

137. *Lloyd's Evening Post*, and *British Chronicle* (Feb. 21–23; Mar. 14–16, 1763); *London Magazine* (Apr. 1763), 223.

138. *Lloyd's Evening Post, and British Chronicle* (Dec. 21–23, 1763).

139. *London Chronicle* (July 21–23, 23–26; Aug. 18–20; Oct. 1763).

140. *Annual Register* (1763), 6, part 1: 67. See also *Lloyd's Evening Post, and British Chronicle* (Apr. 4–6, 6–8, 1763); *London Magazine* (Apr. 1763), 223.

141. *South Eastern Circuit Indictments; Essex Felony; Summer 3d Geo: 3d; 1763*, PRO Assi 35 203/2; *South Eastern Circuit Agenda Book, 1763 through 1765*, PRO Assi 31/7.

142. John Lowther was spared because attempts to attack him were thwarted by "a greater number of peaceofficers [being] got together to prevent his being pelted, than ever were known on the like occasion" (*Annual Register* [1761], 4, part 1: 166). A man named Coleman *was* pelted, but two of those responsible were arrested (*London Evening-Post* [Aug. 10–12, 1779]).

143. *London Evening Post* (Aug. 11–14, 30; Sept. 1, 1764).

144. Burg (1983), 35–36.

145. The *Annual Register, Gentleman's Magazine*, and the *Old Bailey Proceedings* were searched for this period, and other magazines and newspapers from the Burney Collection in the British Museum were searched selectively, as were criminal biographies and other forms of "gallows literature."

146. Howell (1816–28), 17: 287–96.

147. *Universal Daily Register* (Nov. 28, 1785), 3; (Nov. 22, 1786), 3; (Nov. 23, 1786), 2; (Nov. 25, 1786), 2.

148. *Universal Daily Register* (Nov. 26, 1785), 2.

149. J. M. Beattie has identified a London pillory death in 1723 from manuscript records of the Surrey courts. John Middleton died by smothering under the mass of debris with which he had been pelted. He was convicted of making

a false accusation of treason and had probably obtained reward money (Beattie [1986], 467–68).

150. *Gentleman's Magazine* (May 1732), 774; (June 1732), 823; and (Oct. 1732), 1, 29; *R. v Dalton and Griffiths* (1732), *OBP*, sessions beginning Sept. 11; Knapp and Baldwin (1819) 1: 425–26.

151. *Annual Register* (1777), 20, part 2: 191–92; *Gentleman's Magazine* (July 1777), 348; (Aug. 1777), 403; Knapp and Baldwin (1819), 3: 395; *London Chronicle* (July 19–22, 1777), 75; *Morning Chronicle* (July 25; Aug. 4, 1777).

152. Faderman (1981), in *Sexual Underworlds of the Enlightenment*, 38–54.

153. Lynn Friedli (1987), " 'Passing Women': A Study of Gender Boundaries in the Eighteenth Century," in *Sexual Underworlds of the Enlightenment*, 234–60.

154. Her final "marriage" lasted three months, during which she and her partner "bedded, lived together as man and wife." Her relationships were characterized by the "vilest and most deceitful practices." The charge on which Hamilton was convicted is not entirely clear but was probably fraud (Knapp and Baldwin [1819], 2: 125–26).

155. *Annual Register* (1780), 32, part 1: 207; *Gentleman's Magazine* (May 1780), 243; *London Evening-Post* (Apr. 11–13, 1780); *London Chronicle* (Apr. 8–11, 1780), 330; (Apr. 11–13, 1780), 353; (Apr. 13–15, 1780), 362.

156. *Annual Register* (1759), 2: 99–100.

157. People would hang on the legs of a body to hasten the criminal's demise or would assisting in the "turning off" of the condemned (Laqueur [1989], 144–67).

158. Laqueur [1989], 149.

159. Von Archenholz, a German visitor to eighteenth-century London observed: "Unnatural pleasures are held in great abhorrence with the men. In no country are such infamous pleasures held in greater detestation" (quoted in Gordon R. Taylor [1958], *The Angel Makers: A Study in the Psychological Origins of Historical Change, 1750–1850* [London: Heinemann], 274).

160. See Jeffrey Weeks (1981), *Sex, Politics and Society: The Regulation of Sexuality since 1800* (London: Longman), 201.

161. Issues of sexuality are explored further in Simpson (1984).

162. Hay et al. (1975).

163. Lynn Lofland (1973), *A World of Strangers: Order and Action in Urban Public Space* (New York: Basic Books), 56–65.

164. Lee (1869).

165. See the sources cited in note 34 above.

166. Of four people other than pickpockets among the crowds at the pillory, one was the son of a staymaker, one a "laboring man," and two were ticket porters (*Lloyd's Evening Post, and British Chronicle* [Apr. 6–8, 1763]; *London Evening-Post* [Aug. 10–12, 1779]; *Universal Daily Register* [Nov. 23, 1786]). Cobbett,

an eyewitness, described the crowd at the pillorying of Daniel Eaton to be "a speciman of London. . . . Gentlemen, Merchants, Tradesmen of all sorts, artizans and labourers, and a pretty fair proportion of females" (quoted by Thompson [1963], 605).

167. *London Chronicle* (Apr. 11–13, 1780) 353.

Epilogue

Robert J. Kelly and Jess Maghan

Of this nature is the hatred which compounds from the lives of our enemies a fiction which is wholly false. We attribute to them not that state of normal human happiness shot through with the common sorrows of mankind which should move us to entertain for them a feeling of kindly sympathy, but a species of arrogant delight which merely pours oil upon the furnace of rage. It transfigures people no less than does desire. . . . On the other hand, since it can find satisfaction only in destroying that delight, it imagines it, it believes it to be, it sees it, in a perpetual condition of destruction. No more than love does it concern itself with reason, but goes through life with eyes fixed on an unconquerable hope.

—Marcel Proust, Jean Santeuil

No philosopher has ever analyzed the emotion of hatred with greater penetration than Proust displays in this passage. His observations are moral and psychological, suggesting the complex structure of hate. But because his claims do not venture into other regions of filiation and sociability and because of the constraints of his artistic and moral asceticism, he stands astonished before the spectacle of unbridled anger and its consequences. We have chosen to place this phenomenon in historical, legal, psychological, and social landscapes in order to round out the picture.

Phenomena like hate crimes cannot be reduced to simple cause-and-effect schemas. Hate crimes share many of the characteristics of crimes

221

in general, but they also possess dynamic racial, political, ideological, and cultural dimensions that magnify their impact on victims and on the communities in which they occur.

The essays in this volume may have raised more questions than can be answered. We hope that these contributions will enhance our capacities to see something of the nature of the problems that beset many nations and societies. The question, of course, is *how* can one bring others to see that racial and ethnic polarization is widespread, that there exist structures of exclusion operating against gays, women, and others under the guise of "merit" or "qualifications," or "national interest."

One part of the answer must be that it is possible that others will not be moved at all, that some will remain within the circle of beliefs in relation to which the responses they offer are obvious, predictable, and static. Moreover, if they should be moved, if the strategies for change in attitude and behavior should succeed, it is not because those beliefs— those assumptions concerning others—have been discarded or left behind. Rather, it is because they have been altered in ways that are internal to themselves.

It is in the space created by debate and discussion that movement might occur. It was President Clinton who, in March 1992, set the tone and temperament for these discussions when he said before both white and black audiences that there cannot be any more of "them"; there is only "us." Someone for whom sexual orientations and racial identities foreordain certain character traits, abilities, and attitudes is likely to remain obdurate no matter how much evidence is offered to the contrary, but on the other hand, that same someone may just reconsider.

One simply cannot tell in advance what will work a change in someone's views and attitudes; the range of possible change extends far beyond formal argumentation. This does not mean, however, that there is nothing one can do except be passively fatalistic; one acts on the basis of calculations that have at least the probability associated with rules of thumb. For example, an appeal to equal access for women and minorities is likely to receive a serious and respectful hearing from someone with a daughter in professional training. It is certainly possible that some come away from reading and thinking about the issues with a new, perhaps deeper, understanding of their responsibilities as citizens.

What indeed happens when someone changes his or her mind? The temptation would be to say that it marked the achievement of a heightened or raised consciousness, and that such persons who are now "enlightened" had passed from an unreflective state to one of a new and enlarged awareness. But, in fact, awareness is simultaneously a loss: Someone now able to empathize with the victims of prejudice and bigotry is now unable to see any merit in former views; the passing from one point of view to another deprives the individual of whatever certainties flow from the perspective transcended.

We believe that awareness and sensitivity to hate is not a quantity that can be increased or diminished on an absolute scale; rather, it is a name for what is obvious and clear to us, situated as we are within a structure of beliefs. When our beliefs change—when the assumptions within which the possibilities of seeing, acting, and saying are no longer what they were—then what we have taken for granted, and what we have been aware of, will have changed, too. But the change will not be from a confused state of mind or thoughtlessness to a state of awareness; it will be from one state of awareness to another. In short, we are always aware. One's fidelity to a set of beliefs can always be defended weakly or strongly, and when that faith is succeeded by another, a new set of reasons will accompany it, and that set of reasons will be the instantiation of a new awareness.

We question whether it is proper to describe the psychological dynamics involved in mental and emotional shifts in a quasi-theological vocabulary. Yet a shift in the attitudes and mental images individuals possess of each other is a small matter compared to the consequences of a religious conversion. We do not pretend that these articles will raise consciousness, but if all they will have done—and it is no small thing—is change consciousness through logical and moral persuasion by confronting petulant ignorance, our goal will have been accomplished.

At a more general, impersonal level of discussion situated in the historical context of the postimperial period, where tumultuous events unfold almost daily, a general sense of suspicion among formerly colonized peoples has become widespread. Many are caught up in the swirl of events of this transition as great cold war empires dismantle themselves. The post–cold war period envelops both colonialism and the resistance to it. What this means in the thematic structure of this volume is that the Copernican social changes occurring worldwide have challenged some of the most basic assumptions of every national culture.

Throughout newly formed and emancipated states, the peoples who have liberated themselves from subordination are poised to challenge the legacy of imperialism and the hate it occasioned. That legacy was one which incorporated native cultures, histories, and territory into the structures of the great empires. The wave of anticolonialism has produced a revisionist siege on imperialist constructions of reality. Fanon in his powerful *The Wretched of the Earth*, inscribed the anger of the oppressed in words that are prophetic of contemporary events: "Today the Third World faces Europe like a colossal mass whose aim should be to try to resolve the problems to which Europe has not been able to find the answer."[1] As the world was decolonized after World War II, very few in the metropolitan Western cultures thought that violent resistance was in the wind. Still, as Fanon saw, alternatives to imperialism arose and have persisted. Now that the wars of liberation are for the most part over, an ideological resistance to oppression has replaced them.

In many societies, the violence of hatred may draw its inspiration from broad ideological doctrines, but the conflicts tend to be local and involve a built-in, community-inspired chauvinism. It is nativism with a vengeance that sets people on edge. It reinforces distinctions through demagogic claims about character, history, and essences. But it is not the only expression of differences among people: there is the possibility of a more generous and pluralistic vision of the world. Even the great architects of opposition to subjugation and racism argued that violence can never be enough to achieve liberation and respect. The strategies of reason and politics must come into play; there is a need to balance violent force with exigent political and organizational processes. Fanon, the writer who offered one of the more sensational counterideologies to colonialism— which has circulated worldwide and suffused itself into the antiracist rhetoric—asserted clearly that liberation cannot be accomplished simply by seizing power or oppressing the oppressor.

In a time of worldwide change, where colonial subjugation as both a practice and an idea is bankrupt, it is astounding that the Irish problem has continued longer than other struggles. Perhaps it is understood not as a nationalist or imperialist issue, but as a aberration within the British dominions. Yet the facts are otherwise. In 1596, Edmund Spenser, the great English poet, proposed that most of the "barbarian" Irish should be exterminated (see his *View of the Present State of Ireland*). Since that time, a whole tradition of British and European thought has considered the Irish to be a separate and inferior race, usually unregenerately barbarian, often delinquent and certainly primitive. The situation of the Irish entangled in the web of British interests is analogous in many ways with African-Americans in the United States. Dominating the movement for full integration and the end of racism is the psychological effort to gain "respect," a theme echoing in America from W. E. B. Du Bois to Orlando Patterson—a relentless moral insistence that blacks be treated as human beings and citizens.

The legacy of colonialism and imperialism has left in its wake a sense of resentment in the great metropolitan centers of power and a fragmented, deeply divisive colonial wasteland of tribalism, endless warlordism, and horror. Again, the comparisons with racism in the United States are worth noting. As with the colonialist mentality, racism is not merely satisfied with holding victims in its grip and emptying their brains of form and content. By a kind of perverted logic, it turns to the past of a people and distorts, disfigures, and destroys it.

This book comes at a time when intellectuals and social activists in former colonial states and regions are inventing reinterpretative discourses and narratives in order to take a fresh look at their own collective histories. The multicultural movement in the United States, which seems to rescue the past of its diverse peoples, has kindred functions but also reflects the possibility of serving as an antidote to bias crime. It is creating an alternative, richer social history steeped in the complexities of ethnic and minority experiences. Before the 1990s, no discourse had developed in American intellectual communities—including the universities, colleges, and secondary schools—that did anything more than identify with power. For at least two generations, the United States had sided in the Middle East mostly with tyranny and injustice. No struggle for democracy or for the rights of minorities and women had official American support. Instead, one administration after another, Democrat or Republican, propped up compliant and unpopular clients and turned a blind eye and deaf ear to the efforts of oppressed peoples to liberate themselves from military occupation, while subsidizing their enemies. Along with France, Britain, China, and the former Soviet Union, the United States has promoted unlimited militarism and engaged in weapons sales everywhere in the world. All of these external policy initiatives were complemented by a surreptitious cultural war in the United States against Arabs and Islam: appalling racist caricatures suggesting that Arabs are all either terrorists or sheiks, and that the regimes and homelands of Arabs are arid slums.

The new movement has been hotly and sometimes violently contested. However, its key premise may be validated over time, if the diverse peoples of the United Stated insist on reclaiming their own identity, history, tradition, and uniqueness. This may do much to illustrate that, despite their differences, the diverse groups have always overlapped one another, through incorporations, crossovers, conflicts, and the processes of amalgamation and assimilation. Anglo-Eurocentric attitudes still monopolize the presentation of history, and to the extent that they continue to do so, the country will remain brittle with racial, ethnic, and religious tensions.

One theme that seems emergent in this book is that hate crimes are deeply connected to, and expressive of, political, cultural, and racial realities. In the United States, the Middle East, Asia, Canada, Western Europe, and Latin America, it seems socially and politically beneficial to open up and explore history rather than suppress or deny it. There should be no reason to fear such projects—the countries with culturally heterogeneous populations are not likely to unravel into incoherent separatists states like Lebanon. But if the multicultural ethos prevails it may indeed point the way to political changes and changes in the way women, minorities, and immigrants see themselves. Narratives and histories that are enlightening are also emancipating and, in their best and strongest sense, are the bases for integration—not separation.

While the manuscripts were in preparation, the Oklahoma City terrorist bombing occurred in which hundreds were killed and seriously injured. A massive manhunt was mobilized, with an angry president promising the American people—in language that clearly signaled his outrage and shock—that justice would be done. The entire nation turned to Cable News Network to witness the devastation, the heroic and heartbreaking efforts at rescue, and a manhunt that was conducted vigorously on an unprecedented scale.

From the reactions of people in Oklahoma City and across the United States, the bombing was seen as a terrorist act and also as a hate crime. The two notions folded into each other in this horrendous event because it was quickly sensed that more than a political point was being made; gratuitous hatred was painfully evident. Even hardened experts on television wondered about the purpose of the bombing. What could possibly be gained by brutalizing and intimidating the public in such a manner?

We suggest that several purposes, all interconnected, form the basis for the attack: First, the hate crime event was rationally conceived and professionally executed; and by incubating fear indiscriminately, the perpetrators of this crime sought to capture the attention of an audience much larger and relevant to their goals—the government of the United States.

Apparently, the perpetrators of this violence presumed that the pain and fear experienced by the citizens would influence the policies, beliefs, attitudes, and actions of the United States government.

Secondly, the hate crime/terrorist act—the two notions seem inseparably linked in this instance—was ideologically motivated and was not therefore a random, spontaneous event (though it seems like a climacteric for the victims). Instead, it was an action that flowed from a philosophical package of beliefs and ideas. Thus, in the minds of the terrorists, the crime is not irrational but, perhaps, an act of heroism inspired by an ideology that preaches the validity of the cause and the justification of the means.

The images of the bomber and his alleged affiliations among far-right fringe groups is by now familiar and sinister. The blast in downtown Oklahoma City in front of the federal building represents the ultimate urban horror: an anonymous, malevolent destructive device planted and set to do massive damage and harm; the prospective victims temporarily were captured in a concrete execution chamber, as it were, selected by sheer chance, irrespective of age or complicity in the lunatic grievance motivating the attack.

Terrorism and hate crime in the events of the past two years—including the World Trade Center attack in New York City; the genocide in Rwanda; the Tokyo nerve gas incident; and now Oklahoma City—suggest that terrorism and its conjoining fanaticism have finally stepped across a threshold that has been anticipated with dread by many security experts. It is fairly common knowledge that there are groups willing to kill randomly, who are skilled in the use of chemical weapons, ballistic devices, and possibly biological weapons that can destroy far more people than conventional weapons. Considering these factors, the spectrum of danger on a global scale has broadened into threats more terrifying than ever before—and, we must add, far more difficult for governments to forestall or frustrate.

It used to be known or, more accurately, was thought to be known, who the haters and terrorists were: members of handfuls of Middle Eastern, leftist and rightist political movements, sponsored and protected by governments in some cases, bent on achieving their well-advertised ideological goals through death and intimidation. The current generation of terrorists and purveyors of hate are more obscure; their associations appear to be assemblages of disparate fanatics and extremists pursuing unique and mysterious agendas with only the capacity for random violence in common. The outlook is far from optimistic. It looks as if the rise and proliferation of apocalyptic sects and extremist groups has merged with the increasingly easy availability of biochemical weapons that can kill thousands in an attack. This means that the potential for random murder and catastrophic public disruption lies within the reach of small, disaffected, irresponsible groups of—what shall we call them?—"true believers."

Even though extremists have had the power to kill more people than they ever did, the fact that they held back somewhat suggests that they imposed certain restraints on themselves. Most such groups viewed themselves as political activists rather than wanton killers. After all, they had to appeal to potential supporters and sympathizers and had to be wary of producing a backlash had they used the most efficient and repellent methods.

In some ways, the arena of terrorism and hate crime was shaped by the cold war and the rules of terrorism, if we can refer to it in this way, and were governed by the curtailments of larger state power, whose threats of retaliation and withdrawal of support served as a deterrent. But the end of the cold war has more or less ended the sponsorship business. At the same time, however, the collapse of the Soviet empire, the creation of new states, and the breakup of others triggered an explosion of ethnic conflicts with racial and religious hatreds mixed in, giving fresh scope to hate crime and terror. In short, the rules of the game have changed drastically since 1993, when American immunity was swept away in the World Trade Center detonation and the subsequent arrests of conspirators preparing to destroy the United Nations building and other vital structures. In these cases, the motive was apparently religious and without any discernible goal: these were planned attacks on the United States, the "Great Satan" in the ideological demonology of the opposition.

The religious dimension of terrorism—evident in the American right-wing groups who are loosely connected with the Christian Identity Movement—adds a greater danger.[2] Presently, even small, charismatic cults are adopting violent methods as well. These extremist sects and groups appeal to many people in an antispiritual age because they combine their empowering theology with a warm, supportive social environment, at least at first. Once in the close-knit group of believers, they encounter a darker side filled with paranoid delusions about enemies and divine demands for vengeance.

What is apparent in the current wave of terror and hate are dehumanization and enmification—psychological processes that precede violent behavior; for opponents defined as intrinsically evil, as subhuman, killing becomes much easier. In religiously oriented groups, the basis of their faith makes killing not only legitimate but also mandatory. In the United States, as the bombings at the World Trade Center and in Oklahoma City indicate, there are many shadowy groups—militants, survivalists, religious and political cults—with hate-driven agendas of destruction. These groups have a taste for weapons and ballistics of frightening capabilities that can focus the anger of the alienated and disaffected on the government as the symbol of oppression. Members of such groups see themselves as victims of egregious government bureaucracies and politicians exercising tyrannical power. Thus, the perceived belligerence of the government is seen as a declaration of war against its citizenry. How hate groups manage to turn angry people into terrorists is an issue that needs careful study.

Research efforts along these lines are suggestive of the role of psychosocial mechanisms, where at the outset a palliative rationale operates to create an emotional blindness in which destructive conduct seems personally and socially acceptable; violence is portrayed in the service of lofty moral purposes. Individuals then act from a morally inspired agenda of action. The socialization, or brainwashing, activities in hate cults and violent fringe groups are designed along these parameters to selectively disengage internal, self-sanctioning controls by reconstructing conduct, by disregarding or misrepresenting the injurious consequences of one's actions, or by blaming and dehumanizing victims.[3] Thus, the detrimental effects of reprehensible conduct are minimized or ignored, and attribution of blame is foisted upon victim groups. The process involves the subtle diffusion and displacement of responsibility for one's behavior. A sort of "conversion experience" very likely occurs, transforming individuals into dedicated combatants. Because of our focus on hate groups, the impression should not be conveyed that the structured process of release from self-controls occurs only under extraordinary circumstances; quite the contrary. These mechanisms operate in everyday life where decent people routinely perform activities that in furthering their interests or social values may have injurious human effects. Judges, physicians, teachers, bankers, and others engage in actions that at times oblige them to construct self-exonerations and justifications in order to neutralize pernicious psychological effects or denigrating self-prohibitions and self-devaluations.[4]

Can those exposed to extremist political rhetoric in such settings participate in mass murder of the type that occurred in Oklahoma City? We believe that becoming a terrorist does not require a profound alteration of personality structures; nor does it entail the incorporation of very aggressive drives or radical transformations in moral standards. It also does not require profound changes in a individual's "identity kit," as occurs in prisons, seminaries, convents, and in military boot camps. Rather, it can be accomplished by cognitively restructuring the moral value of killing, so that the killing can be done free from nagging self-censure.[5] By morally approving or sanctioning violent tactics, conditioned individuals might imagine that they are protecting cherished values and preserving a way of life under threat. The task of making hate crimes and terroristic violence plausible is facilitated when nonviolent options are determined to be ineffective. The psycho-moral processes being discussed imply further that, in the name of deeply felt convictions, quite ordinary individuals are capable of marshaling the energy to commit extraordinary violent acts in the name of religious, or even nationalist, political imperatives through transformative mechanisms that turn them into zealous militant crusaders against evil. Indeed, in the eyes of supportive groups, risky attacks directed at the apparatus of oppression may be construed as acts of selflessness and patriotic martyrdom.

The process of displacing responsibility for heinous deeds has been gruesomely revealed in socially sanctioned mass executions. As Robert Lifton has documented, Nazi physicians and prison staffs divested themselves of personal responsibility for their monstrous atrocities by facile deference to the axiom of military obedience—that they were simply carrying out orders. Augmenting the mass murder program and blunting its effect on those implementing it was a systematic ideology of dehumanizing the victims; Jews, Slavs, and other stigmatized groups were denuded of their basic humanity. That process weakened emphatic identifications between victims and their victimizers.[6] Clearly, inhibitions against violence and murder, when they are relaxed, expedite the brutalization of those divested of human qualities without serious risk of self-condemnation to the agents of cruelty.

Similarly, the phenomenology of hate crimes and terror pose threats to human welfare that stem primarily from grotesque deliberate acts of principle rather than from irrational impulses. Ironically, while principled violence would be of greatest social interest, it is the most ignored in the analysis of violence and hate. Can cruelty and destructive ventures of great magnitude be controlled? How can social safeguards be implemented that protect us from terror, genocide, and systemic hate?[7] Furthermore, has anything been learned from hate crimes and their accompanying terror that can be exploited in the interest of curbing this violence? These are questions every government and public must continually ask to stimulate interest in the examination of an experience in the search for answers. The cluster of terrorist events in Europe may be instructive as to how a society reacts to systemic violence.

In London in the 1970s, IRA bombings initially produced massive shock and then diffuse fear about the community's collective sense of security. Then came a determination to resist it. Likewise, the Italians, Germans, and Israelis have shown that the recovery process is possible in the face of terror and hate. Anger and frustration mount, but if channeled in productive ways, they can yield positive results. For instance, in Oklahoma City, the tragic event compelled a level of cooperation and coordination at all levels of society—including the private sector, law enforcement personnel, the medical community and emergency assistance services, social workers, firefighters, utility workers, transportation personnel, communication workers, forensic experts, and military and numerous other specialists—to organize around several interrelated goals.

It is clear that politically directed hate speech has become an instrument of bonding for broad sections of white America. Their anger has been stroked by talk radio and exploited for political gain. This phenomenon of violence nestling in many groups that is prompted into action by the hectoring of haters on radio is not unique to the United States: its occurrence has been documented in many conflict-ridden regions of the world. Americans and others around the world can agree with President Clinton that "angry voices" bear some of the blame.

Before the bombing, it was possible to pretend that hate radio was merely "cathartic," a way of venting anger. Yet something is missing in this explanation, especially where the references to the outrage focus on the "paranoid style" of the radical right. In fact, most Americans can draw a line between their resentment of "big government" infringements, as it has come to be called, and the belief that fascist-style federal agents are breaking into homes across the country. It is then the actual agenda of the militias that is harder to face up to. Contrary to much opinion, they are not opposed to government per se; indeed, they cultivate friends and sympathizers at all levels of government. They do not wish to smash the state itself as a political entity but rather specific state governments that enforce civil rights, protect endangered species, promote gender equity, and make gestures toward easing the plight of the homeless, the underclass, and the brutalized. The evidence for this view of the terrorists will become available as it is collected; suffice it to say that the target of the Oklahoma City bombing was probably not just the dreaded and much maligned Bureau of Alcohol, Tobacco, and Firearms but agencies whose tasks include social security, affirmative action, and aid to families with dependent children. This means that the staff people and clients most likely to be in the building when the bomb detonated were women, the elderly, and minorities. Though it is not yet known why the federal building in Oklahoma City was targeted, it seems that the prime suspect is a racist whose military career disintegrated because of those prejudices.

In the aftermath of the bombing, many in the press dwelled on talk radio for its glorification of political violence and sought to formulate an argument that makes morally equivalent the tumultuous 1960s radicalism of the Weathermen and Black Panthers with the radical right and the militia movement. To claim a sociological equation in which the Black Panthers are positioned alongside the militias is a construction that ignores what are very significant differences in the politics of both groups and the status of gaps between blacks and whites, not to mention the power gap between the left and right. It is the case that both groups embrace armed resistance, but when Khalid Muhammed delivered his anti-Semitic tirade, the United States Senate voted unanimously to condemn him. There has been no such reaction to the fulminations of right-wing agitators. Students of the Holocaust readily understand that speech is the principal weapon in the breakdown of democratic society, if only because it shatters the capacity for empathy.

If the Oklahoma City recovery effort shows us anything, it is that survival and interdependence, the connections among people, are not only possible but emotionally and socially beneficial. It is more rewarding to think concretely and sympathetically about others than only about "us." No one can deny the persistent continuities of long, cherished traditions, sustained habitations and cultural geographies, but there seems no reason except fear, prejudice, and hate to keep insisting on separation and distinctiveness, and it is this that strokes the fires of hatred.

And where do these distressing events—from Oklahoma City to the Long Island railroad massacre—leave us? Just where we have always been, debating various agendas, each of which seems accusatory. Policies, proposals, and claims to cope with hate crime do not seem to lead to anything positive. But they have a salutary negative effect. As these essays illustrate, across a range of historical periods, cultures, and issues, we can identify nonfruitful solutions by shifting our attention away from the realm of abstract moral calculation and into the realm of particularized history and cultural settings, where questions are asked in a context and not in a vacuum.

NOTES

1. Frantz Fanon (1963), *The Wretched of the Earth* (New York: Bantam Books), 314.
2. Michael Barkun (1994), *The Origins of the Christian Identity Movement* (Chapel Hill: Univ. of North Carolina Press); Allen Sapp et al. (1993), "Value and Belief Systems of Right-Wing Extremists: Rationale and Motivation for Bias-Motivated Crimes," in *Bias Crime: American Law Enforcement and Legal Responses,* 2d rev. ed., ed. Robert J. Kelly (Chicago: Office of International Criminal Justice, Univ. of Illinois at Chicago).
3. Albert Bandura (1990), "Mechanisms of Moral Disengagement," in *Origins of Terrorism: Psychologies, Ideologies, Theologies, States of Mind,* ed. Walter Reich (New York: Cambridge Univ. Press), 161–91.
4. H. C. Kelman (1973), "Violence Without Moral Restraint: Reflections on the Dehumanization of Victims and Victimizers," *Journal of Social Issues,* vol. 29.
5. Neville Sanford and C. Comstock (1971), *Sanctions for Evil* (San Francisco: Jossey-Bass).
6. Robert Jay Lifton (1986), *The Nazi Doctors: Medical Killing and the Psychology of Genocide* (New York: Basic Books).
7. Efforts to come to grips with the core of hate usually begin with interactive groups who are encouraged to express frankly their fears, grievances, and anger where tensions are high. Once resentments are made explicit, participants are capable in many instances of developing a working trust. From implicit trust, it is possible to suggest ways of dealing effectively with the sensitivities of others and of finding confidence-building measures that eventually can overcome antagonism. The bases of hostility may be rooted in language, history, economics; at the least, sharing knowledge and admitting offensive behavior is a step toward peaceable resolution of conflict.

A philosophical approach to coping with the intense feelings hate crimes arouse may be found in the work of Jurgen Habermas. Habermas's analytical models of what he calls "discourse ethics" might serve as a technique and a set of principles essential in establishing communication strategies to cope with hate crimes and grievances that, if not satisfactorily dealt with, can lead to serious violence (See Habermas [1993], *Justification and Application: Remarks on*

Discourse Ethics [Cambridge: MIT Press]). Habermas's work in the area of discourse ethics, when applied to conflict situations offers a methodology for the possible resolution of seemingly intractable differences among disputants.

The principle of universalization ("U") is intended as a "procedural" instrument in practical situations; it helps to determine what range of issues or aspects of conflicts can be decided in mutually acceptable ways for all parties. Its procedural character may be seen as a reinterpretation of the formal character of Kant's categorical imperative by specifying the conditions that must be met to reach agreements. Habermas's contribution in the articulation of the U principle is to preserve the role of autonomy for those involved in defining the limits, boundaries, and applicability of rules they decide; in doing so, the U principle rejects sources of moral authority external to the wills of rational agents; autonomy is construed in *intersubjective terms*.

The structure imposed on practical argumentation by U compels each participant to adopt the perspectives of all others in examining the validity of proposed norms, for it is the consequences for the needs and interests of those affected that constitute the relevant reasons in terms of which the issue of normative validity must be decided. Clearly, not all practical questions admit of resolution in this manner since common interests cannot always be found or formulated. In the case of bias and hate crimes, feelings may run very deep and differences may have hardened over decades; contributing to the problems of resolution and even empathic understanding among disputants may be the intrusive power of external interests that influence conflicts well beyond the immediacies of particular solvable problems in specific communities.

For Habermas, hate crimes as an expression of group conflict cannot be properly elucidated from the egocentric perspective of the isolated deliberating subject. Coping with social problems such as bias and hate can be achieved through a process of practical deliberation and reasoned agreement among all the potentially affected by proposed norms of justice and reconciliation.

In cases of bias crimes, the dynamical applications of moral/ethical principles and norms may work most effectively in stages. Sociologically, it can be demonstrated that universally grounded moral norms are in need of articulation in particular contexts. The breakdown of preconditions for the general acceptance of legally defined status rights must first be empirically demonstrated prior to the application of adjudication and remediation measures. Thereupon, empirical research can identify populations victimized by prejudice and hate and, by documenting the scope of the problem, create a public awareness of it. Popular attention in society at large and among specific groups victimized by hate or victimizing because of hatred can be heightened by research work and its public dissemination. At this point, the formation of policy strategies for the resolution of the problem may emerge, and it is here where the moral/ethic discourse strategy comes into play. This paradigm would be helpful in the clarification of bias crime problems and attitudes toward them in the public at large and in segments of the population where the problems are most chronic and acute. Lastly, when the mass media popularize research on hate crime problems, general attitudes and policy are more likely to be debated and changed. Also by publicizing bias events, public opinion may consolidate around a set of solutions. In any case, the media exposure of bias crime can do much to precipitate discussion, debate, and policy evaluations one way or another.

An Annotated Bibliography of
Hate Crime Literature

Contributors

An Annotated Bibliography of Hate Crime Literature

Jess Maghan

Hate crimes and related issues of racial discrimination and sexual harassment continue to engender numerous streams of literature from a broad range of legal, political, academic, and professional viewpoints. Hate crime literature consistently carries two general themes: dehumanization and a terroristic effect on individual victims and entire communities.

The purpose of this annotated bibliography is to provide an introduction to the sources and references for specialized readings. It is designed to serve more as a sampling and introductory map to the theme and form of the current literature. The works cited will enable the reader to further surmise the depth of the field and the growing research in the field of hate crimes. As societies become more conscious of the common patterns and deleterious nature of hate crimes to the social order and stability, these writings in research, policy, legislation, and law will become more permanent reference categories for the hate crime field.

Because this topic is both dense and overwhelming, it is useful to break it down into the following manageable set of components. These are: (a) principles and historical context; (b) terroristic and dehumanizing effects; (c) victims and victimizers; (d) controversial issues and legislation; (e) criminal justice concerns; (f) instructional and technical manuals; (g) task force and status reports of civil rights and criminal justice agencies; and (h) hate crimes from a global perspective.

The subject of hate crimes ranges widely over many areas, and it is useful to present important books, essays, research monographs, and general accounts, as these relate to and supplement the chapters and source materials included in this book. Relevant government documents are cited because they provide an additional structural component for understanding how hate crimes are legislatively promulgated.

These materials often describe events that occurred before the conceptualization of hate violence as a crime and act as a bridge from the earlier literature concerning prejudice and ethnoviolence. These give a general overview of the hate crimes and acts of violence and prejudice against particular peoples or minorities. Included in this literature are details on hate crime laws in the United States, statistics on hate crime violence, and important topical events in the development of hate crimes. Literature from an international perspective is increasing, especially in Western democracies, and as the concept of hate crimes becomes more established in a global context.

PRINCIPLES AND HISTORICAL CONTEXT

The legal definition and manifestation of hate crime legislation is of relatively recent origin in the United States, Canada, and other Western democracies and is emerging in the same context in the new democracies in Central and Eastern Europe.

The concept of "hate crimes," as it is employed in the United States, refers to specific criminal behaviors or acts that are motivated by prejudice based upon gender, race, ethnicity, religion, sexual orientation, or other identified categories that vary from state to state, as well as nation to nation. Other terms such as "bias-motivated" and "ethnoviolence" have been utilized to describe these acts.

While writings on prejudice and violence extend back to the beginning of the written word, literature concerned specifically with hate crimes as a legal and legislative movement has only recently appeared in a global perspective. The increase in these writings is strongly influenced by advances in worldwide media technology that allow such crimes to be exposed and the laws or penalty enhancements for committing them.

TERRORISTIC AND DEHUMANIZING EFFECTS

Shuman-Moore, Elizabeth, and Darren B. Watts. 1994. "Bias Violence: Advocating for Victims." Parts 1 and 2. *Clearinghouse Review* (special issue) 14(5): 4–

18. In a two-part essay, the nature of bias violence and a program to assist victims of this type of violence is presented. Part 2 reviews the federal civil remedies that may be available to victims of bias violence and examines applicable state law provisions.

Weisburd, Steven Bennett, and Brian Levin. 1994. "On the Basis of Sex, Recognizing Gender Based Bias Crimes." *Stanford Law and Policy Review* 7(2): 21–47. The authors cite a powerful "in terrorem effect." It is in this context that bias crimes embody the unique capability of threatening an entire community. The article includes a special analysis of gender-related crime; that is, crimes where the victim's gender is a salient aspect of the offense.

HISTORICAL CONTEXT

Hate crimes, as developed in the American context, are directly linked to a strong tradition of free speech that protects even the most offensive form of expression. No other country in the world offers the same kind of protection to offensive speech.

Clarke, Floyd I. 1991. "Hate Violence in the United States." *FBI Law Enforcement Bulletin* 60(1): 11–18. Messages of hate are spread by the latest in today's technology, such as cable television and computer bulletin boards. The FBI's efforts in responding to hate crime are divided into two separate projects: (1) the FBI Civil Rights Program, which focuses primarily on investigating incidents involving individual perpetration of hate-motivated violence; and (2) the Domestic Counter-Terrorism Program, which focuses "on the unlawful use of force or violence by terrorist groups for political or social ends."

Hacker, Andrew. 1992. *Two Nations: Black and White, Separate, Hostile, Unequal.* New York: Scribner. This work gives an analysis of the conditions that keep blacks and whites dangerously far apart in their ability to participate fully in the American dream. Hacker demonstrates that black Americans are unique in their subjugation to an all-pervading portrayal of their inferiority as citizens. This book is an intensive portrayal of the problems of American democratization since the Second World War.

Jost, Kenneth. 1993. "Hate Crimes." *CQ Researcher* 3(1): 718. To combat hate crimes, more than half the states have adopted laws providing longer sentences for certain offenses when they are motivated by specified types of prejudice. Some civil liberties advocates say these laws threaten freedom of speech. The U.S. Supreme Court is reviewing lower-court rulings on the legal test between civil rights and civil liberties.

Levin, Jack, and Jack McDevitt. 1993. *Hate Crimes: The Rising Tide of Bigotry and Bloodshed.* New York: Plenum Press. Hate crimes consist of a wide variety of criminal behaviors with a common foundation in bias or bigotry and a vast difference in their severity and their impact on the broader community. For example, immigrant-bashing hate crime directed at newcomers, Asians, and Latinos is on the increase. Successful intergroup relations and interdiction strategies are also cited.

Mahoney, Kathleen. 1992. "The Constitutional Approach to Freedom of Expression in Hate Propaganda and Pornography." *Law and Contemporary Problems* 55: 77–105. The act of giving meaning to a constitutional guarantee, such as freedom of expression, is juxtaposed in emergent hate crime case law. It is at this juncture where explicit or implicit reliance on the ways in which the interpreter imagines social and political life becomes apparent: pornography and hate propaganda are two such areas examined.

Newton, Michael, and Judy Ann Newton. 1991. *Racial and Religious Violence in America: A Chronology.* New York: Garland. A chronology of eight thousand hate crimes perpetrated on the grounds of racial or religious prejudice from the discovery of the New World (1500s) to the later part of 1989. Trends in racial and religious violence are identified by placing isolated incidents in their historical perspective and demonstrating how modern ethnic mayhem is by no means unprecedented. Taking the question, Are hate crime penalty enhancement laws constitutional? this section presents statements by both supporters and opponents of the issue.

Walker, Samuel. 1994. *Hate Speech: The History of an American Controversy.* Lincoln: Univ. of Nebraska Press. The First Amendment protects even the most offensive forms of expression: racial slurs, hateful religious propaganda, and cross burning. Should it be illegal to call people names based on race or religion? Should it be illegal to publish defamatory materials that incite prejudice against a racial or religious group? This book provides a social and political history of hate speech and includes detailed bibliography and case law citations.

VICTIMS AND VICTIMIZERS

Barnes, Arnold, and Paul H. Ephross. 1994. "The Impact of Hate Violence on Victims: Emotional and Behavioral Responses to Attack." *Social Work* 39(3): 247–52. A sampling of hate crime victims participated in focus groups for this research. The study detailed the type of hate crime committed and the emotional and behavioral responses of the victims. Several emotional reactions such as anger, fear, sadness, powerlessness, and suspicion were identified. This work highlights the need for social workers to be more aware of hate violence in order to appropriately assist in response and prevention.

Comstock, Gary David. 1991. *Violence Against Lesbians and Gay Men.* New York: Columbia Univ. Press. Physical violence perpetrated by heterosexuals against lesbians and gay men is on the increase. Data show that these perpetrators are average young men whose behavior is socially sanctioned rather than intrapsychically determined. Empirical data is presented, including documentation on extralegal violence.

"Hatred Turns Out Not To Be Colorblind." 1993. *Time*, Jan. 18, 22. The article focuses on a January 1, 1993, incident in which a black man was doused with gasoline and set on fire; it also addresses the FBI's first national report on bias crimes. The gravity and urgency of the need for maintaining national reporting of hate crimes is documented. The FBI and its critics both concede that reporting is a process that is far from complete; less than one-fifth of the nation's law enforcement agencies participated.

Horowitz, Craig. 1993. "The New Anti-Semitism." *New York* 26(2): 20–28. Anti-Jewish attacks occurring within a three-month period in New York City fomented enormous discord between the black and Jewish communities. The article describes the response efforts of black leaders to the hate crimes, both on a community-activist and institution-wide level.

Peters, Jeff. 1993. "When Fear Turns to Hate and Hate to Violence: The Persecution of Gays Is Increasing." *Human Rights* 18(1): 22–30. The article includes statistics, federal and state legislative initiatives, and victim accounts that supplement more lengthy treatments of this component. It also explores the various possible motivating factors for the commission of these crimes.

Stanley, Alessandra. 1991. "City College Professor Assailed for Remarks on Jews." *New York Times*, Aug. 7, p. B1. In a lecture on African-American cultural education, City College professor Leonard Jeffries claimed that Jews in the Hollywood movie industry have conspired against black people. The lecture, presented at the Empire State Black Arts and Cultural Festival, cosponsored by Governor Mario Cuomo's advisory committee on black affairs, brought intense controversy and also focused on Dr. Jeffries' work as a consultant to the New York Department of Education.

Zwerling, Martin S. 1995. "Legislating Against Hate in New York: Bias Crimes and the Lesbian and Gay Community." *Touro Law Review* 11: 529. Zwerling's article provides an examination of the current patterns of hate crimes against the lesbian and gay community. Detailed statistical analysis is made with a recommendation that statutes include *sexual orientation* as a protected category, within the constitutionality of hate crime legislation.

OTHER VICTIM GROUPS

In addition to those groups traditionally recognized as victims of hate violence, an increasing number of reports have appeared identifying other groups that have become victims of hate violence.

Chan, Carole. 1991. "Violence and Intimidation: Rising Bigotry Towards Arabs and Muslims." In *Report on a Public Hearing by the Los Angeles County Commission on Human Relations*. Los Angeles: Los Angeles County.

Copeland, Lois. 1991. *Violence Against Women As Bias Motivated Hate Crime: Defining the Issues*. Washington, D.C.: Center for Women Policy Studies. Gender specific bias/hate crimes represent complex and important aspects of the hate crime field. These crimes often overlooked in the context of equal opportunity issues receive scant attention. The specifies issues involved and interdiction strategies are outlined.

"Racial Violence Against Asian Americans." 1993. *Harvard Law Review* 106(8): 339–47. Stereotypes include the perception that Asian-Americans are rich and physically weak and, as the model minority, do not face discrimination. Asians are often viewed as an economic threat, foreign and interchangeable. Countering such stereotypes will help to eliminate racial violence against Asian-Americans.

Reinharz, Shulamit. 1986. "Loving and Hating One's Elders: Twin Themes in Legend and Literature." In *Elder Abuse: Conflict in the Family*, edited by Karl A. Pillemer and Rosalie S. Wolf. Dover, Mass.: Auburn House.

Rutledge, Bruce. 1991. "Hate Crimes: Arab Americans Feel the Heat of Bigotry." *Human Rights* 18(1): 30. The demonization of Arabs in relation to stereotypes of terrorist and radical elements has become commonplace. Concern for media accuracy is addressed. Arab and Muslim citizens in the United States are unfamiliar with channels of communication to redress these situations. Law enforcement and public safety personnel are uninformed on the cultural and religious mores of Arabs.

Solotoff, Lawrence, and Henry S. Kramer. 1994. *Sex Discrimination and Sexual Harassment in the Workplace*. New York: Law Journal Seminars-Press. The dynamic nature of this field of the law presents challenges to those who study or work in the field. Sex-based discrimination and bias practices are anything but routine. No one benefits from acts of abuse and hostility in the workplace directed at one employee or another because of sex, race, color, religion, or national origin.

Waxman, Barbara F. 1991. "Hatred: The Unacceptable Dimension in Violence Against Disabled People." *Sexuality and Disability* 9(3): 185–99.

VICTIMIZERS

The psychological and sociological studies of the perpetrators of hate violence, although comparatively limited in number, are an integral part of the hate crime literature.

Hamm, Mark S. 1993. *American Skinheads: The Criminology and Control of Hate Crime*. Westport, Conn.: Praeger. This book gives a profile of Tom Metzger, former KKK member, and Clark Martell, creator of the first American neo-Nazi Skinheads street gang, as instrumental in formation of the Skinhead movement in the United States. The fact that many Skinheads are employed as productive workers and/or are responsible students is revealed. Factors that have created these "normal, hardworking, responsible student thugs" are considered.

Conceptual Foundations/Controversial Issues

These writings constitute the largest subdivision of the hate crime literature and include works, largely drawn from legal sources, that lay the conceptual foundations for hate crime laws, describe the constitutional and social issues raised by hate crime laws and offer suggestions for alternative approaches for dealing with incidents of hate violence.

Czajkoski, Eugene H. 1992. "Criminalizing Hate: An Empirical Assessment." *Federal Probation* 22(2): 36–38. The article gives a basic description of hate crimes, concentrating on the peculiar mix of incidents in the state of Florida. Considerable details as to the possible indicators of motivation are examined.

Feingold, Stanley. 1993. "Hate Crime Legislation Muzzles Free Speech." *National Law Journal* 15(45), col. 1. Utilizing the Supreme Court case, *Wisconsin v Mitchell*, 92.515 (1993), the author suggests that hate crime laws threaten free speech.

Gerstenfeld, Phyllis B. 1992. "Smile When You Call Me That: The Problems with Punishing Hate Motivated Behavior." *Behavioral Sciences and the Law* 10(2): 259–85. The actual impact of hate crime laws is largely symbolic. These laws have a number of problems. Hate crime laws may violate the Constitution. Hate crime involves the problematical consideration of the offender's motive. Social scientific theories suggest that the laws may actually increase bigotry and disempower minorities. It is recommended that policy makers explore other means of reducing bigotry.

Haiman, Franklyn Saul. 1993. *"Speech Acts" and the First Amendment*. Carbondale: Southern Illinois Univ. Press. Haiman presents an exegesis on the current manifestation of speech acts and the First Amendment. The author presents a comprehensive analysis of the dangers of the trend toward intermingling morality and the law, posing this as a threat to free society.

Hansen, M. 1993. "Hate Crimes, Harassment Split ACLU: Critics Claim Group Ignoring Free Speech Concerns in Quest for Social Justice." *ABA Journal* 79: 17. Hansen gives an analysis of the internal strain among civil liberty groups and the claims of the dangers inherent in ignoring free speech in the quest of hate crime legislation for social justice.

"Hate Is Not Speech: A Constitutional Enhancement for Hate Crimes." 1993.

Harvard Law Review 106(6): 1314–31. Penalties for crimes committed because of the victim's race or similar characteristic are not only constitutional, they are necessary. The interethnic warfare in what was formerly Yugoslavia show the extremes to which hate violence can lead. The author cautions against American jurisprudence distorting the principles of free speech in order to defend hate-inspired violence.

Hentoff, Nat. 1993. "Hate Crimes: Should They Carry Enhanced Penalties?" *ABA Journal* 79(45): 116–21. This brief article takes a look at differing opinions on the issue of enhanced penalties for hate crimes.

Jacobs, James B. 1993. "Should Hate Be A Crime?" *Public Interest* 113: 315. Jacobs sees little crime control benefit in hate crime legislation. Criminal law should not be expected to solve America's social problems, Jacobs asserts. One of the recurring themes in the debate over the validity of hate crime as a separate offense is the problem of motive. Jacobs cites the views of respected academics who argue, among other things, that Americans are to a great extent implicitly racist, having grown up in a racist society. How then can one distinguish the implicitly racist act from the consciously motivated racist act? Wouldn't everything then be considered a hate crime? Ultimately, he concludes that these problems require timely resolution but that criminal law is not the proper venue for it.

Jacobs, James B., and Kimberly A. Potter. 1997. "Hate Crimes: A Critical Perspective." In *Crime and Justice: A Review of Research*. Vol. 22. Chicago: Univ. of Chicago Press. Jacobs and Potter maintain: "Creation of a hate crime category fills political and symbolic functions but is unlikely to provide a useful indication of the state of various prejudices or to reduce crime generated by prejudice. Indeed, deconstructing criminal law according to the dictates of 'identity politics' might exacerbate social divisions and conflict" (83).

Lawrence, F. M. 1993. "Resolving the Hate Crimes Paradox: Punishing Bias Crimes and Protecting Racist Speech." *Notre Dame Law Review* 68(4): 673–721. The author maintains that bias crime statutes are constitutional and represent the highest expression of a societal commitment to racial, religious, and ethnic harmony. They represent modern evolvement of civil liberties statutes and free speech.

Matsuda, Mari J., et al. 1993. *Words That Wound: Critical Race Theory, Assaultive Speech, and the First Amendment.* Boulder, Colo.: Westview. In analyzing assaultive speech, the authors argue for an antisubordination interpretation of the First Amendment. Race theory, as substantive to social reality and a sense of social utopianism, is presented.

Morsch, J. 1991. "Motive in Hate Crimes: The Argument Against Presumption of Racial Motivation." *Journal of Criminal Law and Criminology* 82(3): 659–89. See especially the section entitled, "The Problem of Motive." The suggestion that state legislatures reform current hate crime statutes to ease the prosecutor's burden of proving the accused's motive is viewed as constitutionally flawed. The author advises that states should adopt measures to resolve these "motive requirement" problems.

Stinski, Brent F. 1993. "Can Hate Be Controlled? A Clouded Issue." *Human Rights* 20(2): 26–28. Stinski writes a provocative profiling of the opinions of Supreme Court justices Scalia, Rehnquist, Kennedy, Souter, and Thomas, concerning the St. Paul *Municipal Hate Crimes Ordinance*. The author also includes a review of the Wisconsin Supreme Court's interpretation of "enhancement laws" in the application of hate crime laws.

Strossen, Nadine. 1993. "Hate Crimes: Should They Carry Enhanced Penalties?—Yes: Discriminatory Crimes." *ABA Journal* 79: 44. Strossen argues against the enhanced penalties aspect of "hate speech crimes" as violating the First Amendment. The basic distinction between protected thought and punishable conduct is seen as central to both free speech jurisprudence and antidiscrimination laws.

LEGISLATION

This literature includes the reports and background papers prepared for specific legislation to establish hate crime laws.

Freeman, Steven L. 1994. *Hate Crime Laws: Punishment Which Fits the Crime.* Vol. 13. New York: Legal Affairs Dept., Anti-Defamation League of B'nai B'rith. The current national preoccupation with hate crimes portrays a profound irony: that hate crimes are nothing new. In actuality, a historical synopsis refutes this theory. The author profiles epic cases of racial assaults, cemetery desecrations, gay bashings, and countless other forms of bias-motivated crimes as a sad and living legacy; a very real part of American history.

Goldberg, Marion Zenn. 1992. *Statutes Combat Hate Crimes in Forty-Six States.* ADL Reports. New York: Legal Affairs Dept., Anti-Defamation League of B'nai B'rith. The rising tide of bias-related violence is engendering hate crime statutes. Thirteen states have passed hate crimes statutes in the last year. The Anti-Defamation League of B'nai B'rith (ADL) recently reported forty-six states with having established hate crime legislation.

Jacobs, James B. 1992–93. "Implementing Hate Crimes Legislation, Symbolism, and Crime Control." *Annual Survey of American Law* 4: 541–53. Hate crime laws are viewed as products of "identity politics" and more symbolic issues in society. Jacobs argues that legislators do not pass these laws to necessarily deal with crime but actually to maintain votes by supporting the "victimized" interest groups and reaffirming the American antibigot morality. Problems in implementation of hate crime legislation and the impact on the criminal justice system is examined.

U.S. House Committee on the Judiciary, Subcommittee on Crime and Criminal Justice. 1992. Hate Crimes Sentencing Enhancement Act of 1992: *Report to Accompany H.R. 4797*. Washington, D.C.: U.S. Government Printing Office. H.R. 4797 addresses the growing menace of hate crime in America by directing the U.S. Sentencing Commission to adopt guidelines to increase, by three offense levels, the sentence received for a federal hate crime offense. *Hate crime* is defined under the bill as a "crime in which the defendant's conduct was motivated by hatred, bias, or prejudice, based on the actual or perceived race, color, religion, national origin, ethnicity, gender, or sexual orientation of another individual or group of individuals." Increasing penalty by three severity levels translates into an average sentence enhancement of one-third real time served.

CRIMINAL JUSTICE

With the passage of hate crime laws, the criminal justice system became involved with the reporting, tabulating, investigation, prosecution, and sentencing of hate crime violence. The articles in this section are written with a focus on a specific aspect of the involvement of the criminal justice system with hate crime violence.

Finn, Peter, and Taylor McNeil. 1987. *The Response of the Criminal Justice System to Bias Crime: An Exploratory Review*. Cambridge, Mass.: ABT Associates. The initial consternation within law enforcement agencies over the requirement for developing operational and policy guidelines is discussed. The document includes reviews of training manuals and bias and hate crimes reporting procedures for criminal justice agencies.

Hernandez, Tanya Kateri. 1990. "Bias Crimes: Unconscious Racism in the Prosecution of 'Racially Motivated Violence.'" *Yale Law Journal* 99(4): 845–64. This document focuses on physical injuries that result from bias crimes and redress through criminal statutes. The inadequacy of federal statutes as cause for state statutes is also examined.

Kelly, Robert J., Jess Maghan, and Woodrow Tennant. 1993. "Hate Crimes: Victimizing the Stigmatized." In *Bias Crime: American Law Enforcement and Legal Responses*, edited by Robert J. Kelly. 2d rev. ed. Chicago: Office of International Criminal Justice, Univ. of Illinois at Chicago. The article discusses hate crimes in the language of "bias incidents." Bias crimes, besides leading to fear on the victim's part, may lead to street actions, a highly charged demand for justice, and criticism of law enforcement. This criticism is viewed by the writers as healthy for self-scrutiny and examination of policy and procedures. The paper also addresses the increasing criminal victimizations of gays and lesbians.

Lieberman, Michael. 1992. "Preventing Hate Crime: New Tools, New Expectations for Law Enforcement." *Police Chief* 59(6): 33–36. Race relations and the U.S. criminal justice system have gained national attention following the Rodney King verdict. A renewed commitment by American police departments in enforcing hate crime laws is documented. The importance of effective data collection is outlined as essential these efforts.

Shoop, Julie Gannon, and Nan Levinson. 1993. "High Court Upholds Increased Penalties for Hate Crimes." *Trial* 29(8): 16–18. The authors maintain that laws increasing penalties for bias-motivated crimes do not violate the First Amendment. The authors use *Wisconsin v. Mitchell* in their justification of penalty enhancement laws.

INSTRUCTIONAL/TECHNICAL

Instructional and technical resources for hate violence education programs are becoming more readily available.

Association of State Uniform Crime Reporting Programs. 1992. *Hate Crime Statistics, 1990: A Resource Book Prepared under the* Hate Crime Statistics Act of 1990 *for the Federal Bureau of Investigation*. Washington, D.C.: U.S. Dept. of Justice, Federal Bureau of Investigation. The guidelines define and give examples of hate crimes, requiring that all crimes be evaluated at two levels of review to determine whether or not they are motivated by bias; the guidelines also specify the data police departments are to provide about each hate crime.

Bodingerde-Uriarte, Christina. 1991. *Hate Crime: A Sourcebook for Schools Confronting Bigotry, Harassment, Vandalism, and Violence*. Washington, D.C.: U.S. Dept. of Education, Office of Educational Research and Improvement, Educational Resources Information Center. This is a guide for teacher preparation and classroom presentation of hate crimes within a contemporary social context.

Illinois. Cook County State's Attorney. 1994. *A Prosecutor's Guide to Hate Crime*. Chicago: Cook County State's Attorney's Office. This handbook, written primarily for prosecutors in Cook County, Illinois, cites the different bureaus, divisions, and units within the state's attorney's office relevant to hate crime interdiction. It serves as a "how to" manual on prosecuting individuals who violate hate crime laws.

National Institute Against Prejudice and Violence. 1994. *Prejudice and Violence: An Annotated Bibliography of Selected Materials on Ethnoviolence*. 2d ed. Washington, D.C.: U.S. Government Printing Office. This publication gives a composite listing of publications by The National Institute Against Prejudice and Violence (NIAPV) on ethnoviolence, 1990 to 1994. The data collection goes beyond categorization of offenses to the range of emotional responses felt by the victims.

TASK FORCE/STATUS REPORTS

Anti-Defamation League of B'nai B'rith. 1992. *Addressing Racial and Ethnic Tensions: Combating Hate Crimes in America's Cities.* New York: Anti-Defamation League. The ADL addresses the findings of a national survey conducted in cooperation with the U.S. Conference of Mayors. The publication provides statistical analysis of hate crime incidents, victim profiles, trends, and interdiction strategies. Exemplary programs are cited.

California Attorney General's Commission on Racial, Ethnic, Religious, and Minority Violence. 1986. *Final Report.* Sacramento: Office of the Attorney General of California. The lack of widespread knowledge of hate crime laws or remedies available to victims is generally not known by victims and law enforcement practitioners. The report provides incidence profiles, particularly toward new refugee groups throughout California.

Fernandez, Joseph M. 1991. "Bringing Hate Crime into Focus." *Harvard Civil Rights–Civil Liberties Law Review* 26(1): 261–93. The U.S. Congress passed the *Hate Crime Statistics Act of 1990*, an act created to provide the empirical data necessary to design prevention strategies. This is the first federal legislation requiring the government to collect specific data on hate crimes, including violence against gays and lesbians.

National Research Council. 1989. *A Common Destiny: Blacks and American Society.* Washington, D.C.: National Academy Press. This publication presents data and research on the position of blacks in American society since World War II. Despite evidence of progress, the main aspirations of black Americans are unfulfilled in the areas of equal opportunity and the removal of barriers to employment, housing, education, and political activities.

Protess, David L. 1996. *Chicago Hate: An Analysis of Official and Press Portrayals of Hate Crimes in the City of Chicago in 1995.* A report prepared for the Human Relations Foundation of Chicago. Chicago: Northwestern Univ. Protess provides a profile of hate crimes reporting in Chicago and environs; and he notes disparity of newspaper coverage of city hate crimes vis à vis suburban settings and comments on sources and quality of reporting content.

U.S. Civil Rights Commission. 1992. *Civil Rights Issues Facing Asian Americans in the 1990s.* Washington, D.C.: U.S. Government Printing Office. The report discusses how Asian-Americans, particularly Asians immigrants, face discrimination, prejudice, and denial of equal opportunity, including police protection, education, health care, and the access to the judicial system.

U.S. Federal Bureau of Investigation. 1993. "Hate Crime Statistics 1993: Charac-

teristics of Hate Crimes in 1993, Summary of Hate Crime Data Collection."
Uniform Crime Reports. Washington, D.C.: Criminal Justice Information
Services Division, U.S. Department of Justice. Tables and narratives on bias-
motivated crime reported to the FBI's Uniform Crime Reporting (UCR) system by city, county, and state law enforcement agencies for 1993 are presented.
These incidents are documented by race, religion, ethnicity/national origin,
and sexual orientation. UCR reports that blacks committed hate crimes in
1993 at a per capita rate exceeding that of whites by more than 4 to 1.

OUTSIDE THE UNITED STATES

Hate violence occurring in other countries requires a contextual analysis. The majority of existing reports concern Germany, but an increasing
number of articles discuss hate violence in other European countries. Recently, reports discussing hate violence in non-European countries are occurring. The United Nations and Human Rights Watch of New York
City are primary resources for this emerging data.
Anti-Defamation League of B'nai B'rith. 1992. *Anti-Semitism in Western Europe:
A Focus on Germany, France, and Austria*. New York: Anti-Defamation League
of B'nai B'rith. The collapse of communism and economic stress are seen as
forces undergirding the marked rise in hate crimes. The nationalistic fervor
and search for "simple solutions" throughout Europe and the alarming rise in
right-wing groups in Germany, France, and Austria is discussed, with recommendations for remedies.
"Catching the Plague" (1992). *The Economist* 84(9):63. Antiforeigner violence has
officials concerned that Spain will experience the same frenzy of hate crimes
that many parts of Europe are experiencing. While opinion polls show Span-
iards are more tolerant of outsiders than most other Europeans, experts cau-
tion the government to improve the employment rate and take control over
illegal immigration.
Cooper, Mary. 1994. "Europe's New Right: Are Right-Wing Extremists Gaining
a New Foothold in Europe?" *CQ Researcher* 13(1): 3–8. The reintegration and
economic problems of Germany are providing cause for right-wing extremists to exploit ethnic turmoil, thereby breeding antiforeign violence and sentiment. Germany has seen a high number of antiforeign crime incidents. This
situation is reflective of the European community at large. A bibliography of
topical books, articles, reports, and studies is included.
Greenspan, Louis, and Cyril Levitt, eds. 1993. *Under the Shadow of Weimar:
Democracy, Law, and Racial Incitement in Six Countries*. Westport, Conn.:
Praeger.
Hamm, Mark S., ed. 1994. *Hate Crimes: International Perspective on Causes and*

Control. Cincinnati: Anderson. Case studies of American and European neo-Nazi Skinheads as perpetrators of terroristic ethnic hate crimes are presented, including sociological and psychological analysis of "Nazi occultism and the morality of vengeance."

Hesse, Barnor, et al. 1992. *Beneath the Surface: Racial Harassment.* London: Avebury Press. Originally an inquiry into racial harassment commissioned by the North East London Borough of Waltham Forest in 1988, this work documents relevant literature in criminology, victimology, police research, social policy, and the study of racism.

Marks, John. 1991. "New Germany's Old Fears—Hate Crimes." *U.S. News and World Report* 111(16): 20. Hate crimes against refugees and foreigners have increased in Germany. Sixty percent of German citizens sympathize with the motives behind these crimes, causing even greater social discord.

Nelan, Bruce W. 1991. "As Europe's Ethnic Mix Begins to Change, Some Countries Discover They Are Not As Tolerant of Foreign Cultures As They Once Thought They Were." *Time,* Oct. 8, 36–39. As Europe's ethnic mix begins to change, some countries discover they are not as tolerant of foreign cultures as they once were. The forces of ethnic change and reactionary social responses in Germany, France, Britain, and Italy are engendering hate crimes.

Contributors

Julia Greider-Durango coordinated a variety of international programs for the University of Illinois from 1988 to 1996. Her current research interests include public health policy and child welfare in the United States and Colombia.

Robert Harnishmacher is the editor-in-chief of *Magazin für die Polizei: Internationales unabhängiges Fachmagazin* and an associate professor at the European Academy.

James B. Jacobs is a professor of law and the director of the Center for Research in Crime and Justice at the New York University School of Law.

Robert J. Kelly is Broeklundian Professor of social science at Brooklyn College and a professor of criminal justice at the Graduate School of the City University of New York.

Jess Maghan is the director of the Center for Research in Law and Justice and an associate professor of criminal justice at the University of Illinois at Chicago.

Asad ur Rahman is a professor of English at Brooklyn College of the City University of New York.

Antony E. Simpson is a professor in the doctoral program of criminal justice at the John Jay College of the City University of New York.

Ghada Talhami is the chairperson and an associate professor in the Department of Politics at Lake Forest College.

Suzanne Wilson is a visiting assistant professor in the Department of Sociology at the University of Illinois at Urbana-Champaign.